CYBER SECURITY

BCS, THE CHARTERED INSTITUTE FOR IT

BCS, The Chartered Institute for IT champions the global IT profession and the interests of individuals engaged in that profession for the benefit of all. We promote wider social and economic progress through the advancement of information technology science and practice. We bring together industry, academics, practitioners and government to share knowledge, promote new thinking, inform the design of new curricula, shape public policy and inform the public.

Our vision is to be a world-class organisation for IT. Our 70,000 strong membership includes practitioners, businesses, academics and students in the UK and internationally. We deliver a range of professional development tools for practitioners and employees. A leading IT qualification body, we offer a range of widely recognised qualifications.

Further Information
BCS, The Chartered Institute for IT,
First Floor, Block D,
North Star House, North Star Avenue,
Swindon, SN2 1FA, United Kingdom.
T +44 (0) 1793 417 424
F +44 (0) 1793 417 444
www.bcs.org/contact

http://shop.bcs.org/

CYBER SECURITY
A practitioner's guide

David Sutton

Published by BCS Learning & Development Ltd, a wholly owned subsidiary of BCS, The Chartered Institute for IT, First Floor, Block D, North Star House, North Star Avenue, Swindon, SN2 1FA, UK.
www.bcs.org

ISBN: 978-1-78017-340-5
PDF ISBN: 978-1-78017-341-2
ePUB ISBN: 978-1-78017-342-9
Kindle ISBN: 978-1-78017-343-6

British Cataloguing in Publication Data.
A CIP catalogue record for this book is available at the British Library.

Disclaimer:
The views expressed in this book are of the author(s) and do not necessarily reflect the views of the Institute or BCS Learning & Development Ltd except where explicitly stated as such. Although every care has been taken by the author(s) and BCS Learning & Development Ltd in the preparation of the publication, no warranty is given by the author(s) or BCS Learning & Development Ltd as publisher as to the accuracy or completeness of the information contained within it and neither the author(s) nor BCS Learning & Development Ltd shall be responsible or liable for any loss or damage whatsoever arising by virtue of such information or any instructions or advice contained within this publication or by any of the aforementioned.

BCS books are available at special quantity discounts to use as premiums and sale promotions, or for use in corporate training programmes. Please visit our Contact us page at www.bcs.org/contact

Typeset by Lapiz Digital Services, Chennai, India.
Printed by Hobbs the Printers Ltd, Hampshire, UK.

MRI scanners are noisy, very noisy indeed. So, if ever you find yourself lying inside one and they ask you what music you'd like to hear, insist on one of AC/DC, Deep Purple, Metallica, Led Zeppelin, Guns N' Roses or Hawkwind, because you'll never be able to hear anything that's quieter.

They say that when life throws you lemons, you should always grab Tequila and salt, but sometimes there's none to hand. So, when a straightforward keyhole procedure turns into four-and-a-half-hour open table surgery, once you've come round, you think you've pulled the big handle and that all your lemons have come up together. Then they give you a couple of shots of liquid morphine and it all begins to feel much better. Mind-bogglingly freaky, but much, much better.

This book is for the incredible surgeons, doctors, nurses and support staff at St Richard's Hospital in Chichester, without whose amazing skill and dedication you probably wouldn't be reading this now.

CONTENTS

LIST OF FIGURES AND TABLES

AUTHOR

David Sutton's career spans 50 years and includes radio transmission, international telephone switching, computing, voice and data networking, structured cabling systems, information security and critical information infrastructure protection.

He joined Cellnet (now Telefónica UK) in 1993, where he was responsible for ensuring the continuity and restoration of the core cellular and broadband networks, and represented the company in the electronic communications industry's national resilience forum. In December 2005, he gave evidence to the Greater London Authority enquiry into the mobile telecoms impact of the London bombings.

David has been a member of the BCS Professional Certification Information Security Panel since 2005 and has delivered lectures on information risk management and business continuity at the Royal Holloway University of London, from which he holds an MSc in Information Security, and at which he has been an external tutor on their open learning MSc course.

Since retiring from Telefónica UK in 2010, he has undertaken a number of critical information infrastructure projects for the European Network and Information Security Agency (ENISA), developed business continuity and information risk management training material for InfoSec Skills, and has served on the training accreditation panel for the Institute of Information Security Professionals (IISP).

Other books by the author

Information Security Management Principles (second edition), published by BCS, ISBN 978-1-78017-175-3 (co-author)

Information Risk Management: A Practitioner's Guide, published by BCS, ISBN 978-1-78017-265-1

ACKNOWLEDGEMENTS

I would like to express my thanks to Matthew Flynn, Ian Borthwick and Rebecca Youé of BCS for kindly agreeing to publish this book; to my wife Sharon for yet again putting up with my grumpier moments and for her unceasing encouragement; to 'Fred' (Friend of the Retired, Elderly and Disabled) for the use of wireless fidelity (WiFi) in her bar 'La Brasa' in Oliva; to Louise from the Roald Dahl Museum in Great Missenden for her suggestion regarding Gobblefunk; and finally to Scott Keenan for the sandwich!

ABBREVIATIONS

3G	Third Generation public cellular mobile system
4G	Fourth Generation public cellular mobile system
AES	Advanced Encryption Standard
ATM	Automatic Teller Machine
BC	Business Continuity
BCI	Business Continuity Institute
BCP	Business Continuity Plan
BCS	BCS, The Chartered Institute for IT
BGP	Border Gateway Protocol
BIA	Business Impact Analysis
BS	British Standard
BSI	British Standards Institution
BT	British Telecom
BYOD	Bring Your Own Device
C2	Command and Control
CA	Certification Authority
CAN	Controller Area Network
CBT	Computer-Based Training
CCA	Centre for Cyber Assessment
CCP	Certified Practitioner
CCSC	Certified Cyber Security Consultancy
CCSK	Certificate of Cloud Security Knowledge
CCSP	Certified Cloud Security Professional
CCTV	Closed-Circuit Television
CEO	Chief Executive Officer
CERN	European Organization for Nuclear Research
CERT	Computer Emergency Response Team
CERT/CC	Computer Emergency Response Team/Coordination Centre
CES	Consumer Electronics Show
CI	Critical Infrastructure
CII	Critical Information Infrastructure
CISMP	Certificate in Information Security Management Principles
CiSP	Cyber Security Information Sharing Partnership
CISSP	Certified Information Systems Security Professional
CNI	Critical National Infrastructure
COBIT	Control Objectives for Information and Related Technologies
CPNI	Centre for the Protection of National Infrastructure
CSIRT	Computer Security Incident Response Team
CSP	Communication Service Provider

DARPA	Defense Advanced Research Projects Agency	**HR**	Human Resources
DDoS	Distributed Denial of Service	**HTTP**	Hypertext Transfer Protocol
DES	Data Encryption Standard	**HTTPS**	Hypertext Transfer Protocol Secure
DMZ	Demilitarised Zone	**HVAC**	Heating, Ventilation and Air Conditioning
DNO	Distribution Network Operator		
DNS	Domain Name System	**IA**	Information Assurance
DoD	Department of Defense	**ICT**	Information and Communications Technology
DoS	Denial of Service		
DPA	Data Protection Act	**IDPS**	Intrusion Detection and Prevention Systems
DR	Disaster Recovery	**IDS**	Intrusion Detection System
DRIPA	Data Retention and Investigatory Powers Act	**IEC**	International Electrotechnical Commission
DVLA	Driver and Vehicle Licensing Agency	**IED**	improvised explosive device
ECU	Engine Control Unit	**IETF**	Internet Engineering Task Force
EDR	Event Data Recorder	**IFE**	in-flight entertainment
ENISA	European Union Agency for Network and Information Security	**IoT**	Internet of Things
		IP	Intellectual Property
EU	European Union	**IP**	Internet Protocol
FAST	Federation Against Software Theft	**IPC**	Investigatory Powers Commission
FCA	Financial Conduct Authority	**IPv6**	Internet Protocol Version 6
FIPS	Federal Information Processing Standard	**ISAC**	Information Sharing and Analysis Centre
GCHQ	Government Communications Headquarters	**ISF**	Information Security Forum
		ISMS	Information Security Management System
GDPR	General Data Protection Regulation	**ISO**	International Organization for Standardization
GPS	Global Positioning System		
GSM	Global System for Mobile Communications	**ISP**	Internet Service Provider
		ITU	International Telecommunication Union
HIDS	Host Intrusion Detection System	**JANET**	Joint Academic Network
HIPAA	Health Insurance Portability and Accountability Act	**LAN**	Local Area Network
		MAC	Media Access Control
HMRC	Her Majesty's Revenue and Customs	**MAO**	Maximum Acceptable Outage

MTDL	Maximum Tolerable Data Loss	**SAN**	Storage Area Network
NCSC	National Cyber Security Centre	**SCADA**	Supervisory Control And Data Acquisition
NGO	Non-governmental organisation	**SIE**	Security Information Exchange
NHS	National Health Service	**SLA**	Service Level Agreement
NIDS	Network Intrusion Detection System	**SME**	Small-to-Medium Enterprise
		SPoF	Single Point of Failure
NIS	Network and Information Security	**SSCP**	Systems Security Certified Practitioner
NISCC	National Infrastructure Security Coordination Centre	**SSH**	Secure Socket Shell
		SSID	Service Set Identifier
NIST	National Institute for Standards and Technology	**TCP**	Transmission Control Protocol
NSA	National Security Agency	**TLP**	Traffic Light Protocol
NTP	Network Time Protocol	**TLS**	Transport Layer Security
OS	Operating System	**TOR**	The Onion Router
P2P	Peer-to-Peer	**UAC**	User Account Control
PAS	Publicly Available Specification	**UDP**	User Datagram Protocol
		UPS	Uninterruptible Power Supply
PCBCM	Practitioner Certificate in Business Continuity Management	**VESDA**	Very Early Smoke Detection Apparatus
		USB	Universal Serial Bus
PCIDSS	Payment Card Industry Data Security Standard	**VoIP**	Voice Over Internet Protocol
PCIRM	Practitioner Certificate in Information Risk Management	**VPN**	Virtual Private Network
		WAN	Wide Area Network
PDCA	Plan–Do–Check–Act	**WAP**	WiFi Access Point
PDF	Portable Document Format	**WARP**	Warning, Advice and Reporting Point
PGP	Pretty Good Privacy		
PII	Personally Identifiable Information	**WEP**	Wired Equivalent Privacy
		WiFi	Wireless Fidelity
PIN	Personal Identification Number	**WLAN**	Wireless Local Area Network
		WPA	Wireless Protected Access
PKI	Public Key Infrastructure	**WPA-PSK**	Wireless Protected Access Pre-Shared Key
RFC	Request for Comments		
RIPA	Regulation of Investigatory Powers Act	**WPS**	WiFi Protected Setup
RTO	Recovery Time Objective		

PREFACE

Whilst conducting my research for this book, I have noted literally hundreds of cyber security incidents – some relatively trivial, some rather more serious. What has never ceased to amaze me is not that they keep happening, but that the same kinds of incident keep happening, and that some people do not appear to learn the lessons of others' mistakes and occasionally even of their own.

In the 21st century, we are almost totally reliant upon information technology, and in particular the interconnectedness that allows us to conduct our lives more efficiently. We now regard access to the connected world as a basic utility along with gas, electricity and water; as business, commerce and government continue to place their services online, we have become increasingly dependent upon something that few people truly understand.

It is an unfortunate fact that when the internet was developed (originally as the ArpaNet[1]), its main purpose was to enable information to be shared freely between institutions conducting research for the US Department of Defense (DoD), and because it was essentially a closed network, security was not even considered as a requirement. A consequence of this is that many of the protocols used over the internet are completely insecure, and until recently there has been a general reluctance amongst the software development community to build security into protocols and applications.

That aside, many of the underlying security issues in cyberspace are caused by a lack of understanding of the risks of using cyberspace; by people who have not been adequately trained to do their job; who have not done it correctly; or who were simply unaware that there was anything for them to do in the first place. These issues affect everybody who uses cyberspace – in their personal as well as professional lives – at home, whilst travelling and at work.

When electronic equipment became a commodity product in the late 1960s and early 1970s, enthusiasts began to experiment with modifications – both to hardware and software – and they became known as 'hackers'. Hacking then was a benign activity, intended to encourage learning and to find ways of improving the performance of electronics, but as time progressed the term began to be used by the media in a derogatory way for those who broke into other people's computer resources.[2]

Whilst there are laws, regulations and rules regarding the protection of physical and information assets, there are none that apply to virtual assets within cyberspace. However, in the realm of cyber security, there are some clear objectives:

- to protect the overall security of cyberspace;
- to plan for disruptive incidents and to exercise those plans;

xvi

- to improve the awareness of cyberspace users;
- to share threat and vulnerability information relating to cyberspace;
- to address critical interdependencies within cyberspace.

Much of this work has already begun, but there is considerably more to do, and it will be an ongoing exercise. In July 2016, the UK's National Crime Agency reported that the technical capabilities of criminal gangs are outpacing the UK's ability to deal with their threat, and that there were 2.46 million cyber incidents last year, including 700,000 cases of fraud – with the biggest threat coming from just a few hundred criminals.[3]

The lesson – as many a security professional will tell you – is that if a well-resourced attacker really wants to break into your computer, read, steal or change your information, then they will almost certainly find a way of doing so. It may not be cheap or easy, it may involve using a mix of technology and human agents, but if they think it is worth it, you will find it very, very hard to stop them.

In 2014, FBI Director James Comey said, 'I am convinced that there are only two types of companies: those that have been hacked and those that will be. And even they are converging into one category: companies that have been hacked and will be hacked again.'[4]

We frequently take things at face value, especially in the online world. Why?

If a stranger approached you in a street and said, 'I can do you a really good deal', you would naturally be suspicious, but put the same words online, and people are falling over themselves to take up the offer.

The expression, 'If it sounds too good to be true, it probably is', is frequently quoted in the online world, but it's amazing how many people cannot bear the thought of missing out on the possibility of getting something for nothing, and end up getting nothing. There's one born every minute.

Criminals have always preyed upon human frailty and greed and will doubtless continue to do so until the end of time, but there are simple steps we can take to reduce the chance of being their victims, and to make their lives so difficult that they go hunting elsewhere.

During the early stages of writing this book, my wife and I were visiting friends in Spain. The house they were renting did not have internet access, and I found myself at something of a loss, unable to verify references, look up new information, save my work to the cloud, catch up with the news in the UK, laugh at the daily Dilbert cartoon or check my email.

Fortunately, I was able to achieve some of this by using 'free' WiFi at bars and restaurants in the town but, remembering my own words, used caution in everything I did. To say that it was difficult coping with intermittent access to the internet and taking the extra precautions when using WiFi in a public place would be a gross understatement.

Criminality does not respect national borders or trade barriers. It is too early to tell whether the UK's recent referendum vote to leave the European Union (EU) will result in joy or sorrow for the cyber security community – I live in hope for the former, but strongly suspect it could be the latter. What I believe I can say for sure is that new vulnerabilities will surface at frequent intervals, new threats will arise, and that the world of cyberspace will continue to be populated by the good, the bad and the downright ugly.

We don't really need to know in detail how the connected world works, no more than the driver of a car needs to understand the workings of the internal combustion engine, but hopefully this book will help to make us better drivers!

WHO SHOULD READ THIS BOOK?

The straight answer to this is probably anyone who has an interest in or concerns about cyber security. It is aimed at both the public and private sectors and should have appeal to home users; students studying information security, computer science and other information technology-related subjects; and information security practitioners and their line managers, whether technical or not.

The aim is to inform the reader about the realities of cyber security, detailing the issues faced by both individuals and organisations, the likely targets of cyber-attacks, the vulnerabilities and impacts these attacks may cause, the kinds of threat and how to go about protecting an individual's or organisation's assets against cyber-attacks.

WHAT EXACTLY DO WE MEAN BY CYBER?

Since this book deals with cyber security issues, we should begin by trying to define 'cyber'.

The science fiction author William Gibson coined the term cyberspace in a short story entitled *Burning Chrome*[5] in 1982, but did not define it until two years later in his book *Neuromancer*,[6] in which he describes it thus:

> Cyberspace. A consensual hallucination experienced daily by billions of legitimate operators, in every nation ... a graphic representation of data from the banks of every computer in the human system. Unthinkable complexity. Lines of light ranged in the nonspace of the mind, clusters and constellations of data.

Bearing in mind that this predates the development in 1990 of the worldwide web by Sir Tim Berners-Lee at the European Organization for Nuclear Research (CERN) by six years, it is quite a startling piece of insight.

The UK Cyber Security Strategy, 2011[7] offers this definition:

> Cyberspace is an interactive domain made up of digital networks, that is used to store, modify and communicate information. It includes the Internet, but also the other information systems that support our businesses, infrastructure and services.

Perhaps the most meaningful definition can be found in the present-day definition of Cyberspace from the International Organization for Standardization (ISO) of a:

> complex environment resulting from the interaction of people, software and services on the Internet by means of technology devices and networks connected to it, which does not exist in any physical form.[8]

Cyber security therefore refers specifically to information security as applied to cyberspace, and in this respect, it is slightly different from the wider concept of information security, which includes non-electronic information as well. It is sometimes also referred to as computer security or IT security. Again, the ISO standard has a simple definition 'preservation of confidentiality, integrity and availability of information in the Cyberspace.'

It notes that 'In addition, other properties, such as authenticity, accountability, non-repudiation, and reliability can also be involved.'[9]

Finally, the standard defines cybercrime as:

> criminal activity where services or applications in the Cyberspace are used for or are the target of a crime, or where the Cyberspace is the source, tool, target, or place of a crime.[10]

OVERVIEW OF THIS BOOK

Whilst there is a logical layout to this book, although helpful, it is not necessary to read through it sequentially – the reader should feel free to dip in and out of chapters in any order they wish.

TERMINOLOGY AND DEFINITIONS

Some of the following definitions are taken from ISO/IEC 27000:2014 [1] and ISO Guide 73:2009 [3], with some from ISO 22301:2012 [2], BS ISO/IEC TR 18044:2004 [4] and ISO/IEC 27032:2012 [5]. A few are not defined in any standards, so I have suggested my own.

While this book was in its latter stages of production in mid-May 2017, the 'WannaCry' virus made an unwelcome appearance. Threats such as viruses and ransomware are covered in detail in Chapter 5 of this book, and methods of preventing and/or dealing with them are covered in Chapters 8 and 9.

News of the attack was not a great surprise, but the scale of it was – I had expected it to have a considerably wider impact, and it is to the credit of the IT and security specialists around the world that its spread was limited and dealt with so quickly, although a great many people had a thoroughly frustrating and exhausting weekend.

Let us hope that the lessons have been learned; that out-of-support software is replaced, patches are applied and the recommendations in this book are followed. It is not a question of if another attack occurs, but when; and when it does, it may well be far more aggressive.

NOTES

1. For an excellent description of how the ArpaNet/internet began, read *Where Wizards Stay Up Late* by Katie Hafner and Matthew Lyon, (New York: Touchstone, 1998).

2. An early example of this can be found in *The Cuckoo's Egg* by Clifford Stoll (London: Pan Books, 1991).

3. See www.bbc.co.uk/news/uk-36731694

4. See https://www.fbi.gov/news/speeches/combating-threats-in-the-cyber-world-outsmarting-terrorists-hackers-and-spies

5. *Burning Chrome,* William Gibson. Harper Voyager, New edition (27 Nov. 1995).

6. *Neuromancer,* William Gibson. Harper Voyager, New edition (27 Nov. 2015).

7. See https://www.gov.uk/government/publications/national-cyber-security-strategy-2016-to-2021

8. See ISO/IEC 27032:2012 p. 4.

9. ibid

10. ibid

GLOSSARY

Access control The means to ensure that access to assets is authorised and restricted on business and security requirements. [1]

Asset Any item that has value to the organisation. [1] Assets may be tangible, such as network equipment, systems, etc. or intangible, such as software or intellectual property.

Attack An attempt to destroy, expose, alter, disable, steal or gain unauthorised access to or make unauthorised use of an asset. [1]

Audit The systematic, independent and documented process for obtaining audit evidence and evaluating it objectively to determine the extent to which the audit criteria are fulfilled. [1]

Authentication The provision of assurance that a claimed characteristic of an entity is correct. [1]

Availability Property of being accessible and useable upon demand by an authorised entity. [1]

Business Continuity (BC) The capability of the organisation to continue delivery of products and services at acceptable predefined levels following a disruptive incident. [2]

Business Impact Analysis (BIA) The process of analysing activities and the effect that a business disruption might have upon them. [2]

Confidentiality The property that information is not made available or disclosed to unauthorised individuals, entities or processes. [1]

Consequence An outcome of an event affecting objectives. [3] Consequences are also referred to as impacts.

Control A measure that is modifying risk. [3] Controls come in a number of forms – at the strategic level, they can be to accept the risk; to modify or reduce it; to avoid or terminate it; or to transfer or share it. At the tactical level, control choices are preventative, to stop something from happening; corrective, to fix something that has happened; detective, to discover when something has happened; and directive, to put processes and procedures into place. Finally, operational controls can be physical, such as locks and barriers; procedural, such as change control mechanisms; and technical, such as antivirus software.

Cyber-attack Aggressive cyber action taken against people, organisations, networks, systems and services and which is intended to cause loss or damage.

Cyber bullying Cyber bullying or cyber harassment is simply the act of harassing or bullying a person or group of people using cyber-based methods such as social media, text messaging and the like.

Cybercrime Criminal activity where services or applications in the Cyberspace are used for or are the target of a crime, or where the Cyberspace is the source, tool, target, or place of a crime. [5]

Cyber espionage Covert surveillance activity conducted over cyberspace.

Cyber hacktivism Includes individuals or groups who may be stalking someone in an act of revenge for a perceived grievance, looking to expose some wrongdoing, or a business trying to place their competitors on the wrong foot.

Cyber security Preservation of confidentiality, integrity and availability of information in the Cyberspace. [5]

Cyberspace Complex environment resulting from the interaction of people, software and services on the internet by means of technology devices and networks connected to it, which does not exist in any physical form.

Cyber terrorism Includes cyber-attacks by terrorists against nation states, business and commerce. It may also include a terrorist group trying to turn people against their own government, or a nation state trying to unbalance another government. One way or another, it's all just a form of terrorism designed to induce fear or to stir up hatred.

Cyber theft Theft or a fraudulent activity conducted over cyberspace.

Cyber warfare An attack on another nation state's information or infrastructure conducted over cyberspace.

Data A collection of values assigned to base measures, derived measures and/or indicators. [1]

Disaster recovery (DR) A coordinated activity to enable the recovery of IT systems and networks due to a disruption.

Event The occurrence or change of a particular set of circumstances. [3]

Exploit A particular form of attack that takes advantage of one or more vulnerabilities, and in which a tried and tested method of causing an impact is followed with some rigour. Exploits are similar in nature to processes, but whereas processes are generally benign, exploits are almost always harmful.

Hazards A source of potential harm. [3] They are frequently viewed as being natural, as opposed to man-made, events, including such things as severe weather and pandemics.

Impact An outcome of an event affecting objectives. [3] This is also referred to as consequence.

Information An organised and formatted collection of data.

Information assurance The process of ensuring that data is not lost when critical events or incidents occur. It is generally associated with computer, cyber or IT security rather than the somewhat wider meaning of 'information security'.

Information security The preservation of confidentiality, integrity and availability of information. [1]

Information security incident An information security incident is indicated by a single or a series of unwanted or unexpected information security events that have a significant probability of compromising business operations and threatening information security. [4]

Integrity Property of protecting the accuracy and completeness of assets. [1]

Level of risk The magnitude of a risk expressed in terms of the combination of consequences and their likelihood. [1]

Likelihood The chance of something happening. [3] The terms likelihood and probability are often used interchangeably, but likelihood is a rather general term denoting a degree of uncertainty, whereas the term 'probability' has a more statistical underpinning. The term 'possibility' is generally not used, since many things are possible, but the term gives no indication whether or not the event is actually likely to take place.

Monitoring Determining the status of a system, a process or an activity. [2]

Non-Repudiation The ability to prove the occurrence of a claimed event or action and its originating entities, in order to resolve disputes about the occurrence or non-occurrence of the event or action and involvement of entities in the event. [1]

Objective A result to be achieved. [1]

Organisation A person or group of people that has its own functions with responsibilities, authorities and relationships to achieve its objectives. [1]

Policy The intentions of an organisation as formally expressed by its top management. [1]

Probability The measure of the chance of occurrence expressed as a number between 0 and 1, where 0 is impossibility and 1 is absolute certainty. [3]

Process A set of interacting activities, which transforms inputs into outputs. [1]

Resilience The adaptive capacity of an organisation in a complex and changing environment. [3] Although this definition refers to organisations rather than to information assets, the definition holds true in that where an information asset is properly protected, it is able to resist certain threats. However, to make an information asset fully resilient may be a very complex task and require several different methods of protection.

Review An activity undertaken to determine the suitability, adequacy and effectiveness of the subject matter to achieve established objectives. [1]

Risk The effect of uncertainty on objectives. [3] Risk is the product of consequence or impact and likelihood or probability, and is not the same as a threat or hazard. In the context of information risk management, risk is usually taken to have negative connotations. In the wider context of risk however, it can also be seen in a positive light and referred to as 'opportunity'.

Risk acceptance The informed decision to take a particular risk. [3] Risk acceptance (or risk tolerance) is the final choice in risk treatment once all other possible avenues have been explored. This is not the same as ignoring risks – something that should never be done!

Risk analysis The process to comprehend the nature of risk and to determine the level of risk. [3] This is the part of risk assessment where we combine the impact and the likelihood (or probability) of a risk to calculate the level of risk in order to plot it onto a risk matrix, which allows us to compare risks for their severity and to decide which are in most urgent need of treatment.

Risk appetite The amount and type of risk that an organisation is willing to pursue or retain. [3]

Risk assessment The overall process of risk identification, risk analysis and risk evaluation. [3] This includes identification of the information assets and their owners; impact assessment; threat and vulnerability identification; likelihood assessment; risk analysis; production of the risk matrix; and finally risk evaluation.

Risk avoidance An informed decision not to be involved in, or to withdraw from, an activity in order not to be exposed to a particular risk. [3] Risk avoidance (or risk termination) is one of the four strategic options for risk treatment. Avoiding the risk should normally remove the risk completely, but may leave the organisation with other challenges.

Risk evaluation The process of comparing the results of risk analysis with risk criteria to determine whether the risk and/or its magnitude is acceptable or tolerable. [3]

Risk identification The process of finding, recognising and describing risks. [3]

Risk management The coordinated activities to direct and control an organisation with regard to risk. [3]

Risk matrix A graphical representation of impact versus likelihood used to assist in the prioritisation of risks.

Risk modification Risk modification (or risk reduction) is the process of treating risk by the use of controls to reduce either the consequence/impact or the likelihood/probability. Sometimes the term 'risk treatment' is used in this context, but risk treatment is really a generic term for all four kinds of strategic control. Strangely, ISO Guide 73 does not attempt to define risk modification or reduction, although it does refer to it under the definition of 'control'.

Risk reduction See 'Risk modification' above.

Risk retention The acceptance of the potential benefit of gain, or burden of loss, from a particular risk. [3] Once risks have undergone the risk treatment process, there may be some outstanding risk that cannot be further reduced, transferred or eliminated. This is referred to as 'residual risk', and risk retention is the ongoing process of accepting and managing this.

Risk review The activity undertaken to determine the suitability, adequacy and effectiveness of the subject matter to achieve established objectives. [3]

Risk sharing A form of risk treatment involving the agreed distribution of risk with other parties. [3]

Risk termination An informed decision not to be involved in, or to withdraw from, an activity in order not to be exposed to a particular risk. [3]

Risk tolerance An organisation or stakeholder's readiness to bear the risk after risk treatment in order to achieve its objectives. [3]

Risk transfer Risk transfer (or risk sharing) is a form of risk treatment involving the agreed distribution of risk with other parties. [3] One of the strategic risk treatment options is to transfer the risk to or to share it with a third party. Transferring or sharing the risk, however, does not change ownership of the risk; it remains with the organisation itself, regardless of who else shares the risk.

Risk treatment The process to modify risk. [3] Whilst this may be technically correct, risk modification is just one form of risk treatment, and alternatively may involve risk transference or sharing, or risk avoidance or termination.

Stakeholder A person or organisation that can affect, be affected by, or perceive themselves to be affected by a decision or activity. [3]

Threat The potential cause of an unwanted incident, which may result in harm to a system or organisation. [1] Whereas hazards are generally viewed as natural events, threats are usually man-made, whether accidental or deliberate, and may include such things as sabotage and cyber-attacks.

Threat actions The actual attacks. These are often not a single isolated event, but can consist of many discrete activities, involving surveillance, initial activities, testing and the final attacks.

Threat actor or threat agent An individual or group of individuals who actually execute a cyber-attack.

Threat analysis The process of understanding the level of threat – this is referred to in more detail in Chapter 6 – Risk management overview.

Threat consequences or impacts The results or impacts of a cyber-attack, which we deal with in Chapter 4.

Threat source A person or organisation that wishes to benefit from attacking an information asset. Threat sources often pay or otherwise pressurise threat actors to attack information assets on their behalf.

Threat vectors or attack vectors Tools, techniques and mechanisms by which an attacker conducts the attack on their target.

Vulnerability The intrinsic properties of something resulting in susceptibility to a risk source that can lead to an event with a consequence. [1] Vulnerabilities or weaknesses in or surrounding an asset leave it open to attack from a threat or hazard. Vulnerabilities come in two flavours – intrinsic vulnerabilities, which are something inherent in the very nature of an information asset, such as the ease of erasing information from magnetic media (whether accidental or deliberate), and extrinsic vulnerabilities, which are those that are poorly applied, such as software that is out of date due to a lack of patching.

Sources of standards information:

1. ISO/IEC 27000:2014 – *Information technology – Security techniques – Information security management systems – Overview and vocabulary.*
2. ISO 22301:2012 – *Societal security – Business continuity management systems – Requirements.*
3. ISO Guide 73:2009 – *Risk management – Vocabulary.*
4. BS ISO/IEC TR 18044:2004 – *Information technology – Security techniques – Information security incident management.*
5. ISO/IEC 27032:2012 – *Information technology – Security techniques – Guidelines for cybersecurity.*

Note: Permission to reproduce extracts from British and ISO Standards is granted by the British Standards Institution (BSI).

British Standards can be obtained in PDF or hard copy formats from the BSI online shop: www.bsigroup.com/Shop or by contacting BSI Customer Services for hard copies only: Tel: +44 (0)20 8996 9001, Email: cservices@bsigroup.com

The chapters of this book are organised as follows:

Part I – Cyber security problems

Chapter 1 – Introduction – what cyber security is all about, and a summary of the expectations of individuals and organisations who would be affected by a cyber-attack.

Chapter 2 – The big issues, including privacy, security (and privacy versus security), confidentiality, integrity, availability, non-repudiation, big data and data aggregation and the likely vulnerabilities that could allow an attack to be successfully conducted.

Chapter 3 – Cyber targets, including finance organisations, commercial businesses, critical infrastructure, manufacturing, academia and research organisations, industrial control systems and government and military targets.

Chapter 4 – Cyber vulnerabilities and impacts, including policy, process and procedure vulnerabilities, technical vulnerabilities, people-related vulnerabilities, physical and environmental vulnerabilities; personal impacts and organisational impacts.

Chapter 5 – Cyber threats, including types of attacker, types of attack, the motivations for and the benefits of launching an attack, the risks involved in doing so, and how attacks typically are conducted.

Part II – Improving cyber security

Chapter 6 – A brief overview of information risk management, including identifying assets, risk identification, analysis and evaluation and options for risk treatment.

Chapter 7 – The benefits of business continuity and disaster recovery.

Chapter 8 – Steps that can be taken by both individuals and corporate users to improve their cyber security.

Chapter 9 – Additional steps that can be taken by organisations, including cyber security policies and operational actions.

Chapter 10 – How users can be made aware of cyber security risks, and how training may be required for those more closely involved in securing the organisation.

Chapter 11 – Information sharing, including information available to assist in the management of cyber security issues; warning, advice and reporting points (WARPs); computer emergency response teams (CERTs) and computer security incident response teams (CSIRTs); security information exchanges (SIEs) and Information Sharing and Analysis Centres (ISACs) and the UK's Cyber Security Information Sharing Partnership (CiSP).

Appendices

Appendices – Lists the national and international cyber security standards, good practice guides, legislation that is relevant within the UK, information on aspects of cyber security training, and finally links to other relevant organisations.

PART I
CYBER SECURITY PROBLEMS

1 INTRODUCTION

If you spend more on coffee than on IT security, you will be hacked. What's more, you deserve to be hacked.

Richard Clarke, author and former Special Advisor for Cyberspace to the US President

In this chapter, we will examine the fundamentals of data and information, since these lie at the very heart of cyber security. Although the two are frequently used interchangeably, it is important to understand the essential difference between the two. We shall also consider the wider context of cyber security, and provide an overview of the remainder of the book.

BACKGROUND

Anyone born after the late 1980s will have little or no concept of life before mobile phones and the internet. They have grown up accustomed to searching the world-wide web for resources; sending emails; shopping without leaving the house; listening to music and watching films online; keeping in touch with friends using social media and a hundred and one other things. If we took away their smartphones and computers, they would find it almost impossible to conduct what some of us will remember as a 'normal' life.

Whilst many of us may have experienced difficulty with the transition from writing letters, visiting the library, going to the cinema and buying records, the connected world remains a fact of life and is accepted as such – and it's going to become even more widespread. Services will increase in capability whilst becoming more intuitive, and they will become faster and cheaper – future generations will accept ubiquitous connectivity and availability of information as the norm.

In recent years, it has become increasingly apparent that many of these services and applications are completely insecure, and whether by accident or design, can often leak our personal information, location and credentials.

This has resulted in a paradigm shift in the criminal world. The American serial bank robber Willie Sutton (no relation) was once quoted as saying that he robbed banks 'Because that's where the money is.' Whilst this may still be true, it is much less risky for a thief to steal money from a computer on the other side of the world than it is to break into a bank or hold up staff with a shotgun. As we shall see later in this book, it can also be much more lucrative.

We worry about privacy, yet we willingly give out our home address, email address and credit card information to a company we have never heard of in anticipation of getting a bargain. Most of the time we are lucky: the company turns out to be genuine and we get what we paid for. But sometimes we might not be so lucky – either the offer might be a scam, or rather more seriously, the company's records might be stolen, including the personal information we have provided, and now an unknown third party has this, and can use it, abuse it or sell it on.

When we hear of a new Act of Parliament in which the law appears to give the police and security services the unconditional right to snoop into our private lives we feel threatened; when we hear that the security services have used the same legislation to intercept communications between terrorists and have prevented an attack, we are encouraged. We understand that there must be such surveillance, but we don't want it to apply to us – after all, we have done nothing wrong.

In 2016, the UK Office for National Statistics estimated that in the previous year there had been 5.1 million cases of fraud and cybercrime in England and Wales alone.[1] The upshot of this is that most people in the UK are now far more likely to be the victims of cybercrime than good old-fashioned burglary.

When we purchase goods on the internet, especially software for our smartphones and computers, we have to accept the terms and conditions dictated by the seller, but do we ever read them before clicking 'Agree'? In 2014, F-Secure, a provider of security software, arranged for a free WiFi network to be deployed in the Docklands area of London.[2] Anybody wishing to use the network had to accept the terms and conditions, and a number of people did so, being completely unaware that they had committed themselves to 'assign their first-born child to us for the duration of eternity'.

This so-called 'Herod clause' was inserted as a light-hearted way of establishing whether or not anyone had actually read the terms and conditions, and later an F-Secure spokesperson said, 'We have yet to enforce our rights under the terms and conditions but, as this is an experiment, we will be returning the children to their parents.'[3]

We assume – often wrongly – that terms and conditions will be fair and will comply with legitimate and reasonable trading standards, but often they are so lengthy and written in legalise that even if we begin to read them we soon lose interest. Of course, if you don't click 'Agree', you can't use the facility or the software – or maybe can only use a heavily cut-down version of its functionality. We download 'apps' for our smartphones and tablet computers that are designed to make our lives more fulfilling, but many of these use the device's location whether they need to or not, and this data can be collected, aggregated and sold on to others.

So, when things do go wrong, we must accept at least a part of the blame – after all, whether knowingly or unknowingly, we have given away information that can be used to identify us and the chance for someone else to take advantage of opportunities for gain at our expense.

The problem, however, is much wider than that of our own failings. Attackers will try to take advantage of insecure applications and web-based services to gather information about us, and in this case, it is the organisation that hosts the service and holds the information rather than the consumer that must shoulder the responsibility.

Whilst most organisations who suffer hacking attacks fix the problem (shutting the stable door after the horse has bolted), some change their terms and conditions in such a manner as to place the onus back on the consumer in the event that their website contains vulnerabilities. An example of this is the cyber-attack on the toy maker V-Tech in December 2015, following which the company made this addition amongst others to its terms and conditions:

> You acknowledge and agree that any information you send or receive during your use of the site may not be secure and may be intercepted or later acquired by unauthorised parties.[4]

Whether this would stand up in a court of law is highly debatable, but we can all draw our own conclusions as to how secure we think this website is and whether or not we would use it again – that is if we had bothered to read the terms and conditions in the first place!

Failing to secure our computers, smartphones and tablets, and wilfully handing over our credentials to strangers is the cyber equivalent of leaving the house unlocked when we go on holiday, with the keys left in the car on the driveway, and we wouldn't dream of doing that, would we?

The knowledge hierarchy

As a first step towards understanding the knowledge hierarchy, we begin the journey by collecting *data* – facts and figures, as shown in Figure 1.1, The journey of data. We then combine these to construct meaningful *information* that informs us and provides *knowledge*. Using this knowledge, we can make inferences and deductions, predictions and recommendations, resulting in meaningful decisions.

At the data level, volumes are high, but the value of each individual item of data is low. As we move up the scale, through information and knowledge to decision-making, the volumes are greatly reduced, but the value increases dramatically.

Figure 1.1 The journey of data

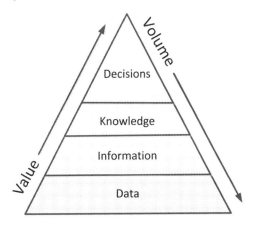

Examples of the sources of data

There are so many sources of data that it would be difficult to list them all, but let's look at some examples of those that would affect us in our everyday lives in the context of cyber security:

- call data records from our mobile phones that itemise who we have called, when, from where and for how long;
- social networks – text and photographs from the likes of Facebook, Twitter and LinkedIn;
- Global Positioning System (GPS) location recovered from mobile phones and photographs we have posted;
- travel cards, such as the Oyster card used in London and the surrounding areas;
- fitness tracking data from running shoes and body monitors;
- number plate recognition data including data from congestion charge cameras;
- credit and debit card transactions;
- PayPal transactions and withdrawals from automatic teller machines (ATMs);
- airline passenger name records and loyalty cards;
- company ID cards, especially where used for physical access control;
- computer device MAC addresses and IP addresses;
- Bluetooth and wireless network (WiFi) identifiers;
- passport scanners;
- store loyalty cards;
- user identification names and associated passwords.

You may be able to add considerably to this list, but just think – if someone could gain access to all or even a large proportion of this information, they would know a great deal about you, your movements, your relationships, both business and personal, your spending habits, your religion, sexual orientation and/or gender, political views and your general health.

They could also increase their store of knowledge by comparing some of your data with that of other people – your Facebook friends for example.

This information has value – not only to you, but also to those who might wish to make use of it, whether for legitimate purposes or otherwise. When we sign up for a 'free' service, it is anything but free. We are trading some of our personal information in exchange for that service, and once we have given it away, we have completely lost control over it.

The critical information security issues

When we consider the security of information (including the requirements of cyber security), there are some fundamental terms that should be understood. These begin with what is often referred to as the information security triad – confidentiality, integrity and availability. However, there are two additional terms – authentication and non-repudiation, which are now considered to be equally important.

Confidentiality

Confidentiality is concerned with ensuring that information is neither disclosed nor made available to those who are not authorised to have access to it. Loss of confidentiality can either be considered as an end in its own right, as in the case of the formula for a new drug, for example, or as a means to an end, as in the example of a password or PIN that gives someone access to a bank account.

In either case, the loss of confidentiality can have a profound impact on the person or organisation that suffers a cyber-attack.

Integrity

Integrity is concerned with securing the accuracy of information, however it's stored or transmitted. Integrity involves ensuring that only authorised people can create, change or delete information, and is very closely linked with confidentiality, since it is usually people who have unauthorised access to information that will also cause integrity issues.

Integrity failures can also have a profound effect, for example the unauthorised changing of a student's grades from a 'fail' to a 'pass', or the unauthorised changing of a user's access level from 'guest' to 'administrator'; changing a criminal sentence from a custodial sentence to a fine; altering a mortgage applicant's credit rating; or removing details of previous illness from someone's medical records.

Availability

Availability is concerned with ensuring that systems and the information stored on them is available for use when required, and by whatever means have been agreed. For example, a bank's customers would reasonably expect to be able to access their accounts, either online or via telephone banking, at any time of the day or night.

Failures of availability almost invariably result in inconvenience, such as the 2012 failures of the Royal Bank of Scotland systems that left customers without access to their accounts and prevented many inter-bank transfers; but in extreme cases could be instrumental in life or death situations, for example in the case of access to a hospital database containing details of an unconscious patient's allergies.

Although the above three factors have long been considered to form the 'triad' of information security, the two following factors (authentication and non-repudiation) are also strong contenders.

Authentication

Enabling a system to identify users with a high degree of confidence is rapidly becoming the norm. The old-style username and password has long been considered to be insufficient to make a positive identification, so additional methods have been introduced – one such is so-called 'two-factor' authentication, in which the usual username and password (something you know) are supplemented by another form of identification, such as a token or smartphone app that generates a time-dependent one-time random number (something you have) or a biometric factor such as a fingerprint or iris scan (something you are).

Non-repudiation

Despite the fact that someone has authorised access to a system or information, in the case of a breach of confidentiality, integrity or availability, they can deny having taken the action that resulted in the problem occurring.

Non-repudiation is concerned with ensuring that suitably authenticated users cannot deny having carried out a particular action. This invariably means that a precise audit trail is kept of every action that the user undertakes.

It is also worth taking a little time to explain some of the more common terms that we frequently take for granted.

Security

Security is a term generally used to include both confidentiality and integrity, and to a somewhat lesser extent, availability. It implies quite simply that something is protected from unauthorised access or harm, but the definition really goes no further.

We feel that we, or our property, is secure when it is protected against unwanted intrusion, whether by the use of physical locks or by some purely electronic mechanism that forbids entry to those without the right keys.

Security is not only a mechanical or physical condition, but also a state of mind – an emotional condition.

Privacy

Privacy on the other hand, has a slightly different meaning. Whilst the same considerations as security apply, privacy brings in a more personal view, in that the subject matter, rather than being general in scope, is much more personal to us, for example someone living under a repressive regime might value highly the privacy of their political opinions.

On face value, we may think that security and privacy are very similar, and in some instances, they are. However, there is also a tension between the two – for example, we rely on the government to keep us secure, both individually and as a nation – but in order to do this, we may feel that they have invaded our privacy by intercepting our internet transactions and emails. Security can come at a cost.

This conflict of ideals is covered in the next chapter under 'Surveillance'.

Trust

The Oxford online dictionary definition is that trust is 'the firm belief in the reliability, truth or ability of someone or something'.

Trust is rather like a raw egg. It is extremely easy to break and almost impossible to rebuild. We place our trust in people, organisations and systems, sometimes without thinking or pondering the possible consequences.

Sometimes, when trust is broken, the party responsible suffers irreparable reputational or financial damage, for example when an online trader 'loses' our credit card details along with those of thousands of other customers. However, on some occasions, the share price eventually recovers to normal or near-normal levels.

Big data and data mining

We have heard increasing reports about big data in recent years. The term itself is not particularly informative, since it simply suggests large volumes of data. In fact it refers not only to large volumes, but also to multiple data sources and their aggregation, and implies both an ability and a will to sift through the records and establish trends – turning information into knowledge.

For example, one could imagine that a major supermarket chain holds big data – its databases contain the registration and payment details for millions of customers; tens of thousands of products; the combination of which customers have bought which products; and when, where, how much they paid and how they paid.

The value of that data to the supermarket is immense, but it is only its ability to make sound business use of it that will determine its eventual value to both the supermarket and the consumer.

Data aggregation

Data aggregation describes the way in which big data is acquired. Some big data (as in the example above) has just one source, but other uses will require additional data sets to be included. These may be acquired directly by the organisation requiring the data, or if they are not available from within the organisation, they may be brought in from outside.

If carried out properly, data aggregation can be a very powerful tool in combining seemingly unrelated data sets into one that can be used to provide a detailed profile of a subject. However, data aggregation is much more than simply a means of acquiring big data. It creates a whole set of challenges in the world of security – for example combining low classification data sources can result in a gold mine of personally identifiable information (PII).

THE EXPECTATIONS OF USERS AND ORGANISATIONS

Individual users, as well as those who work for organisations, together with the organisations for whom they work, all have an implicit expectation that they will not be impacted by the issues described above. For example, people have a right to expect that an organisation handling information about them will treat it in confidence, with respect and in accordance with the appropriate legislation such as the Data Protection Act (DPA), and will not allow it to be made available to those who have no entitlement to see it.

This includes the 'selling on' of users' information, much of which is completely illegal. In January 2017, the UK's consumer magazine *Which?* published an article in which it claimed to have been in a position to purchase personal details including names, addresses and credit card details from 10 legitimate 'list broker' firms for as little as £0.04 per unit. People have not only an expectation, but also a right to know that their personal details will not be sold on in this way.

People also have a perfectly reasonable expectation that information they access will be correct (integrity), and available to them when they require it (availability). Recently, a major retail company that operates its own credit card upgraded its systems over a weekend at the end of a month. The upgrade was fraught with problems, and customers were not only unable to access their account details, but also because of the scale of the problems were unable to contact the company's customer service operation due to the high level of calls. And all this at a time when many of the credit card customers were trying to pay their account.

CYBER SECURITY IN THE WIDER CONTEXT

Cyber security overlaps with several other aspects of security, and Figure 1.2 shows these relationships pictorially:

- Information security, which is concerned with the protection of confidentiality, integrity and availability in all areas of information, not just that which exists in cyberspace.

- Application security, which is concerned with the introduction of controls and measurements to an organisation's applications, whether software, hardware or information.

- Network security, which is concerned with ensuring the protection of an organisation's networks, within the organisation, between organisations and between the organisation and its users. Network security can also include server operating systems (OS) and increasingly the virtualisation layer and associated management systems.

- Internet security, which is concerned with protecting the availability and reliability of an organisation's internet-based services, and protecting individual users both at work and in their home environment.

- Critical information infrastructure protection, which covers the cyber security aspects of elements of a country's critical information infrastructure (CII) elements as discussed in greater detail in Chapter 3.

Figure 1.2 Relationship between security domains

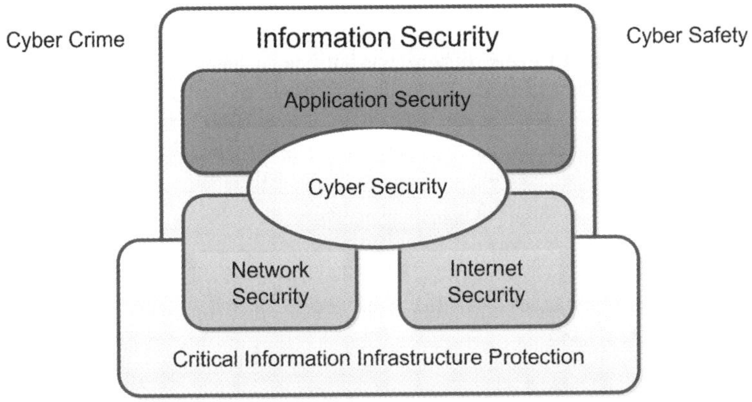

NOTES

1. See www.ons.gov.uk/ons/rel/crime-stats/crime-statistics/year-ending-june-2015/sty-fraud.html

2. See http://safeandsavvy.f-secure.com/2014/09/29/danger-of-public-wifi/

3. See https://fsecureconsumer.files.wordpress.com/2014/09/wi-fi-experiment_uk_2014.pdf

4. See www.telegraph.co.uk/technology/2016/02/10/vtech-says-it-is-not-responsible-for-security-after-hack-exposed/

2 THE BIG ISSUES

Cyber weapons provide the tantalising possibility of being able to cripple the enemy without inflicting lasting damage on them.

Philip Hammond MP, 2016

In this chapter, we will examine the key cyber security issues that concern us, both as individuals and organisations, regardless of the inherent threats, vulnerabilities or the actual impacts or consequences. These will be discussed in later chapters.

When you look at all the issues, they tend to resolve themselves into one of four areas of cyber security:

- cybercrime;
- cyber harassment or cyber bullying;
- cyber warfare;
- cyber surveillance.

CYBERCRIME

The first big issue we will examine is that of cybercrime. Many cybercrimes will also be recognisable as 'ordinary' crimes, but each of these will have a cyber element to it – either as a means, using cyber systems or networks to achieve an end, or where cyber systems or networks are both the means and the target.

Cybercrime can affect anybody, regardless of whether or not they are online. Once a criminal acquires your bank or credit card details, they can spend your money, even if you have never used a computer.

Financial theft

Financial theft is the most widespread type of cybercrime. Unlike a conventional bank robbery, where hard cash is stolen, this type of crime requires little or no risk to the thief – no guns, masks or getaway cars – and can deliver a significantly greater reward.

One downside of financial theft by cyber means is that there may well be an audit trail, indicating where the money came from and where it was transferred to. Cyber thieves have tried to address this weakness in their plan by money laundering,[1] and also by distancing themselves from the criminal act itself by using intermediaries.

Increasingly, cyber criminals are taking less interest in acquiring individual personal details in order to commit the crime – not that we should be complacent about this – but are looking to acquire details of thousands or millions of individuals' personal details so that they can maximise their return on investment, since each item of information will have a value.

They may often achieve this by selling the data to larger criminal gangs whose resources make them better placed to make use of the information in wide spam campaigns such as those that purport to sell high-end watches and mobile phones.

Alternatively, criminal gangs are targeting specific groups of individuals by advertising on legitimate websites non-existent vehicles for sale. After agreeing to purchase the vehicle via email with the fraudsters, buyers then receive an email purporting to be from an organisation such as Amazon stating that their money will be held in an escrow account, and that once the buyer has confirmed that they agree with the arrangement, the money will be released to the seller, therefore offering 'buyer protection'. In reality of course, once the money has been transferred by the buyer into the 'escrow account', the transaction ends with no vehicle in sight.

Website defacement

The term 'hacker' originally referred to someone who was inquisitive about how things worked, took them apart to understand them and put them back together again in a way that made them work better.

A later definition of a hacker was someone who wrote software that would perform a useful action in an elegant manner. When computer memory was an incredibly expensive commodity,[2] a piece of code that was reduced to run in a very small memory space was considered to be 'a great hack'.

Some of the greatest inventions have come through this benign activity, but sadly the term 'hacking' has been altered by the media to become something rather uglier in recent times, referring to those who have less honourable intentions and break into other people's computers for fun, revenge or to make a statement of some form – often on political, ethical or environmental matters, and some hackers will simply deface a website (usually its 'landing' page) in order to make their point.

Planting the flag

Some hackers will simply break into a system 'because it's there', and 'because they can'. There is little merit in this, other than to demonstrate to their peers how clever they are and how poor the target's security is. This intrusion, sometimes called 'planting the flag', is to show they have been successful, and will (they hope) gain them the admiration of their peers.

On occasion, this form of hacking is relatively benign, and can result in defacement of website pages. Hackers of this type are often so-called 'script kiddies', who take advantage of software and techniques they have discovered in the darker areas of the world-wide web, and although they may mean no real harm, serious damage can easily result since their knowledge and ability to use the software and tools may be very limited.

However, script kiddies can graduate into fully blown cyber criminals if they are encouraged and able to develop their skills, and this can cause a great deal of damage.

Many organisations affected by this type of hacking accept they have been less than careful about their cyber security and respond by tightening their security practices, whilst others may press for arrest, prosecution and even deportation, as in the case of George McKinnon, who was accused of hacking into almost 100 NASA and US military computers over a 13-month period in 2001 and 2002.[3]

Exploitation

Exploitation takes intrusion to another level entirely. A hacker who exploits a system they have penetrated may well exfiltrate, delete or corrupt information, and the impact of this can be extremely serious, not only for the target organisation, but potentially for its customers and system users.

In 2013, the American chain store Target was hacked and the personal details, including credit card details, of 40 million customers were stolen.[4] The hackers almost certainly gained access by using the stolen credentials of a maintenance supplier before planting the malware in the cashiers' terminals. Their technical security measures (intrusion detection software) spotted the attack, but failure to follow processes and procedures resulted in nothing being done to prevent the information from being stolen. The cyber-attackers were to blame for the original crime, but the company was equally culpable for failing to act and protect its customers' data.

Denial of service (DoS) and distributed denial of service (DDoS)

Although they can be used for other purposes, denial of service (DoS) attacks are usually mounted in order to prevent legitimate users from accessing an organisation's website. The reasons for this will vary – some will be used as a weapon of blackmail (pay us money and we'll stop); some will be due to political or other activism (usually known as hacktivism), and will simply be to cause financial loss and/or public embarrassment; whilst others will be in revenge for some action, real or perceived.

Some DoS attacks are designed to crash a website by overloading it to a point at which it can no longer function at all, whereas others will simply block legitimate access, leaving the supporting applications unable to receive and process requests for service. Either way, the end result is that response from the website will slow dramatically, and will usually stop completely.

DoS attacks can also target an organisation's email service, for example by a disgruntled employee, causing the Exchange server to overload and stop handling valid email traffic.

Nowadays, the most seen kinds of DoS attack are the distributed (DDoS) attacks, in which multiple computers work together to overload the target website. Attackers frequently use botnets (discussed in Chapter 5) in order to assemble sufficient capability, since very few stand-alone systems are capable of successful attacks against very large websites.

A recent example of a successful DDoS attack was on 31 December 2015,[5] when a hacking group calling themselves New World Hacking claimed responsibility for attacking the BBC's website, causing problems for other services such as its iPlayer video service. The group claimed that they were only testing their capability.

Copyright violation and intellectual property (IP) theft

Copyright violation is a major industry, but often brings little direct reward, other than 'free' goods for the recipient. Infringement of copyright can include music, films, books, photographs and computer software.

Whilst the copyright holder normally still retains ownership of the material, illegal copies are made and the owner therefore is deprived of the benefit they may have earned from it.

Copyrighted material is often distributed using file sharing websites, such as The Pirate Bay, using so-called 'torrent' files that link users back to the particular file or files to be downloaded. As more users join the sharing process, the downloaded material becomes shared between them and distribution is on a peer-to-peer basis.

This also makes it impossible to identify the individual who originally hosted the material, since many copies will have been made in a very short space of time.

Whilst exchanging files by torrent is not illegal, the content may well be, especially if it is someone else's copyright and they have not agreed to its being shared in this way. Losses to various industries are estimated to be in excess of US $50 billion per annum.

Various organisations exist to protect copyright[6] – these include:

- the Copyright Licensing Agency;
- the UK Copyright Service;
- the Performing Rights Society;
- the British Association of Picture Libraries and Agencies;
- the Intellectual Property Office;
- the Motion Picture Licensing Corporation;
- the Design and Artists Copyright Society;
- the Federation Against Software Theft.

Whilst the theft of intellectual property is similar in many respects, its subsequent sale or distribution is usually not. Whereas copyright violation generally allows a wide audience to benefit from free software, music or video material for example, IP theft is more generally carried out to order for one or a few select customers, and rarely becomes more widely distributed. In the past, this would have commonly been referred to as 'industrial espionage'.

The consequential financial loss to the owner, however, can be significantly greater, especially in cases where, for example, a pharmaceutical company has developed a ground-breaking drug, only to lose its formula to a competitor who can then sell it with merely the production, packaging, marketing and distribution costs.

Use of dark patterns[7]

The use of so-called dark patterns, whilst not actually a crime, does tend to come very close to the line between fairness and dishonesty.

Occasionally when you access an internet website you will find that because the text on web pages was unclear, you have agreed to download software or accepted an offer when you did not intend to do so. Sometimes, web page designers deliberately place selection boxes in unusual places or make the choices complex so that you are driven to making their choice rather than yours.

Entire businesses exist that use psychological analysis to identify the shapes, sizes and colours of buttons, click boxes and text that a user is most likely to click on – and those that they are least likely to – when accessing a web page. The results are sold to organisations developing new websites or upgrading existing ones with the intention of encouraging users to select the organisation's choice rather than making their own.

In extreme cases, items you did not request might be added to your online shopping basket, and if you aren't sufficiently aware, you may inadvertently purchase something you simply don't want as well as the items that you do.

This process of making web pages confusing is referred to as dark patterning, and the techniques are extremely subtle, relying on known aspects of human behaviour. For instance, if you are trying to book a flight, you may find that the airline or travel agency offers to sell you travel insurance, and that unless you deliberately opt out of the offer as opposed to opting in, you will discover that you have bought it and may have some difficulty in obtaining a refund.

There is nothing technically illegal about these dark patterns, but to many people's minds, they represent sharp practice. Pressure groups are now developing that try to combat this by setting out a code of conduct for web developers, but it is possible that only legislation will fully resolve the issue, since the sales and marketing policies of the offending organisations are likely to drive the practice for the foreseeable future, especially where it increases that organisation's revenue.

CYBER HARASSMENT OR CYBER BULLYING

Cyber harassment or bullying is simply the act of harassing or bullying a person or group of people using cyber-based methods such as social media, text messaging and the like. I have chosen to separate this from cybercrime, since some aspects of cyber bullying are not actually offences under either criminal or civil law, but which do represent a major issue in today's society. However, some jurisdictions have introduced legislation that extends the offences of conventional harassment to include cyber harassment as well. The difference between cyber harassment and cyber bullying is usually that with cyber harassment, anyone or any organisation can be the victim, whereas cyber bullying generally refers to children as being the victims.

Cyber harassment or bullying can begin in the same way as conventional harassment or bullying, where one person makes a negative comment about another, causing offence. The bully (who may well be a control freak) seizes upon this effect and continues to exploit it, often encouraging others to join in. The results can be devastating, and some people who have been persistently harassed or bullied have been driven to take their own lives. Cyber harassment or bullying is no less aggressive and dangerous, and it may take a number of forms.

Cyber harassment is intended to make the victim aware that something very specific might happen to them. The person making the threats might be known to the victim, or they may be unknown, and targets can be widened to include organisations that the person making the threats feels have caused them or someone else some injustice.

Cyber stalking

As with conventional stalkers, cyber stalkers operate in two slightly different ways. First, they can follow the movements and activities of their victim by stealth, and not alert them to the fact that someone is following them. Second, they can still follow the movements and activities of their victim, but this time rather more openly, with the victim being aware they are being stalked, but usually without knowing the identity of the stalker.

Sometimes the victim will be a person known to the stalker – a relative, former partner or neighbour; but on other occasions the victim will be completely unknown to the stalker – perhaps a celebrity, the chief executive officer (CEO) of an organisation or a politician. Whoever is the target of cyber stalking, its main objective is usually to cause distress, and it is frequently successful.

Cyber stalking is sometimes concerned with intimidation of the victim by letting them know that the stalker is watching them, but that is normally where it stops.

Cyber trolling

The activity of cyber trolling is a form of verbal abuse designed to intimidate or offend the victim in some way. Cyber trolls make confrontational or abusive statements online and differ from cyber stalkers in that cyber trolls rarely make much effort to hide their identity. Cyber trolling also differs from cyber bullying or harassment in that it is carried out quite openly, possibly in the hope that others will support the cyber troll's point of view, designed to cause distress to the victim.

Cyber trolling also differs from free and intelligent discussion, since it neither provides nor invites a rational interchange of views, and focuses purely on the cyber troll's negative and usually strongly expressed and frequently irrational opinions.

Cyber trolls will often use social media or online discussion forums to post inflammatory comments, designed to provoke a reaction or response from the victim, which will invariably seed the troll with further opportunities for posting comments, and this can easily escalate into a full-blown online fight.

Current wisdom suggests that ignoring comments posted by cyber trolls is by far the best way of dealing with them, since their activities will soon peter out if there is no reaction, response or exchange. Alternatively, on many discussion forums, offensive users can be blocked so that victims of trolling no longer see their comments. Cyber trolls can also be reported to the forum administrator and may have their accounts deleted as a result.

CYBER WARFARE

The term cyber warfare describes the process by which one nation state or politically motivated group conducts an attack against some aspect of another – possibly its critical infrastructure (CI), its government's political process or indeed the offensive or defensive capability of its armed forces.

Until recently, warfare was a relatively straightforward affair. One nation state picked a fight with another nation state, and their two sets of armed forces attacked each other with gusto until one nation state capitulated and the war was over. This was only ever really complicated when more nation states joined in on either side, but the net result was usually the same. This kind of warfare is often referred to as symmetric warfare, since both 'sides' are usually evenly matched.

With the rise of terrorism however, the boundaries became less clear. A militant group could declare war on many nations – frequently being quite indiscriminating about whether some of those nations supported the same religious or ideological concepts. Since terrorist groups rarely have the same purchasing power as nation states, the weapons they use are often home-made – improvised explosive devices (IEDs) for example – but since they can be used in unconventional ways – not in a straight battle – they tend to be deployed as roadside devices, or detonated by suicide bombers.

This kind of warfare is termed asymmetric warfare, since one side may be extremely small in numbers in comparison to their opposition, but can still deliver devastating results.

However, a cyber-attack or cyber incursion by one nation state against another does not technically mean that they are actually at war, and the attack could simply be seen as an act of aggression as opposed to a full declaration of hostilities.

Cyber warfare adopts both symmetric and asymmetric methods, since it can be used by one nation state against another, or by small groups – even by individuals – against a significantly larger adversary. Cyber warfare can be conducted just as easily from an armchair, a stool in a cyber café or an office chair in a government building, and carries few of the dangers of conventional warfare, unless the other side can locate the attacker and direct a drone to deliver lethal ordnance.

If they work for the government or military, or are a highly skilled and experienced individual, once a 'cyber warrior' has completed their daily or nightly shift, they can walk home safe in the knowledge that they are unlikely to be shot at, despite possibly having caused their adversary significant cyber havoc.

Espionage

Espionage is the capability to obtain secret information without either the permission or the knowledge of its owner. Governments routinely spy on one another. They have done so for centuries and will doubtless continue to do so for many more. Sometimes, the espionage is concerned with finding out what another government has – for example, its nuclear missile capability – whilst at other times it is concerned with another government's intentions, which may be more difficult to discover, but which might be deduced, given sufficient data.

Cyber espionage is no different, but whereas conventional espionage involves agents who place themselves in some danger by operating in enemy territory, cyber espionage can be safely conducted from a comfortable office with no risk whatsoever to the agent.

If a field agent is captured and exposed as a spy from another nation state, the diplomatic repercussions can last for months or years, but because the cyber espionage departments of nation states take great care to conceal their identities, and frequently disguise the attack as originating from somewhere else, it is difficult, if not impossible, to prove absolutely who carried out an attack, and assumptions, even if correct, do not constitute sufficient evidence.

Surveillance

Surveillance is slightly different from espionage – perhaps not in the way it is carried out, but in its aims and objectives. Surveillance focuses on keeping track of people's activities, communications and contacts, and in cyber warfare terms, could be described as being more akin to investigations into terrorism.

This is where there is a particular crossover in the techniques used by security agencies and the military, since both need to co-operate in order to track down suspected terrorists.

Surveillance has played a key role in identifying and locating individuals and groups who have clear intentions to carry out acts of terrorism, and although the details remain secret, the government has made it clear that a number of potentially lethal attacks have been prevented by careful surveillance, and they are using this argument to make the case for legislation that makes it less demanding for the security services to be able to monitor the activities of the population – that unsteady balance between security and privacy we mentioned earlier.

Non-military surveillance is also discussed in greater detail in the section on cyber surveillance later in this chapter.

Infiltration

Although governments and security services do not publicly discuss this area of cyber warfare, one of the best (but risky) methods of conventional surveillance has been through infiltration of activist groups, allowing agents to identify possible targets and the leaders of these groups.

Cyber infiltration is no different in terms of its objectives, and agents must be able to infiltrate online groups just as easily, and because of their physical separation from the rest of the group they are much less at risk if their activities are identified and there is the possibility of their being 'outed'.

Sabotage

When we consider sabotage, we often think of war films in which a small group of saboteurs destroy something the enemy holds dear. Usually one or more meet a grisly end or are captured and interrogated, but usually the film ends with success.

Cyber sabotage is again much less risky for its teams of saboteurs. Operating remotely, they will identify and surveil their target from afar, and by one of the methods of attack we have already described, will carefully position their weapon, which will then wreck the enemy's infrastructure.

By far the best example of this is the Stuxnet attack on the Iranian nuclear research programme. It was believed to have been conducted by a joint US–Israeli team,[8] who developed software that would identify a very specific laboratory – Natanz in Iran – which used Siemens SCADA[9] systems to control the centrifuges. The malware they were able to deploy caused the control system to repeatedly speed up then slow down the rotation of the centrifuges, whilst hiding the fact from the monitoring systems, resulting in destruction of the machinery.

Whilst it was not 100 per cent successful, the action did at least temporarily slow down Iran's nuclear programme.

It has also been shown to be possible to commit sabotage on elements of critical infrastructure. The Idaho National Laboratory in the USA ran a test in 2007 in which it repeatedly opened and closed the circuit breakers connecting a 50 MW generator to the grid out of synchronisation, causing the generator to shake itself to pieces.[10] On a larger scale, the impact on a major power station generating hundreds of megawatts of power could seriously impact the country's economy.

Psychological cyber warfare

Psychological cyber warfare differs only from cyber harassment or bullying in one key aspect – that of scale. Whereas cyber bullies are generally individuals or small groups, psychological cyber warfare is conducted by much larger groups, for example terrorist organisations, and by nation states.

Psychological cyber warfare generally has one of two main objectives. First, it is used by one organisation or government to demoralise the population of another country, with the ultimate objective of them withholding their support for the current regime.

During World War II, both the Allies and the Axis forces used psychological warfare radio broadcasts in attempts to cause antagonism towards the opposing governments. In this respect, psychological cyber warfare simply takes the medium from broadcast radio to the internet.

The alternative objective is subjugation and repression of the population by its government – often an oppressive regime – which can use cyber techniques to deter the population from standing up to it and to spread the fear of the possible penalties for doing so.

By not only using the internet as a weapon in this way, such regimes frequently also control how the population can use the internet by preventing access to websites that do not support the regime, or that actively oppose it.

Negative news stories in the foreign press about a regime can be suppressed, and glowing accounts of its leadership and their achievements can be substituted – all whilst the population lacks the basic amenities that less repressed societies enjoy.

Deception

Declarations of war are very public. When one nation state actively and openly declares war on another, the event is fairly obvious; the outcome can be witnessed by everybody; the participants are easily identified; and an open attack by one nation state against another may be the trigger for war to be declared. However, in asymmetric warfare, the question of 'sides' is less easy to visualise, and many nation states may be targets, whilst a few individuals may be waging their war.

Does then a cyber-attack by one nation state against another nation state or its infrastructure qualify as an act of war? It is often very difficult to establish and prove exactly which nation state or which terrorist group has initiated the attack, and although it may appear obvious on the surface, things are not always as they seem.

One nation state may obscure the origin of a cyber-attack against another by planting 'evidence' in the attack vector that would lead one to infer its origin, but who is to say that it is not the work of yet another nation state that wishes to take advantage of a possible breakdown in diplomatic relations?

Whatever the reason, establishing the source of an attack will always remain an extremely difficult challenge, and for that reason, the term 'cyber war' is perhaps somewhat misused.

CYBER SURVEILLANCE

Whether or not we are conscious of the fact, we are continually under surveillance. There are two quite distinct types of cyber surveillance. The first that readily springs to mind is that of intrusive or invasive snooping, which particularly since the Snowden revelations[11] is usually associated with surveillance by the security services. The second, which on the surface is much less intrusive, is the collection and use of data about us by organisations with whom we interact on a daily basis.

Targeted surveillance

This will usually be because the subject has come to the attention of the authorities, who are taking an active interest in his or her activities. Such people are normally (but not always) criminals or terrorists, and we are content to know that the appropriate police or security services are giving them their full attention.

However, if we gain the impression that we are being snooped upon we tend to take a rather different view, and it is in this that we are conscious of the problem that the police and security services constantly experience when they do not have a definite target – they have to collect far more data than they need and then (in theory) throw away the data that is not relevant and which they don't need to retain.

Because the cost of storage media is continuing to fall rapidly, data collection and storage is costing less as time goes on, and therefore organisations will collect and store as much as they can and keep it until they can understand how best it can be used.

Catch-all surveillance

In the aftermath of the Snowden leaks, we hear that the security services on both sides of the Atlantic are monitoring telephone calls, emails, internet searches and transactions without necessarily having the legal right to do so, and this gives us serious cause for concern, since we have absolutely no control over this.

The National Security Agency (NSA) has its own interpretation of the word 'collect'. We might think of this as simply involving monitoring, interception and storage of data, but the NSA considers that it also includes analysis of data.

It is also worth noting that the USA does not currently have any data protection legislation, which means that should your personally identifiable information be hosted there (for example on Facebook) you have no control whatsoever over it.

Alarmed by the recent spate of requests by the American security services for operators to hand over personal correspondence, and following the unsuccessful attempt by the FBI to force Apple to weaken the security settings of an iPhone, in April 2016 the authors of WhatsApp introduced end-to-end encryption[12] of users' messages so that they can only be decrypted by the recipient.

However, in January 2017, it came to light that the WhatsApp service may not be as secure as claimed, since the company has the ability to reset the encryption key, and in certain circumstances, attackers can pose as the recipient of a message and force WhatsApp to reissue keys. Sophisticated manipulation of this system would let attackers intercept and read messages, and unless the sender has selected the 'Show Security Notifications' option, they might never know that a new key had been generated.

However, Apple refused to comply with the FBI's request,[13] and the FBI later withdrew it, claiming that they had been able to successfully break the security of the iPhone in question, possibly with the assistance of the Israeli security company Cellebrite.

We shall deal with the state aspects of surveillance later, but for now, let us consider the theoretically more benign aspect of surveillance undertaken by organisations with whom we interact on a day-to-day basis making use of the data they collect when that interaction takes place. For example, whenever we make an internet search, along with our anticipated search results, the search engine will deliver advertising material that matches either our current or previous searches in order to help us make informed decisions. Well, that's their story anyway!

In practice, of course, the operators of the search engines are not completely altruistic. They earn revenue from advertisers and the more often they can place an advert in front of the potential customer, regardless of whether or not it is actually read, the more revenue they are likely to earn.

It's all about someone else making money on information that they acquire (legally or otherwise) about you or your preferences, and usually without your knowledge or active consent.[15]

Internet search

When you search for something on the internet, how much personal information are you giving away freely? Probably more than you think. Let's just take Amazon as an example. They keep an accurate record of everything you've bought from them, so that if you need the same thing again, with a couple of clicks you can order more and not have to try and remember who supplied it.

They also keep a record of every item you've searched for in the recent past, so in spite of the fact that you're trying to locate a mint vinyl copy of Dark Side of the Moon, you will still see 'recommendations' below your search results for the camera lens you looked at last week, a book you thought about buying a month ago and a DVD similar to the one you bought for your partner at Christmas.

They know what interests you and they want to sell you more. They know how often you actually buy compared with simply browsing; they know that if you look at an item more than a number of times, you will probably buy it; they know how you like to pay; and they know whether you will save up items so that you get free delivery. What don't they know?

When you use an internet search engine, your search request is stored. The links that you subsequently click on are stored. The search engine stores details of every website you search on regularly and automatically makes it a 'favourite'.

In December 2016, the UK's Investigatory Powers Act obtained Royal Assent and became law. One of its more controversial aspects is that the records of any website and mes-saging service visited by UK-based citizens from any device must now be retained by the communications company providing the service.

It has been reported that a total of 48 government departments[15] will be able to view this data, and whilst many, including the police and security agencies, would appear to have a legitimate need to do so, it is difficult to imagine why the Foods Standards Agency might.

Apart from the increased invasion of privacy that this introduces, one of the chief concerns, voiced by the chairman of the Internet Service Providers' Association,[16] is that 'it only takes one bad actor to go in there and get the entire database'.

Cookies

It's not only search that leaves a digital trail – whenever you visit a website, it can leave a small file on your computer known as a 'cookie'. Many cookies are essential to being able to use the website – for example, when you are shopping online, the store needs to be able to link your shopping basket with your computer so that you buy what you actually want. Other cookies are less helpful to you, and may record which pages you have opened, which flights you've examined or which camera you've investigated.

These may not seem to be particularly awful things, but when you next visit the website selling airline tickets, it may just use the fact that you've been there before to hike the ticket price or advise you that the cheaper flight is full and that you must choose another more expensive one. This form of surveillance – and subsequent manipulation – is very subtle, and we are not usually aware of it.

Other cookies record these things so that advertisers can place their adverts in prominent parts of the screen. If you use one of the main search engines or shopping websites and subsequently examine a particular type of camera, when you revisit the site you will almost certainly see an offer from one of the photographic suppliers for that very camera. Again, this is relatively benign in its own right, but remember that the search engine or website may well have recorded every single item you've looked for. This kind of information enables advertisers to build a very accurate profile of you as an individual, and (in theory) to deliver highly relevant advertising to you. In practice of course, the advertiser will be advertising what they want to sell you, not necessarily what you might want to buy.

In 2011, an EU directive required owners of websites to obtain consent from users before placing cookies on their computer. However, although this seems at first like a great idea, there are two fundamental flaws.

Most websites do not allow you to say 'No' to cookies. They frequently allow you to click on 'I understand' or something similar, click on 'Tell me more', or simply ignore the message.

Many websites operate a system of 'implied consent', which means that if you ignore the cookie message described above and continue to use the website, you have implicitly given your permission for the placement of cookies.

Both of these failings are morally reprehensible.

Email

When you send or receive an email, a copy is stored by default on your provider's server in case you ever need to find it again. You can disable this, but how many of us actually take the trouble to do so?

Analysis of emails, whether these are obtained by interception or by access to an ISP's servers, can provide a surveillance organisation with a wealth of information, since there may well be a complete archive of all emails in the 'conversation', and every email sent and received will contain details of the sender and recipients.

Email can be just as pernicious as website cookies. Unless you delete every copy of every email you have sent or received, including those that you have forwarded to other people, the message will still exist in some form somewhere, and emails can also reveal many facts about you, just as web searches can.

Unless you encrypt all your emails containing personal information (again, how many people actually do this?) they can be read just like a postcard, copied, printed, forwarded to others and used in evidence against you if they contain either something derogatory you have said or that implicates you in a crime.

Email can be an extremely powerful tool in the cyber surveillance world, since not only can the content provide valuable information to the security services and law enforcement agencies, but also the 'to' and 'from' fields in an email can yield additional targets for surveillance.

Far from being a blessing, email can be a curse, and many of us will look at our inboxes and wonder how and why we have accumulated so much junk. This is similar to keeping all the letters, postcards, advertising material and free newspapers we receive in the post: we would drown in a sea of paper!

Email can also attract cyber-attacks through the receipt of spam, and this is perhaps the worst aspect of this so-called 'modern miracle'.

Smartphones

Many people now have moved away from the conventional mobile phone. All it can do is make and receive calls and text messages. Along came the iPhone and changed all that. Now all the major mobile phone vendors have jumped on the smartphone bandwagon, and the amount of data they can collect from you is absolutely staggering.

The term 'smartphone' is probably a misnomer. The device is actually a very small computer that runs applications, take photographs and just happens to make and receive calls and text messages as well, so in those terms, it is not too different from your laptop – just much smaller and often no less powerful.

Unless you have switched your phone off, your network operator always knows roughly where you are so that it can route calls and text messages to you. Unless you have ventured into the security settings on your smartphone, you will probably be recording your GPS coordinates and this will pinpoint your position to within a metre or two.

Every application on the smartphone that makes use of your location is now able to track your movements. This will be absolutely fine if you're using a mapping application, but are you as happy to have your location sent back when you're playing a game or reading a book? Of course, the application developer is not particularly interested in where you are, but they might be selling your location along with thousands of others to a third party.

Have you taken a photograph on your smartphone? The location was recorded in the photograph's metadata, known as the exif data. When you upload that photograph to the internet, that exif data became available as well. The exif data will also contain details on when the photograph was taken and probably also the serial numbers of the camera and lens you used!

Facial recognition

Facial recognition permits the identification of individuals either live from a modern camera or smartphone, or from a previously taken photograph. The image is compared with those held in a central database, and sophisticated algorithms are used to match features such as the eyes, the mouth, the shape of the head and so on. Once a match has been made in this way, additional information about the individual may be acquired, either from the same database, or from a wider search of the internet.

The police and security services must make considerable use of this in tracking down and monitoring suspected criminals and terrorists, but as individuals, we must face the fact (no pun intended) that if someone's photograph is posted on the internet, they can be identified and possibly traced regardless of whether or not they have committed a crime.

However, if facial recognition is used as a means of authentication, it could be possible to falsify the matching process by wearing a mask, so this should not be used in isolation.

Consider, for example, someone who was photographed whilst taking part in a peaceful demonstration in a country where the government exercises total control over its population. The demonstrator might subsequently receive a visit from the secret police and vanish forever.

Terms and conditions

Terms and conditions are potentially a major issue as we discussed earlier in this book. Few of us even glance at them. Due to their general length and complex 'legalese' wording, hardly anyone will have read any of them from start to finish, and will have simply clicked on the 'Accept' button, potentially committing themselves to signing away any control they might have had over their personal information. Of course, the software vendors give us no choice – there is no negotiation involved, and if we want the software, we have to revoke all rights we may have had.

Additionally, and possibly more worryingly, is that by signing away our rights by accepting the terms and conditions, we may leave ourselves open to some form of surveillance, such as providing our location when using a smartphone.

When you first use an application on your smartphone or tablet computer, you will have had to accept the terms of use, which invariably will include that the application author's organisation can store, use and sell on the details of what you have done. Not only that, because many of us don't turn off the GPS facility in our smartphones, the application can contain the ability to track your location and report it back to the provider – sometimes even when you are not actually using it.

Even if you do read the terms and conditions when you initially load an application or purchase goods in the internet, the seller may at some stage update them (their ability to do this without telling you may be enshrined in the original terms and conditions), so you may never know that they have changed. If the supplier does inform you there has been a change, the privacy bar may have been lowered, but will you read them this time?

Store loyalty schemes

Are you enrolled in a store loyalty scheme? Many of us are, and this allows the store to record the fine details of everything we buy there, how much we have paid for it, where and when. Store loyalty schemes are a wonderful invention. The deals the store subsequently offer us usually represent good value for money, and often helps the store to dispose of goods it might not otherwise be able to sell. We might be able to enjoy a discount on some products; a free coffee and cake on our next visit; an invitation to the 'special' pre-Christmas shopping event; or jump the queue when a new product is announced. Some stores now produce a smartphone application that gives you access to their website, your account and many other things.

Do you collect Nectar points or Avios? Think of the volume of data they can collect based on your spending habits.

Have you ever received an email out of the blue from a company you have never dealt with online and wondered how you came to receive it? It is highly likely that when you signed up for a loyalty scheme, you failed to tick one of the opt-out boxes on the form – or was it an opt-in box? Many companies use dark pattern methods to trick you into making the wrong choice when completing such a form, and since you didn't actually read the terms and conditions, you find that you have agreed to the store selling your contact details to a third party. Of course, you can try and change this, but often it is either too much trouble or the means of doing so are too difficult to find on the company's website, so you just put up with it.

Is this a cyber security issue? Definitely, since now a third party has all your details as well as the store that offered you the loyalty scheme, and when the third party's network is hacked, those details could go anywhere.

Credit cards

What about credit and debit cards? In the UK, billions of pounds are spent annually using credit and debit cards rather than cheques or cash, and much of this spend is online. The UK Card Association reported that in 2015, £210 billion was spent online, representing 32 per cent of total card spending, and of that, approximately 51 per cent of all online transactions were completed via a mobile device.[17] They allow us to make spontaneous purchases when we might not have sufficient funds in our bank account; as long as we pay off the outstanding balance each month on our credit cards there is no financial charge; and they even act as protection if something goes wrong when we make some purchases.

The same applies to newer forms of payment. mPay, ApplePay, AndroidPay and travel money cards such as Caxton all represent benefit to the provider as well as to the consumer, but with similar levels of risk.

Combine a credit or debit card with a loyalty scheme and things begin to look very rosy indeed for the provider. Combine them yet again with their smartphone application you downloaded that tracks your movements and you could find that the next time you are shopping you receive a text message as you pass a particular supermarket aisle that offers you extra discount. Possible? Absolutely.

Combine them further where retailers provide the SIM card for your mobile phone (and therefore know your regular contacts and movements), and where you accepted the terms and conditions, you may have agreed to allow the retailer to include the fact that their banking service is aware of all your current account financial transactions.

Travel cards

Do you travel in a major city like London? If you do, you will probably use an Oyster card or something similar. You load the card with money and use it whenever you need to – on the Underground, the buses, the river and even on some over-ground train services.

Again, the card provider knows exactly when you have travelled, your route, how long it took (except on buses, where you only use the card when you board and not when you leave) and where, how and how often you top up the card.

All this is seemingly quite harmless, since we benefit from much of the technology and services, but to go back to one of the original points of this section – if the security services wanted to build up a profile of you, it would be extremely easy to pull together the credit/debit card, store card, travel card, email messages, internet searches and combine them with closed-circuit television (CCTV) images.

Data aggregation and analytics

We have mentioned data aggregation in an earlier chapter, but now we have had an opportunity to examine some of the types of data that organisations hold on us, and over which we have absolutely no control, we can see that a data aggregator could build up a very detailed picture of our daily lives.

They would know where we lived; where we work, and possibly the kind of work we do; who our partners and friends are; when and where we shop; what and where we eat and drink; where we go on holiday; what music and films we like; what newspapers and magazines we read; what television shows we watch; what kind of car we drive and where we go in it; and what our hobbies are. In short, there's very little about our private lives that is actually private any more.

Home entertainment systems

In recent years, home entertainment systems have become increasingly sophisticated. Televisions are able to connect to the internet, not only to allow the downloading of viewing material, but also to provide the manufacturers with statistics relating to viewing habits. In theory, this form of remote monitoring should only be carried out with the viewer's express permission, but there have been cases in which manufacturers have uploaded viewing information without the viewer being aware of it.

In March 2017, following a Wikileaks publication, it was reported that the CIA was using software developed in-house to remotely enable the microphone on certain televisions, even when the viewer believed that the set was switched off. The report stated that the programme 'Weeping Angel' also allowed audio to be recorded whilst the set was in standby mode, the recording being uploaded once the set was switched back on again.

Whilst this form of information gathering may be less common than others, it is considerably more intrusive, and suggests that George Orwell's *1984* has come a step nearer.

WHY WE SHOULD CARE

From a personal point of view, we should always be concerned that our personal information is being stored and used in a proper manner. When our credit card provider calls us to query a transaction that appears to fall outside our normal spending profile, we are delighted that they have taken the time to do so in order to protect us.

Proactively therefore, we should take greater care over the information we give out to others – information that can be abused or misused for their gain and our loss; and reactively, if we detect abuse or misuse of our information or credentials, we should take immediate steps such as changing passwords and notifying financial institutions.

From a business perspective, there are four key reasons why we should take notice of cyber incidents, plan to defend ourselves and our organisations against cyber-attacks, and be prepared to respond to them if they occur.

- It is nothing less than good practice to manage risk, and that includes the risks of cyber-attacks, whether these are accidental or deliberate; whether as individuals or businesses. Indeed, there are fiduciary responsibilities for corporates (and board members) to do this.

- Customers have a right to expect organisations to safeguard their information when they provide it to them for whatever reason, and they need to trust that they will not misuse it – in other words, robust adherence to data protection legislation. When the General Data Protection Regulation (GDPR) (described in greater detail in Appendix C) comes into force in 2018, these expectations will be considerably extended.

- In highly regulated sectors, organisations may need to be able to demonstrate compliance with national or EU law; international standards, such as ISO/ International Electrotechnical Commission (IEC) 27001, and sector standards, such as the Payment Card Industry Data Security Standard (PCIDSS),[18] the US Health Insurance Portability and Accountability Act (HIPAA),[19] and the Sarbanes–Oxley Act.[20]

- Organisations should be able to demonstrate good security practice as a means of achieving competitive advantage. Some larger organisations may make use of the ISO/IEC 27001 certification as a means of demonstrating this, whilst smaller organisations that use small-to-medium enterprises (SMEs) may adopt the Cyber Essentials and/or Cyber Essentials Plus schemes,[21] promoted by the UK government.

Under an EU ruling, C131-12,[22] we now have the right to be forgotten should we choose to have information about us removed from websites, especially if we feel that it is no longer relevant. This is also enshrined in the forthcoming GDPR legislation, which the UK government has stated will be enacted regardless of Britain's exit from the EU.

We keep our memories in digital form now rather than exclusively on paper. Letters, postcards and photographs are all just another group of files on our computer, and when we compare information about us to footprints in the sand or the vapour trail of an aircraft, the digital footprint we constantly generate remains, possibly forever, whilst physical footprints are washed away by the tide and vapour trails evaporate.

In 2014, a group founded by Max Schrems, an Austrian privacy activist, launched a case in the Irish High Court, claiming that Facebook had handed personally identifiable information to the NSA, and this had placed the company in breach of EU data protection law, since its European headquarters are in Ireland, and the data was supposedly protected by the 'Safe Harbor' agreement.

Although the case is pending appeal at the time of writing, it effectively rendered the Safe Harbor agreement worthless (the European Court of Justice ruled it to be invalid in 2015), and efforts to replace it with the EU-US Privacy Shield Agreement have so far been unsuccessful. In April 2016, the European Data Protection Supervisor rejected the proposals stating that 'as it stands it is not robust enough to withstand future legal scrutiny'. Time alone will tell whether our personally identifiable information is safe from the likes of the NSA or Government Communications Headquarters (GCHQ). You can draw your own conclusions.

WHAT MAKES CYBER SECURITY DIFFICULT?

Unfortunately, life is not as simple as we would like it to be, and there are a number of inhibitors or barriers to our achieving our expectations about privacy and security, especially for individuals, smaller organisations or SMEs.

Cyber security knowledge and skills

- Cyber security is often seen as a highly specialised subject, and many individuals and smaller organisations believe that they do not possess the necessary knowledge or skills to understand or undertake the necessary work to protect themselves from cyber-attack. This is not necessarily the case, as we shall see in Chapter 8.

- Organisations of all sizes frequently do not possess the people resources they can allocate to this kind of work.

- The organisation's senior management team may not fully understand the need for good cyber security, and how it might be beneficial to their business, and also generally do not understand that the data and thus the information held by the organisation belongs to them and not the IT department.

- When we examine the standards produced in the cyber security field, it appears that many of them are geared more towards larger organisations and multinationals. However, the Cyber Essentials scheme does address this for smaller organisations.

- Many SMEs outsource their IT and in many cases the outsourced companies themselves are also SMEs and often lack good cyber security skills.

Cyber security capabilities

- If an organisation is able to allocate resources to internal IT work, it is often assumed that those members of staff will also take on the responsibility for cyber security. This is a major mistake, since it may conflict with one of the main principles of cyber security – that of the segregation of duties.

- The organisation must define the cyber security requirement, because it owns the data, information and the strategic direction. The IT function must use good security practice to turn the requirement into technical policies. The human resources (HR) function must then, in consultation with the IT function and the business function, develop staff training and education to support the requirement.

- In cases where the IT function is outsourced, there is a tendency to overlook or underplay the need for good cyber security in the outsourced contract, since those undertaking the negotiation may not have sufficient understanding of the requirement, or they may remove it, since they see it as an unnecessary cost.

- When the security function is outsourced, it may very often have been a form of abrogation of responsibility rather than of delegation. The principle that must be applied is that whilst organisations can outsource the information security implementation and management, they cannot outsource the responsibility for ownership.

- There will be additional financial burdens on the organisation in developing and implementing a cyber security framework that will be suitable to protect it, and obtaining capital or operational budget approval may prove a challenge.

- The ability to develop a sound cyber security strategy is somewhat dependent upon the organisation having a clear understanding of information security risk management, and in some cases, this will not be the case.

- Organisations can also consider their cyber security capabilities in terms of any of the Capability Maturity Models,[23] often used for software development, but which have many parallels in the cyber security environment.

Cyber security standards and implementation

As you will see in the appendix, there are literally dozens (if not hundreds) of standards in the information and cyber security domains. Some of these are largely generic, and apply to a wide range of security topics, whilst others are highly specific, being applicable to a single technology.

Unfortunately, many of the mandatory requirements of the existing standards are more relevant to larger organisations and therefore difficult for individuals and SMEs to use effectively.

There is also a danger, especially for larger organisations, to believe that gaining certification to ISO/IEC 27001 means that they are fully secure and that all they now have to do is to 'keep turning the handle'. This could not be further from the reality of the situation, since complacency is often the cause of both organisations and individuals missing a new threat or vulnerability, and being successfully attacked as a result.

- Although there are many excellent standards (mainly the US National Institute for Standards and Technology (NIST), BSI and ISO/IEC standards) in the cyber security field, few of them are easily adaptable to SMEs. This is where the UK government's Cyber Essentials scheme comes into its own.

- Implementation guidelines tend also to be more suited to larger organisations, and therefore SMEs will find it challenging to adapt them to their own situation.

- Many of the international standards carry the implication that organisations will have implemented some higher-level processes and procedures that many smaller organisations will not have been able to undertake.

- SMEs may not feel able to commit to the level of expenditure that might be required to achieve ISO/IEC 27001 accreditation.

Although these may appear insurmountable, in Chapters 8 and 9 of this book, we shall cover many of the recommendations that both individuals and SMEs can undertake without the need for extensive knowledge or skills, and without resorting to expensive work in interpreting and implementing the international standards.

NOTES

1. Transferring the proceeds of criminal activity through bank accounts in countries that have a more relaxed attitude to crime and are happy to turn a blind eye.

2. I recall my employer paying around £100,000 for a 128 kilobyte memory cabinet in the late 1970s. It took up the same space as a double wardrobe and consumed more than a kilowatt of power.

3. See www.bbc.co.uk/news/19959726

4. See www.bloomberg.com/news/articles/2014-03-13/target-missed-warnings-in-epic-hack-of-credit-card-data

5. See www.bbc.co.uk/news/technology-35213415

6. Links to each of these are provided in Appendix E on Standards and Good practice guidelines

7. For more information on dark patterns, please visit http://darkpatterns.org

8. See http://spectrum.ieee.org/telecom/security/the-real-story-of-stuxnet/

9. Supervisory Control And Data Acquisition

10. See www.securityfocus.com/brief/597

11. See https://www.theguardian.com/us-news/the-nsa-files

12. See https://www.whatsapp.com/security/

13. https://www.apple.com/customer-letter/

14. Just because you click 'Accept' on the Terms and Conditions it does not mean that you agree with them, but usually that you have no choice but to accept them if you wish to use the application or service.

15. See https://yiu.co.uk/blog/who-can-view-my-internet-history/

16. See www.bbc.co.uk/news/technology-38068078

17. See www.theukcardsassociation.org.uk/2015-facts-figures/internet_card_use_2015.asp

18. See www.theukcardsassociation.org.uk/security/what_is_PCI%20DSS.asp

19. See www.hhs.gov/hipaa/for-professionals/privacy/

20. See www.soxlaw.com/

21. See https://www.cyberaware.gov.uk/cyberessentials/

22. See http://ec.europa.eu/justice/data-protection/files/factsheets/factsheet_data_protection_en.pdf

23. See https://www.tutorialspoint.com/software_testing_dictionary/capability_maturity_model.htm

3   CYBER TARGETS

With any large network, persistence and focus will get you in.
Rob Joyce, Tailored Access Operations, NSA, USA, 2016

In this chapter, we shall examine the various potential targets of cyber-attacks. I have tried to separate the various types of organisations into the following categories since the motives for these attacks may vary:

- individuals;
- businesses;
- critical national infrastructure (CNI);
- buildings;
- academia and research;
- manufacturing and industry.

INDIVIDUAL TARGETS

Whether we like it or not, we are all potentially the target of cyber-attacks. In the case of individuals, attack is most likely to come from cyber criminals who may not target us directly, but they will certainly do so as part of a larger plan – for instance, acquiring credit card details of thousands of individuals that they can then sell on to other criminals who will target us more directly.

This means that our personal information and to a certain extent, we ourselves, have become a commodity – a product to be bought and sold.

There is little, if anything, we can do about the criminals' larger game plan, but we can take ownership of our individual part of the problem by securing our computers, smartphones, tablets and networks, being careful to whom we give personal information, avoiding scams and generally being more aware – just as we hold a bag close when walking through cities where pickpockets have a reputation for preying on tourists.

We will deal with that in Chapters 8 to 11, when we examine methods of improving our security.

BUSINESS TARGETS

Businesses are a major target for attackers, since there are rich rewards to be gained if attacks are successful. There are two slightly different situations:

- Where the actual target is not the business itself, but something the business has, such as a database of customers and their credit card details; something the business has developed, such as a new product or service; something the business is planning, such as the takeover of a rival organisation; or simply details of the organisation's financial position if they were the object of a possible takeover.

- Where the target is the business itself, and it is the intention of the attacker to cause immediate financial or reputational damage.

Businesses, both large and small, may be much better placed than individuals to understand cyber risks, but may often ignore them, thinking either that they're too small or uninteresting to attract an attacker, or believing that they have nothing that might be of value to one. This is potentially a major mistake, since attackers may not target a specific business, but might gain some benefit if an employee unwittingly provides them with a way in to the organisation's network.

A successful attack on a small maintenance company might for example allow an attacker to gain access to a larger organisation for which it is working and which is actually the attacker's real target. For example, it is believed that when the Stuxnet attacks took place against the Iranian nuclear research programme, the attack was conducted by delivering the malware to five of the research centre's strategic suppliers, at least one of whom then unknowingly took the malware into the centre, probably on a Universal Serial Bus (USB) memory stick. This illustrates that regardless of an organisation's security arrangements, malware can be introduced by a third party, and demonstrates the need to ensure that all software entering the organisation is verified.

Another example of a situation in which a business might be attacked is if the attacker perceives that the organisation had committed some offence or injustice and needs to be publicly exposed or rebuked. The media are occasionally complicit in this kind of activity, since they can (and frequently do) add fuel to an already burning fire.

Businesses are not always targeted directly for perceived actions of this kind – in recent years, dissatisfied customers and disgruntled employees have adopted the use of social media to spread the word, often resulting in damage to the organisation's brand and reputation, loss of business and more.

Does this type of action qualify as a cyber-attack? Maybe not in the strictest sense perhaps, but since the action takes place in cyberspace, I submit that it does qualify as a form of cyber-attack, and that organisations should consider the possibility as part of their response strategy.

CRITICAL NATIONAL INFRASTRUCTURE TARGETS

Attacks against critical national infrastructure organisations are extremely common, and may often originate not from cyber criminals, but from foreign nation states or terrorist organisations, since their objectives are usually to disrupt the target nation in as many ways as possible.

The UK's Centre for the Protection of National Infrastructure (CPNI) has defined the following areas of critical infrastructure, and the CNI sectors in other countries, if not identical, will be very similar:

- communications;
- emergency services;
- energy;
- financial services;
- food;
- government;
- health;
- transport;
- water;
- defence;
- civil nuclear;
- space;
- chemicals;

Communications

The communications portion of the CNI consists of several different areas. The public fixed (landline) and public mobile networks are the most obvious manifestation, but additionally, some private networks are included as well, especially the Airwave network that provides communications for the emergency services and related government and some non-government organisations.

Although less used in the UK, satellite communications are also a part of the CNI, and these tend to be used for both public and private communications in areas where the public fixed and mobile networks do not provide complete or reliable coverage.

Last, but not least, is the internet, which although provided nationally and occasionally locally by Internet Service Providers (ISPs), is centrally connected through a number of so-called 'peering points', which make the interconnections between ISPs at a national level and with ISPs in other countries.

Two particularly fragile components of the internet are occasionally subjected to cyber-attack. The first is the Border Gateway Protocol (BGP), which determines how data packets travel between one part of the internet and another. Once one gateway router is hijacked, it can, for example, advertise the fastest route as being to a malware site. The second is called Domain Name System (DNS) cache poisoning, in which a cyber-attacker makes changes to the domain name system to redirect traffic to another destination.

Emergency services

The next CNI area is that of the emergency services. This covers not only the police, fire and rescue and ambulance services, but also mountain rescue and the Maritime and Coastguard Agency.

People who do not necessarily intend to commit cybercrime, but who intend to undertake some other form of criminal activity can attack the networks and systems of the emergency services. They may realise that by causing some form of distraction, they are able to carry out their intrusion, robbery, or whatever, and feel that it is perfectly within their right to do so. Whether undertaking a DDoS attack on the website of any branch of the emergency services would aid them is uncertain.

Alternatively, they may hold some form of grudge against one of the services and feel that a cyber-attack is a perfectly justified response.

The principle target of such an attack is always likely to be the police, but no service would be immune to a determined attacker, including fire and rescue, ambulance, maritime and coastguard or mountain rescue services.

The fact that a cyber-attack might potentially cost someone their life might not even occur to them. Fortunately, however, the incidence of this type of attack appears to be very low.

Energy

Next, we move to the energy sector, which is split into three distinct areas, each of which has slightly different arrangements:

- electricity
- gas;
- oil.

Electricity

The electricity sector consists of three separate components – generation, which may be from a variety of sources; fossil fuels, including coal, oil and gas, and nuclear, all of which are non-renewable sources; and renewable resources such as hydropower, biomass, biofuels, wind, solar and geothermal.

The second component of the electricity sector is the transmission of power from the generation point through the national grid to the various distribution network operators (DNOs) around the country.

Finally, the distribution network operators then sell the electricity to homes, businesses and industry.

Since just about everything we do on a personal, business, commerce and especially critical infrastructure level depends ultimately on the supply of electricity, cyber-attacks are most likely to target the electricity generation facilities, since there are many of them and therefore there is a chance that some may not have as strong a cyber security management process as others. The transmission management centres, however, would come a close second, since considerably more damage might theoretically be achieved with just one attack.

In December 2016, it was reported that hackers had planted malware on a computer in the Burlington Electric Department – the electrical grid provider in the US state of Vermont.[1] Whilst the computer was reported not to have been connected to any part of the grid, the presence of malware (attributed to Russian hackers) does raise the point that critical infrastructure is potentially a major target.

Gas

Supplies of gas come from natural (non-renewable) resources below ground, known as onshore resources, and beneath the oceans, so-called offshore resources, and increasingly, gas is imported from overseas.

The transmission and distribution work in much the same way as electricity, with a central body delivering the supply to DNOs who then sell the gas to homes, businesses and industry, but the onshore gas storage facilities are likely to be the major targets.

Oil

Oil has similar beginnings to gas – indeed, the acquisition of the raw product uses almost identical techniques, but that is where the similarity stops, since crude oil must be refined and turned into useable products such as heating oil, petrol and so on.

On leaving the refineries, as with gas, much of it is delivered by underground pipes, and is delivered to storage depots from which distribution is either by road or rail, or again sometimes by underground pipes as in the case of distributing aviation spirit to major airports.

Although it did not result from a cyber-attack, the explosions in December 2005 at the Buncefield oil storage depot at Hemel Hempstead in the UK resulted in considerable disruption to the supply as well as to local residents and businesses.[2]

Offshore oil production platforms and smaller onshore production facilities are likely targets as well as the storage and distribution sites.

It is worth adding at this point a brief note about a technology used in the energy, water, civil nuclear and chemicals sectors of critical infrastructure regarding the use of a technology known as SCADA (Supervisory Control And Data Acquisition), which is widely used both to monitor the state of elements of the generation, production distribution systems, and to control their operation.

The generation and distribution networks themselves tend not to have actual connections to the internet, but the SCADA systems that monitor and operate them do. Hence, attacks against these sectors may well commence with an attack on the SCADA systems. This is discussed in greater detail later in this chapter.

Financial services

The finance sector has to be one of the most serious targets. Cyber thieves who can find ways of extracting funds from banks and financial services companies stand to make a killing. Finance organisations therefore take cyber security extremely seriously, since a successful security breach could cause them to go out of business, regardless of any potential fines levied by the Financial Conduct Authority (FCA).

Increasingly, banks are making use of one-time passkey generators in order to secure access to customers' bank accounts. The customer places their bank card into the calculator-like device, enters their private PIN, and the screen displays the eight digit passkey that they must then enter onto the bank's website in order to provide authentication.

The passkey has a short useful life, usually measured in minutes, after which it becomes useless and another passkey must be generated. This greatly lessens the risk to the customer unless the attacker can either manipulate the system and conduct a man-in-the-middle attack, discussed later, or can persuade the customer to part with both the card and PIN by whatever means.

Denial of service attacks against financial institutions are also on the increase. The implication of this is that not only would customers be unable to access their accounts, but in a worst-case scenario, inter-bank transfers could be affected. Whilst this might appear unimportant to many people, recent instances of banks making changes to their (often legacy) systems have resulted in services being badly affected for days at a time; property purchases failing because monies are not transferred in time; salaries and accounts unpaid; and many more.

As an example, in 2014 the Royal Bank of Scotland was fined £56m by the regulator after a 2012 software issue left millions of customers unable to access their accounts.[3]

Food

Cyber-attacks on organisations in the business of growing, importing, producing, distributing and retailing food are not particularly frequent, but occasionally we read of situations in which an activist group decides to take on a multinational organisation related to food, whether this is to cause denial of service or to steal.

In 2014, the Target group in the USA was infiltrated by hackers who stole the details of 40 million credit card users. The company had been prepared for such an eventuality and had an intrusion detection system (IDS) installed that actually detected the attack, but the company failed to respond. The incident cost the group tens of millions of US Dollars.[4]

Government

Government departments and agencies have always been a target for attackers. Fortunately, in the UK a government department, a part of GCHQ called the National Cyber Security Centre, known simply as NCSC,[5] has responsibility for providing guidance to all government departments – national, regional and local – and also to official government websites such as the Driver and Vehicle Licensing Agency (DVLA).

Beginning in October 2016, there were concerns that state-sponsored hackers from Russia were attacking the American Democratic National Committee's network, and that attempts were being made to influence the outcome of the November 2016 presidential election. Following the election, the media[6] reported that the CIA had declared 'high confidence' that the hackers were Russian, but, unsurprisingly, there is no mention of this on the CIA website.

The NCSC brings together and replaces CESG (the former information security arm of GCHQ), the Centre for Cyber Assessment (CCA), Computer Emergency Response Team UK (CERT-UK) and the cyber-related responsibilities of CPNI.

Its purpose, outlined on its website, is:

> to reduce the cyber security risk to the UK by improving its cyber security and cyber resilience. We work together with UK organisations, businesses and individuals to provide authoritative and coherent cyber security advice and cyber incident management.[7]

The NCSC's Certified Cyber Security Consultancy (CCSC) acts as the accreditation agency for government cyber security professionals (CCPs).[8] The scheme is outsourced to three private certification bodies and CCPs offer their services via a CCSC unless they are employed directly in a government department.

Government departments and agencies operate their own cyber security standards and processes, and NCSC also provides highly useful advice and guidance to private sector organisations through their website.[9]

Another government organisation that has a significant input to the UK's cyber security strategy is the CPNI,[10] which maintains strong links with all the sectors described in this part of the chapter.

Health

The health sector deals primarily with the public-facing services – hospitals, health centres and general practitioner surgeries – but also ties in closely with the need for medical research, investigating all health matters and researching new medicinal and surgical treatments for patients.

Hospitals, health centres and general practitioner surgeries

Why would anyone want to attack a hospital? Well, it seems that some attackers simply don't care who their targets actually are. In March 2016, the Medstar group, which runs ten hospitals in Washington DC and Maryland, was the subject of a ransomware attack that blocked staff access to many of the group's IT systems.[11] Several other hospitals in the US have also reported this kind of attack, and some pundits have speculated that there is also the possibility of an attacker taking control of life-critical systems, which puts an entirely different perspective on the issue of cyber security.

There is another potentially sinister aspect to this area – that of internet-connected health-related devices. It is not difficult to imagine that the administration of some drugs and medicines could be achieved remotely, and that the mechanisms could be connected to the internet to enable this. Delivery of too much or too little medication could be life-threatening, and if we ever reach the stage where heart pacemakers become part of the Internet of Things (IoT), security will have to be absolute.

A successful attack on National Health Service (NHS) systems could allow an attacker to obtain details of our medical history, which could potentially be sold to an interested party – an insurance company or a drug manufacturer for example. We normally consider these types of organisation in the UK to be beyond reproach, but those overseas might not be so honest. Additionally, if an attacker was able to access our medical records, they could alter the content either to improve or worsen the history, the results of investigations and tests, recommendations for treatment and the prognosis.

In January 2017 Barts Health Trust, the largest NHS trust in England, was hit by a cyber-attack that resulted in file sharing across its four main hospitals being turned off in order to limit the spread of the impact.[12]

Finally, if a hospital's systems were compromised as part of a larger physical terrorist attack, the result would certainly be panic amongst the general population.

Medical research

One of the areas in which there is massive scope for cyber-attacks, especially where the theft of intellectual property is concerned, is that of medical research. The amount of time, effort and money that pharmaceutical organisations invest in the development of new drugs and medicines is enormous, and this goes some way to explaining the cost of new medical treatments as the developers try to make a return on their investment.

If attackers were able to steal the formula for a new cancer drug for example, they could potentially sell this to less honest manufacturers who would naturally undercut the developer's selling price.

In an even worse scenario, between the testing of a new drug and its final production, an attacker could potentially alter the list of ingredients or change the process by which the drug is manufactured. The result could at the very least be contamination, and could bring about serious side-effects, or threaten lives.

Transport

The transport sector covers commercial air transport, road, rail and merchant shipping for both passengers and cargo.

Air

Increasingly, commercial aircraft are fitted with monitoring systems (especially for jet engines) that allow maintenance teams to see in real time how they are performing, and to understand when to have spare parts delivered to an airport, often before a problem has actually manifested itself, since there is no value to an airline in keeping an aircraft on the ground when it could be earning its keep filled with passengers or cargo.

Fortunately, current standards do not permit control of commercial aircraft from the ground (unlike drones), and it is to be hoped that the events of 11 September 2001 (9/11) will dissuade manufacturers from combining control with monitoring, since the prospect of the more frequent use of a civil airliner as a weapon of mass destruction is too horrible to contemplate.

There was also an unverified report in 2015 of a cyber security expert taking control of an aeroplane's flight control systems via the in-flight entertainment system (IFE) whilst it was airborne.[13] Whilst this is currently just a theoretical possibility, it remains to be seen whether this eventually becomes a practical form of attack.

Another aspect of cyber targets in the transport area of critical infrastructure would be that of the infrastructure that supports air traffic control. At any one time, there are thousands of civil aircraft in the skies, each one of which relies on an air traffic control centre to direct it out of the flight path of other aircraft by ensuring physical separation both horizontally and vertically. If this infrastructure were to be successfully attacked, it could turn aircraft into weapons of mass destruction without the need to target individual aircraft.

Road

The European Commission has placed a requirement that by March 2018, manufacturers of all vehicles sold in the EU must be provided with a system known as eCall,[14] which will automatically alert the emergency services in the event that the vehicle is involved in a collision. On the surface, this appears to be a highly noble undertaking, since faster response to an accident could save lives, and many vehicle manufacturers have pre-empted the requirement, and in addition to eCall systems, have installed event data recorders (EDRs) in their vehicles.

The EDR has the ability to store a large number of parameters, including location, speed and direction of travel, throttle position and cornering data. The driver has no knowledge of exactly what data is being collected, or what might be done with it. Whilst this would be helpful to the police investigating an accident, it follows also that the vehicle manufacturer is likely to be using that data to help in developing better vehicles – again, a positive development.

The driver has no control whatsoever over this data, and there is also the potential that the vehicle manufacturer could be selling that data to insurance companies. The potential for abuse of this has yet to be fully debated, since one could reasonably argue that the data was collected without the agreement of the driver.

Far worse, in 2015, security experts were able to demonstrate their ability to take over control of a Jeep Cherokee under controlled conditions in the USA.[15] They were able to enter through the vehicle's cellular phone connection to access the entertainment system, from which they broke out into the vehicle's Controller Area Network (CAN) and took over control of a number of the engine control units (ECUs). If this type of attack becomes commonplace, the implications are frightening.

Rail

Although driverless trains are something of a rarity, they do exist. On the London Transport system, there are driverless trains on the Victoria underground line and on the Docklands Light Railway. Rather less obvious examples exist at airports such as

London Gatwick, where driverless trains shuttle passengers between the north and south terminals.

Railways rely totally on electronic signalling to control the movement of trains, and should the infrastructure become internet-connected, one could imagine that considerable chaos, damage and potentially loss of life could ensue.

More recently, railway companies in a number of European countries have been installing train monitoring systems that can report information on passing railway stock about weight distribution, wheel loading, wheel defects and noise emission. Identification of the type of rolling stock is carried out by measuring the distance between axles.

An interesting software bug discovered in 2016 was that if a train running on the Swiss railway network has 256 axles, the monitoring system will reset the truck count to zero, indicating that there is no train on the particular stretch of line.[16] It is rumoured that the company work around this problem by connecting additional trucks to 256-axle trains to ensure that they always show up!

If an attacker wishing to cause a major accident was able to penetrate the monitoring system and tamper with the code that counts axles, a great deal of damage could be done.

Water

Cyber-attacks against water companies do not appear to be too widespread, but it has been reported that in 2016, a hacktivist group associated with Syria attacked a water treatment works in the USA.[17] Although their exact motivation is unknown, it appears to be that they wanted to alter the balance of chemicals added in the drinking water treatment process, with the aim of contaminating the supply.

Similar attacks could take place against treatment works for foul water, in which an attacker could again conceivably alter the balance of chemicals used in the treatment process, rendering the resulting output harmful to human and animal life alike, or in extreme cases, could release untreated sewage into rivers and water courses.

Defence

The defence sector is made up primarily of the armed forces – nominally army, navy and air force – and also organisations providing research and development or supply services to the military.

Armed forces

Any individual or organisation that conducts a cyber-attack on the armed forces of a major nation can probably expect swift and painful retribution. However, this does not prevent nation states from trying their hand as a means of testing the strength of the opponent's cyber security, and occasionally conducting intrusive attacks.

Some people define these attacks as acts of cyber warfare, and in part this is true, since one nation state (or terrorist group) has conducted an attack on another; but at the same time, since the origin of the attack may be unclear or even point to another possible attacker, a state of war does not necessarily exist between them.

Military suppliers

Cyber-attacks against military suppliers are very common, and have two fundamental purposes:

- First, they are conducted in order to steal intellectual property such as the designs of new technology used in weaponry and defence systems. An example of this is the attack (attributed to China) on Lockheed Martin, in which designs for the F-35 fighter jet were taken.[18]

- Second, they may be conducted in order to change the way in which military software operates or to plant malware in weapons or defence systems. It is not difficult to imagine what might result if the engine management system of a fighter jet cut out when the pilot was making an attack run, or the effect of a radar system suddenly failing to display incoming bombers.

This might sound like fantasy, but you can be certain that many countries will have thought of the idea, and that some countries may have actually succeeded in making it happen.

The so-called arms race that took place in the latter part of the 20th century was a serious affair. East and West spent vast sums of money in trying to develop weapons and defence systems that would allow them to defeat their enemies – often relying on the element of surprise and leaving their opponent with little or no time or capacity to retaliate, and it was eventually concluded that the end result of this could be nothing less than 'mutually assured destruction'.

This has not prevented or even slowed down the development of conventional weaponry or defence systems, but it has become clear that in the event of another worldwide conflict, conventional ground, sea and air forces would be heavily supplemented by pre-emptive cyber-attacks in an attempt to reduce the enemy's ability to operate their command and control structure.

Nation states have therefore invested heavily in developing cyber weapons and cyber defences, and there is a distinct possibility that another major war could actually be conducted without a single shot being fired.

Civil nuclear

Although we normally think of civil nuclear activities as being in the realm of power generation, there are many requirements for radioactive products used in medicine, where it is utilised in some calibration sources, radioactive drugs and bone mineral analysers; and in engineering where radioactive isotopes are used in the detection of pollution, carbon dating and the quality control of welding operations.

Although the Chernobyl incident in 1986 was not triggered by cyber means, a cyber-attack against a nuclear power station remains a real possibility in an attempt either to degrade electricity generation or to drive the reactor core into instability, resulting in a devastating explosion with radioactive material being dispersed over a wide area.[19]

Attacks on other nuclear facilities might result in a significantly less dramatic impact, but could result in hospitals unable to diagnose illnesses or treat them; and in major engineering projects unable to progress.

Space

The UK is not normally the first country that springs to mind when we talk about space, but in fact we are one of the leading countries that design and manufacture satellites used for communications and research, and we are an active partner in the European Space Agency.

Similar cyber-attacks to those discussed in the air transport section of this chapter are not beyond the bounds of possibility, and although there are no officially confirmed incidents in which one nation state has attacked the space technology of another, it remains a real possibility, especially if viewed as being part of cyber warfare.

Chemicals

Chemical plants produce many of the items that we use in everyday life, giving us food products such as sugar, agricultural products such as fertilisers and chemicals used both in the home, such as cleaning agents, and in industrial processes, such as acids and alkalis.

As with other areas, the impact of cyber-attacks on chemical production facilities could be highly harmful, with compounds being incorrectly mixed, resulting in poisoning of products, crops and people; or with dangerous toxic or explosive mixtures being generated, resulting in widespread pollution. Therefore chemical manufacturing and storage remains a strong potential target.

BUILDING TARGETS

One does not always think of the potential for buildings to be targets for cyber-attacks, but they are becoming increasingly internet-connected for the purposes of management, mainly for heating, ventilation and air conditioning (HVAC), in which the management of systems is outsourced to suppliers who are better equipped to manage them centrally, and only send out an engineer when something cannot be fixed remotely.

Access to the HVAC systems would permit an attacker to raise or lower internal temperatures to unacceptable levels, causing staff to have to leave or causing the temperature of critical environments to exceed operational requirements – an entire data centre could be taken out of service in this way.

Also, an attacker might be able to gain entry to the building's access control system, allowing doors to be locked or unlocked, preventing staff from entering or leaving, or providing them with the opportunity for physical ingress.

The types of building that might be attacked in this way include:

- factories, such as car manufacturing plants where an attacker might take control of an assembly line;
- warehouses and distribution centres, especially where high value goods are stored;
- transport hubs, such as airport terminals and railway stations;

- operational buildings, such as call centres, telephone exchanges and air traffic control installations;

- office buildings;

- hotels, where an attacker could lock or unlock guests' doors at will and steal guests' credit card details;

- sports and recreation buildings, with the potential to access scoring systems as well as HVAC;

- retail properties, including shops, shopping malls, petrol stations and restaurants.

Private houses

There has been much recent interest in home automation, with the ability to connect to a central heating system online from an application on a smartphone; to control curtains and windows; and also for manufacturers of white goods to receive alerts of potential failure of appliances.

Unfortunately, the manufacturers of home automation systems hardware are not always as skilled as they should be in writing secure code (discussed in greater detail in Chapter 4 – Cyber vulnerabilities and impacts). As the market for home automation devices continues to grow, attackers are ideally-placed to target well-publicised vulnerabilities in these systems.

There have been cases where baby video monitors have had little or no security software included, resulting in unauthorised people being able to watch a child remotely.[20]

Ironically, some security systems are also vulnerable. CCTV systems that make use of a digital video recorder to record images may allow an attacker to gain access to an organisation's data network through backdoors in the recorder, and so-called 'smart' TVs equipped with a camera and microphone can also present a means of an attacker gaining access.

We are being made increasingly aware of the Internet of Things and how it has the power to transform our lives. Many of the interconnected devices already being sold in the area of home automation have been implemented with little or no security, thus presenting an attacker with almost unlimited opportunity to cause mayhem and render our homes vulnerable to burglary.

Smart meters are now being installed by energy companies around the UK. However, it has been discovered that there are a number of fundamental flaws in the design, rendering the meters susceptible to cyber-attack. It could be possible for a cyber-attacker to under- or over-report the usage of energy, or to remotely shut off the power to the building.[21]

ACADEMIA AND RESEARCH TARGETS

Many universities have been the victim of cyber-attacks. In December 2015, a major DDoS attack was launched against the Joint Academic Network (JANET), resulting in much reduced connectivity.[22] Universities have suffered infiltration of exam results, and in cases where universities undertake programmes of research for business and industry alike, intellectual property has been exfiltrated.[23]

Academic networks present tantalising opportunities for attackers. Many networks (or network segments) are poorly secured, due partly to the spirit of openness that exists in the academic world, and partly through the efforts of students to secure unauthorised network access off campus as well as on.

Additionally, academic networks frequently have links into organisations that conduct commercial research and to government organisations, meaning that they can be used as a stepping stone to rich pickings.

It is thought that not all of these attacks originate from outside the universities themselves, but often from within, with students testing their hacking skills. The first example of a form of malware known as a worm was released in 1988 by Robert Morris, a student at Cornell University in the USA, and caused devastation on the early internet. Morris was eventually identified and prosecuted under the USA Computer Fraud and Misuse Act.

As a result of this, the Defense Advanced Research Projects Agency (DARPA) funded the establishment of the Computer Emergency Response Team/Coordination Centre (CERT/CC) at Carnegie Mellon University.

In his book *The Cuckoo's Egg*,[24] Clifford Stoll describes the events that began with a loss of 75 cents in inter-departmental accounts at the Lawrence Berkeley National Laboratory in California, and ended up catching a spy working for the Soviet Union who was hacking into American universities and military systems in an attempt to steal military development secrets.

MANUFACTURING AND INDUSTRY TARGETS

Industrial systems, whether involved in planning and design, development or actual manufacturing, have been a target for cyber-attacks for many years. Some attacks are used to conduct industrial espionage, whilst others are designed to cause disruption to industrial processes.

Manufacturing and industrial control systems

SCADA is the most commonly used method of monitoring and controlling industrial processes. It was developed in order to permit the monitoring and control of diverse manufacturers' hardware in the form of programmable logic controllers by a single management system using standardised automation protocols.

SCADA systems consist of five discrete levels:

- Level 0, containing the devices to be controlled, such as sensors and control valves;
- Level 1, containing the input/output modules that report the sensor readings and control valves referred to above;

- Level 2, containing the computer systems that integrate the sensor readings, generate alerts and apply control instructions;
- Level 3, containing the production monitoring and targeting systems;
- Level 4, containing the production scheduling systems.

The attacks, such as the Stuxnet attack described earlier, targets Level 1 and Level 2 devices, so that false data are passed up from Level 1 to Level 2, and incorrect instructions are passed back down as a result.

Other attacks against SCADA-based industrial control systems have been reported, but this was the highest profile case.

Attacks on industrial control systems can be used against any area of the CNI, such as water treatment plants, power stations, oil production platforms and the like.

In recent years, the move from largely manual construction and assembly in the manufacturing industries to automated manufacturing has been a major industry in its own right. Although some of the more delicate aspects of production still require manual (and often highly skilled manual) labour, machines are able to carry out repetitive work without tiring and often with much greater accuracy than a human.

The concept of an assembly line being hacked and aspects of the production being altered were unwittingly suggested by a Citroën car advertisement from 2012 in which the robot spray painting systems begin to make unplanned changes to the design on the production line.[25]

Whilst this was simply a tongue-in-cheek reference, a cyber-attack on an assembly line could easily result in locking nuts not being sufficiently tight or wiring looms wrongly connected, either of which could cause significant rework in the factory, or might not show up until the vehicles were on the road, with potentially fatal results.

There is also the possibility of a cyber-attacker making changes to the operating software of computer-based products whilst in production. Many devices nowadays rely on microprocessors to control their basic and more complex functions, from washing machines to cars, and from network routers to fighter aircraft.

If there is no highly rigid system of control over software between initial development and deployment, these areas become an easy target for an attacker.

NOTES

1. See www.bbc.co.uk/news/world-us-canada-38479179

2. See www.hse.gov.uk/comah/buncefield/buncefield-report.pdf

3. See www.bbc.co.uk/news/business-30125728

4. See www.bloomberg.com/news/articles/2014-03-13/target-missed-warnings-in-epic-hack-of-credit-card-data

5. See https://www.ncsc.gov.uk/guidance

6. See www.bbc.co.uk/news/world-us-canada-38370630

7. See https://www.ncsc.gov.uk/about-us

8. See https://www.ncsc.gov.uk/scheme/certified-professional

9. See https://www.ncsc.gov.uk

10. See www.cpni.gov.uk

11. See www.healthcareitnews.com/news/medstar-attack-found-be-ransomware-hackers-demand-bitcoin

12. See https://www.theguardian.com/technology/2017/jan/13/london-nhs-hospital-trust-hit-by-email-cyber-attackers?CMP=share_btn_link

13. See www.telegraph.co.uk/news/worldnews/northamerica/usa/11611058/Cybersecurity-researcher-made-plane-climb-after-hacking-in-flight-entertainment-system.html

14. See https://ec.europa.eu/digital-single-market/en/news/ecall-all-new-cars-april-2018

15. See www.computerworld.com/article/2951489/telematics/hacker-hundreds-of-thousands-of-vehicles-are-at-risk-of-attack.html

16. See https://www.reddit.com/r/softwaregore/comments/4s755a/trains_in_switzerland_must_not_have_exactly_256/

17. See www.theregister.co.uk/2016/03/24/water_utility_hacked/

18. See http://freebeacon.com/national-security/nsa-details-chinese-cyber-theft-of-f-35-military-secrets/

19. See www.world-nuclear.org/information-library/safety-and-security/safety-of-plants/chernobyl-accident.aspx

20. See www.bbc.co.uk/news/technology-34138480

21. See www.bbc.co.uk/news/technology-29643276

22. See https://www.jisc.ac.uk/news/ddos-attack-disrupting-janet-network-08-dec-2015

23. See www.independent.co.uk/life-style/gadgets-and-tech/news/janet-uk-university-cyber-attack-internet-down-a6765056.html

24. *The Cuckoo's Egg*, Clifford Stoll. London: Pan Books, 1991.

25. See https://www.youtube.com/watch?v=6vuZWx11RLM

4   CYBER VULNERABILITIES AND IMPACTS

Anything that thinks logically can be fooled by something else that thinks at least as logically as it does.
Douglas Adams, *The Hitchhiker's Guide to the Galaxy Trilogy*

In this chapter, we shall examine the reasons why cyber-attacks succeed – cyber vulnerabilities – and the damage or consequences that can result from a successful attack – the impacts. These include policy, process and procedure vulnerabilities, technical vulnerabilities, people-related vulnerabilities, physical and environmental vulnerabilities; personal impacts and organisational impacts.

CYBER VULNERABILITIES

Any weakness that can be exploited to mount an attack on a network, system or service is termed a vulnerability.

Whilst we may be unable to take preventative action to ward off threats and hazards, vulnerabilities are things that we can often take steps to reduce or even eliminate altogether.

Some vulnerabilities reflect the nature of the asset, for example the ability of data on magnetic media to be overwritten or deleted; whilst others result from some accidental or deliberate action or inaction, for example failure to undertake regular backups.

The vulnerabilities themselves, and indeed the controls we may use to treat them, come in many shapes and sizes. Most of them arise from failures to have or to adhere to policies, processes and procedures. Significantly less frequent, but also potentially serious, are the technical vulnerabilities. People-related vulnerabilities are also a major area of concern, as are environmental vulnerabilities.

Policy, process and procedure vulnerabilities

Whilst many organisations have robust policies and procedures in place – either to ensure that the right things happen, or to ensure that the wrong things don't happen – they are occasionally either overlooked or simply given lip service. This section highlights some of the key policies and procedures that organisations should undertake as a minimum.

Failure to have an overall information security policy

The failure of an organisation to put in place an overall information security policy comes right at the top of the list of vulnerabilities. Security policies do not need to be lengthy or complex, but should state clearly and simply what formalities the organisation requires to be in place, and makes it clear that people must adhere to them.

The lack of, or poorly written, access control policies

A formal access control policy or one that is inappropriate for the needs of the organisation is the next port of call, and the lack of suitable policy, or one that is not properly communicated to staff will cause severe repercussions. Access to systems, applications and information should only ever be given on the basis of the user's business need, and should always be approved by their line manager.

Failure to change user access rights when changing role or leaving the organisation

Another vulnerability connected with this is that of poor access control for users changing roles or leaving the organisation. Their access to systems, applications and information is frequently overlooked when an individual changes role. A method of combating this is that of role-based authentication, in which the user gains access by means of both their job function and their identity, rather than by their identity alone.

On leaving the organisation, the user's access rights should be immediately revoked so that they can no longer access the organisation's network and systems.

Inadequate user password management

One of the most frequent vulnerabilities is that of poor password management. In the past, this included the failure to enforce regular password changes together with a test of password strength. However, NIST has recently deemed that frequent changes are unhelpful to users and that strength checkers may not be sufficiently robust. Instead, new guidelines are being developed[1] that rate password length and hashing method[2] as being more user-friendly by placing the burden on the verifier rather than the user.

The continued use of default system accounts and passwords

An extremely common vulnerability is the continued use of default factory-set accounts and passwords for new and upgraded systems. Many individuals in the hacking world are aware of these and circulate them around the community. The failure to change or hide wireless network identities or service set identifiers (SSIDs) will allow an attacker to pinpoint target networks, and if the default administrator passwords have not been changed, or the security level enhanced, these provide a highly attractive entry point into an organisation's network.

The continued use of inbuilt system accounts and passwords

Worse still than the continued use of default settings, there may sometimes be a tendency to allow one system to connect to another by embedding user IDs and passwords within applications. This is a highly dubious practice, since a change on one system or another can easily result in application failures.

The lack of security of mobile devices

Many organisations fail to secure mobile devices, whether these are supplied by the organisation, or brought in by the users themselves (bring your own device; BYOD). Unless properly configured, mobile devices generally are relatively insecure and easily lost, mislaid or stolen, making both the device and the network to which it can connect equally vulnerable.

The lack of network segregation

Network segregation is commonplace in larger organisations, in which different networks are constructed according to the business requirement, and particularly according to their confidentiality, integrity and availability requirements. For example, an organisation with a significant research capability might well place this on a different network than that for finance or general administration use.

Failure to restrict access to networks according to use is a very common vulnerability, and may allow people to reach resources to which they have no entitlement.

Failure to impose a clear desk and clear screen policy

The lack of a clear desk and clear screen policy again is a very common vulnerability. Some organisations make it a disciplinary offence for an employee to leave confidential materials in plain view or for failing to log out of or secure their workstation when they are away from their desk.

Restriction of administration rights usage

Unwarranted access to administration accounts is a frequent vulnerability. Only trained and authorised personnel should have administration rights and that should include user computers as well as central systems. Also, administrators should have two accounts, one with the administrator rights for undertaking such work and a second 'standard' user account for day-to-day activities such as email, internet access and office work.

The use of untested software

It is good practice for organisations to test new or updated software, including the testing of patches before they go into a production or general use environment. Untested software may not only cause operational issues if it fails to work as expected, but in cases where it is used in conjunction with other applications, it can have a knock-on effect resulting in an embarrassing chain of consequences.

Failure to restrict the use of system utilities

Although a relatively minor vulnerability, the failure to restrict the use of system utilities such as a terminal console application – normally by setting access privileges within the user's profile – can result in users carrying out activities that are detrimental to their own device or to other systems, applications or information within the organisation.

Separation of duties

In some situations, it is possible for staff to allow attackers to take advantage of access to information that they might not normally have. This ties back into access control, in which access to information might benefit from being role dependent.

Staff should not be placed in a position, for example, where they can not only raise requisitions for orders, but also authorise them for purchase.

Inadequate network monitoring and management including intrusion detection

Inadequate network management, including the monitoring of hacking and intrusion attacks, will mean that successful attacks and intrusions are overlooked, and little or nothing is known about their occurrence until much later.

The use of unprotected public networks

Many attacks are caused by unprotected public network connections, which allow an intruder to gain easy access to an organisation's network, including the use of shared computers in public environments such as internet cafés and the use of unauthorised and possibly unsecured wireless access points (WAPs).

The uncontrolled use of user-owned wireless access points

Occasionally, users of an organisation's networks will discover ways of subverting the organisation's security procedures and will attempt to connect their devices to parts of the network to which they have no entitlement. One way in which this is achieved is by connecting in a 'rogue' wireless access point to which they have unrestricted access. One of the main issues with this is that the security settings of such wireless access points might not be as strict as those of the organisation itself, and whilst the users may be able to access the network, so might an attacker.

Poor protection against malware and failure to keep protection up to date

Malware protection software, especially antivirus software that is not kept up to date will make an attacker's job much easier. Attackers will take advantage of any means of access available to them, and often are aware of vulnerabilities in applications and operating systems long before a fix is available. Delays in updating these applications leaves an organisation wide open to attack.

The lack of a patching and updating regime

In the same way as the regular updating of malware protection software, the failure to install manufacturers' software patches will leave operating systems and application software open to attack.

Inadequate and untested backup and restoral procedures

Most organisations nowadays carry out regular backups of user data. However, it is far rarer for them to verify that these backups are actually fit for purpose and that information can actually be successfully restored from the backup media. This again presents a serious vulnerability, since backup media that does not fulfil its objective is just as bad as having no backup regime at all.

Improper disposal of 'end of life' storage media

Once storage media has reached its end of life, it should be properly disposed of or wiped before reuse. There are numerous stories in the press regarding people who have bought second-hand computers only to find that the hard drives still contain sensitive or personal information that had not been securely removed prior to the sale. Some organisations will not allow magnetic media of any kind to be resold, and insist that disposal is irreversible.

There are examples of computers that have been bought with the original user's data still intact, as well as computers left on trains without password protection.[3]

The lack of robust 'bring your own device' (BYOD) policies

The concept that an organisation's staff can bring their own device has become very popular, since it can reduce the IT hardware costs to an organisation. However, the lack of appropriate policies for its use and the lack of enforcement can bring about serious breaches of security, especially in situations where other members of a user's family have access to the same device.

In 2010, one organisation was badly affected by a virus that was brought in on a user's own personal computer. The machine had been used over a weekend by the user's teenage son, who had unwittingly accessed a website that contained malware. The resulting infection spread throughout a large part of the organisation's network, and took its entire IT department several days to clear up. The user (a senior manager) was cautioned, but unfortunately the same event happened the following week, and the user was then banned from bringing in his own machine.

Inadequate change management procedures

Inadequate change control can lead to software and patches being rolled out to the user population, new systems and services and network connections being made and redundant systems removed without full consideration (and risk assessment) of the consequences. In smaller networks, change control can easily be vested in one or two people on a part-time basis, but as an organisation's network grows, it may be necessary to employ a full-time team with representatives from multiple business units.

The lack of audit trails, non-repudiation of transactions and email messages

In some sectors, it is vital that online transactions and email correspondence are subject to detailed logging and non-repudiation. In many applications, this audit trail is built in to the operating software, and in the event of a dispute regarding 'who did what', or 'who said what', those organisations that are able to produce evidence in their favour will greatly reduce their risk profile.

The lack of segregation of test and production systems

Those organisations that employ large-scale systems and application testing prior to roll out are open to problems if they fail to separate test and operational facilities, since users may inadvertently connect to a test system resulting in failed transactions.

Acceptable use

It is not only good practice for organisations to include acceptable use statements in contracts of employment, but it should be mandated, whether for hiring permanent staff or taking on external contractors, so that staff members and contractors have no excuse for not knowing that they may not visit inappropriate websites, send or receive inappropriate emails or post inappropriate material on social networks or web blogs.

The uncontrolled copying of business information

Operational management should limit the uncontrolled copying of information by users who have no need to access it – again, this is also largely an access control issue, but the identification of such activity may fall into a different management area. This includes the use of USB memory sticks and shared network drives.

Technical vulnerabilities

Technical vulnerabilities are perhaps less obvious to spot, but are frequently highly dangerous. These could also be considered to be failures of policy, process or procedure, but are sufficiently significant to warrant their own section.

Poor coding practice

Poor coding practice is potentially one of the most serious issues around today. The Internet of Things has brought us an increasing number of internet-connected products such as baby monitors, CCTV systems, home entertainment systems and environmental control systems. Many of these have been shown to have little or no security within the application software that runs within the IoT device itself, and frequently in any application that is used to control it.

Such failings will undoubtedly have drastic consequences, since an attacker can not only attack and take control of the device itself, but may well use it as a stepping stone to other devices on the network. Even if a vulnerability is discovered and hopefully fixed, the chances of it being possible to roll out the corrected code to the entire user base are not great, especially if a device has already been compromised.

In January 2017, it was announced at the Consumer Electronics Show (CES) that a number of manufacturers are developing routers with inbuilt security software designed to protect IoT devices that have inadequate security.[4] This might be a possible solution to the problem, since consumers will only have to place their trust in one system to protect all their IoT devices and applications, but it will almost certainly encourage laziness from the manufacturers of IoT devices and applications as they will feel there is no point in trying to make their product secure.

Indeed, poor coding practice is not limited to the IoT environment – it affects operating systems and applications as well, and combined with back doors that allow a programmer to test code more easily, these types of vulnerability are amongst the oldest in the book!

Poor specification of requirements

Poor coding practice often originates from poor specification of requirements for the product or service. It is a long-held view that it is always better to design security into a product from the beginning rather than trying to patch it in later on, but many organisations still persist in this bad practice.

Poor quality assurance and testing

Hand in hand with poor coding practice runs poor quality assurance and testing. It is easy to imagine that a programmer developing the software for an IoT device might well also be responsible for its functionality testing, in which case (given the lack of a security requirement in the product's specification), the problem will be exacerbated.

People-related vulnerabilities

There are numerous people-related vulnerabilities, some of which arise from the lack of training and awareness provided by the organisation, whilst others arise from people's inability to think and act logically or to follow instructions.

Social engineering

Social engineering may best be defined as an act that influences a person to take an action that may not be in their or their organisation's best interest. This includes persuading them to divulge personal or confidential information.

People are frequently susceptible to social engineering or to coercion, when an attacker who may have carried out research on the individual is able to gain their confidence through flattery or by offering some inducement that the individual is likely to accept.

Social engineering is a skill that many cyber-attackers work hard to develop, since assistance from inside an organisation can save them a great deal of time and effort.

One example of social engineering is the use of so-called 'dark patterns', in which the user is lured into carrying out an action they had not intended. These are discussed in greater detail in Chapter 5 – Cyber threats.

Lack of awareness

An extremely effective technique for delivering malware is to provide people with free memory sticks infected with malware. Not only can this be achieved by handing them out at conferences and exhibitions, but also by leaving them on the ground near a target user's house or place of work.

Thinking they're getting something for nothing, people will happily plug these into their computers without contemplating the possible consequences.

Failure to comply with company policies and good practice

This is one of the most common forms of vulnerability. Computer users, especially in a corporate environment, find that they are constrained by the organisation's policies, processes and procedures, and they will try to find ways of defeating or working around them. Sometimes this is due to sheer laziness on their part, because doing something properly requires effort; at other times they simply don't see the point or disagree with the requirement.

Typical amongst this type of vulnerability is people writing down key passwords, especially passwords for root access to systems, and sharing passwords with colleagues who either have forgotten their own, or more frequently should not have access in the first place.

Simple passwords

Occasionally, users will choose a simple password (for example, 1234) when using an application or service. Good password management techniques should prevent this, but occasionally users will still find ways of circumventing this. Other vulnerabilities in this area include passwords that can be easily guessed or cracked, such as one's mother's maiden name.

Poor response to training and awareness

In Chapter 10 we will cover techniques for training and raising awareness. It is important that this is not a one-off event, but an ongoing process, so that users are regularly updated on security matters they need to be aware of, and that they continue to be trained in the correct way of doing things. However, some aspects of user behaviour will continue to require line management action when they fail to comply, and some organisations penalise staff who repeatedly ignore their training.

Physical and environmental vulnerabilities

There are some areas in which physical and environmental vulnerabilities will have an effect, and the impact of these can be dramatic.

Building and equipment room access

It may sound obvious that physical access to key buildings and sensitive areas within them should be carefully controlled, but all too frequently this is not the case, leaving the way clear for an intruder to enter unobserved. Theft is frequently a motive for this kind of entry, sometimes enabled by careful social engineering and sometimes by distraction of security staff, but it may also provide an attacker with the opportunity to introduce malware into a system.

Physical access to individual items of equipment

In addition to equipment room access, poor security can also allow an intruder to gain access to the individual systems where malware can be introduced. This often happens when a number of systems are located within a single rack space, so that having physical access to one automatically gives an intruder physical access to all the others.

Locking equipment cabinets is an obvious solution, but all too frequently keys are left in the cabinet lock.

Single points of failure

Any organisation that delivers services over the internet, or indeed internally to its staff, must consider the possibility of single points of failure (SPoFs) as a major vulnerability. These SPoFs include the main computer system, its operating system, software applications, firewall technology, network connectivity, web servers and any front-end load balancing systems. The service design must take into account the possibility of failure of any one of these components, leading to an overall failure of service, and the design must be planned so that this does not happen.

Heating, ventilation and air conditioning (HVAC)

Key systems are invariably located in controlled environments such as computer and equipment rooms, but these bring about a potential single point of failure, since all will rely on the environmental controls to maintain a steady temperature and humidity.

Provided that these are maintained within specified limits, the risk is minimal, but once the temperature changes, especially increasing beyond recommended levels, equipment can cease to operate. However, some data centres now run their equipment rooms at slightly higher temperatures than those that are comfortable for humans, realising that a few degrees increase in temperature will not cause problems, but will save a considerable amount of money in the long term.

Power

The loss of or interruption to power is the main vulnerability of all systems, and whilst the loss for any long period of time can cause severe problems, equipment is rather more vulnerable to being powered off and on again repeatedly and is much more likely to suffer catastrophic failure.

These days, no self-respecting organisation with a major IT infrastructure would consider anything but an uninterruptible power supply system to run their essential computer room or data centre, and this would normally be backed up by a system of standby generation. Such systems often also provide power to other essential services such as those used by the supporting operations staff.

CYBER IMPACTS

Cyber impacts or consequences are the result of some unwanted event – when a vulnerability has been exploited by a threat. Impacts come in many shapes and forms, but all require some sort of decision to be made. Some impacts can be tolerated because they are not serious, but many cannot be tolerated and require some form of countermeasure, control or treatment in order to remove or minimise them.

Many impacts will be felt on a personal or individual level, whilst others will have a much wider impact on organisations. We'll take a look at personal impacts first.

Personal impacts

This section covers many of the impacts that will affect individuals in the home or SME environment as well as individuals working in larger corporate organisations.

Loss of or unauthorised changes to personal information

One of the most worrying impacts on individuals is the loss or exposure of personal information. This could be almost anything about our private or professional lives that we would prefer to keep to ourselves, but for whatever reason could become awkward or embarrassing if it became public knowledge.

It is amazing how much information you can accumulate about someone without either ever having heard of them before, or without them being in any way aware of the fact.

There are quite a number of people around the UK who share the same name as me, and who apparently have a very similar email address. I regularly receive emails intended for them. Over a period of time, and quite unintentionally, I have built up a fuzzy picture of some of them. I know most of their full name; often their occupation; roughly, and in a couple of cases, exactly where they live; occasionally, their interests; and some of their shopping habits.

I am sure that if I put my mind to it I could find out much more, but the more important fact is that they either are completely unaware of this, or are totally unconcerned that much of their personal information has reached a person for whom it was never intended.

This is due to one simple fact – they, or the person sending them an email, has typed their email address incorrectly. Within the space of 48 hours, I found it necessary to contact a gardening company who needed authorisation to carry out work, a theatre where my namesake had tried to register for an account on their booking system, and a company selling car wheels that my alter ego had ordered. These are just recent examples – in the past, I have incorrectly received highly confidential cancer patients' medical records and demands to pay armed services mess bills.

I always attempt to contact either the individual or the person who has emailed them, but whilst they could at least apologise for the inconvenience and thank me for pointing out their error, sadly all too frequently there is no response at all. Whatever happened to good manners when we joined the connected world?

Sometimes people give my mobile phone number instead of their own, and I have received numerous text messages from various organisations advising of delivery times and appointments. These too have told me where someone lives and what they have ordered, but I have (so far) resisted the temptation to text back and make changes!

We happily join social networks and post information about ourselves. Facebook, Twitter and LinkedIn are just three examples of social networks where an enormous amount of information can be discovered about us, including our earlier education, university life, job history, interests and hobbies, family life and much, much more.

It's not only individuals who can cause problems for themselves. Take the case of a CEO who was having regular meetings with the CEO of another organisation with a view to a merger. On one occasion he took his family with him and his teenage daughter posted a photograph of the town they visited, together with a comment about her father being in a meeting at a particular company.

Someone following her on the social network put two and two together and made a couple of telephone calls, which resulted in the fact of a highly sensitive discussion becoming public knowledge, affecting the companies' share prices, and effectively ruining the entire project.

This is perhaps an extreme example, but it does illustrate the possible consequences of seemingly innocent actions.

Loss of or unauthorised changes to personal credentials

Individual people's credentials are big business. Details of bank and credit card accounts, usernames, email addresses, passwords and the like are bought and sold on the internet for surprisingly little money.

An attacker who can acquire these in bulk can monetise the data in a number of ways – either by using the credentials himself to mount attacks on the individuals concerned, or by selling on these credentials in bulk to others who are better equipped to mount the attacks.

The impact on the individual can be far-reaching, depending upon the type of credentials discovered. If the individual is lucky, they may discover the attack early on, and may just lose a small sum of money. If they are unlucky, it can be much more devastating.

Loss of money and other financial instruments

Money is a major motivator for cyber-attackers, so naturally they will try to steal as much as they can if the opportunity presents itself. In some situations, where the individual can show that they have taken due diligence over their credentials and have protected their computer and bank cards as well as they reasonably can, the finance organisation will accept responsibility for covering the losses, but where individuals have been careless or negligent, they have the potential to lose considerable sums of money.

A knock-on effect of this is that one's financial standing or credit worthiness might also be affected, if, for example, the loss empties one's bank account immediately prior to a direct debit being taken for a mortgage payment, and this is subsequently marked against the individual's credit rating.

Damage to personal reputation

Cyber-attacks can easily ruin reputations. If you consider the example of someone whose email account is stolen, or whose account username is used by an attacker, it is quite simple to send out malicious emails that could destroy their reputation overnight. More often however, especially if the recipients know the individual well, they accept that the account has been abused, but the repercussions of having malicious communications sent to someone you don't know are potentially far more serious.

Reputations are rather like eggs – very easily broken, and very difficult to piece back together again.

Loss of personal trust

Trust goes hand in hand with reputation. People with a sound reputation tend to be trustworthy and vice versa, and the loss of trust in an individual implies that their word is no longer reliable.

The importance of trust cannot be overstated, whether this is in connection with conventional business or with online transactions. We shall talk more about trust in Chapter 11 – Information sharing.

Loss of or unauthorised changes to intellectual property

The theft of IP is closely related to the theft of money, since although no actual money is stolen, the potential to have earned it through sales will have been denied to the IP owner. A secondary and rather more serious loss of IP is when an attacker steals the original material and claims it as their own, in which case the original IP owner will be at a very serious disadvantage.

An example of this type of loss reported by the Intellectual Property Office in its 2015/2016 IP Crime Report[5] is that of the abuse of the set-top boxes designed to allow users to collect music, videos, photographs and games in a single application. Illegal third party add-on software can allow users to download pirated material from film companies and television companies. The report flagged this kind if IP theft as being one of the top three it is investigating.

Identity theft

Some years ago, a colleague was targeted by an organised group, who used her email address to send out hate mail to everybody in her list of contacts, stole money from her bank account, ran up credit card bills, and almost destroyed her personal and professional life.

However, she was actually extremely fortunate, as she discovered what had happened at an early stage and took remedial action to limit the damage, but whilst the perpetrators were identified, they were never brought to justice since they were beyond the jurisdiction of the European security services.

She believes that the reason for targeting her was that on several occasions she had been publicly very outspoken about the integrity of a large overseas organisation.

Identity theft is often closely coupled with cyber theft, since an attacker may reveal their identity if they carry out too many actions using the stolen identity, whereas in the case of a quick 'smash and grab', the attacker can discard the identity as soon as they have the money.

Personal injury

This aspect of cyber security is rather new. In December 2016, in response to an article he had posted, Newsweek journalist Kurt Eichenwald reported having received a tweet containing flashing images that caused him to suffer an epileptic attack. Clearly the sender was aware of Mr Eichenwald's medical condition, and the matter is under investigation by police in the USA.[6]

Such conduct raises the question as to what might be the consequences, for example, for patients undergoing kidney dialysis at home with equipment that is internet-connected.

Organisational impacts

Many of the impacts that affect individuals will also affect organisations. However, because of the scale of organisations, both in terms of numbers of people and in the amounts of finance involved, the overall impacts will potentially be significantly greater. These could easily include partial or complete failure of an organisation or severe job losses.

Brand and reputation

The organisation's brand will invariably suffer a major impact when a cyber-attack is successful, especially if it became clear that the organisation concerned had not taken appropriate steps either to prevent the attack happening in the first place, or because it had failed to deal with it effectively once it had occurred. On occasions, it is because both of these have resulted in the organisation losing intellectual property, or customer information.

Organisations that suffer this kind of impact may find that customers no longer trust them and decide not to do business with them in the future.

Financial impacts

The impact on an organisation's revenue streams can be devastating. Cyber-attacks frequently result in an organisation being unable to trade online since customers will be unable to place orders. This will not only cause an immediate loss of revenue, but can often also result in downstream losses later on, as customers take their business elsewhere.

Following a successful cyber-attack that results in damage to the organisation's brand, the organisation's share price may well suffer a sharp decline. Under normal circumstances a reduction in share value is a day-to-day occurrence and would not be a major cause for concern, but in these unusual circumstances it might take an organisation months or years to recover its share price.

Additionally, cyber-attacks can cause an organisation to be unable to order goods from its suppliers, pay them for goods already received, or be unable to pay staff their wages or salaries.

Under certain circumstances, and particularly in highly regulated sectors, organisations can be fined for mismanagement of customer data, especially if their actions contravene data protection legislation. They can also suffer further financial losses with interest being charged for late payments, especially to Her Majesty's Revenue and Customs (HMRC) for late payment of corporation tax.

On top of any revenue losses, organisations will find that there are costs involved in putting matters right after a successful cyber-attack, which may include the introduction of remedial information security controls.

Also, as discussed earlier in this book, there is the possibility that an organisation will be subjected to a ransomware attack, and will have to pay the ransom to decrypt their data. The alternative would be for the organisation to face expending considerable effort in recovering all its affected systems. In some cases, the cost of such a recovery process could well exceed the ransom demanded.

Operational failures

If an organisation's operational systems, such as development systems, production control systems, stock control systems and the like are impacted by a cyber-attack, the impact would be potentially catastrophic, as the organisation may be completely unable to operate for the duration of the problem.

Most, if not all of these, failures will inevitably link back to financial impacts, since the organisation's ability to provide its customers with products or services will result in loss of revenue, and quite possibly in damage to the organisation's brand and reputation.

An example of this is the case of the failure of a software upgrade at the Royal Bank of Scotland in June 2012, which resulted in 6.5 million customers being unable to access their online accounts, receive incoming payments and make transfers to either other accounts within RBS or other banks. The bank was fined a total of £56 million by the various regulatory bodies.[7] Whilst this is not a specific cyber security incident, it does illustrate what can happen when system upgrades are not tested prior to roll out.

People impacts

The final impact that organisations might suffer following this kind of event is the loss of staff who have to be laid off due to the financial losses or operational failures, or who choose to leave the organisation because they have lost faith in its ability to adequately plan for and respond to cyber security disruptions.

NOTES

1. See https://pages.nist.gov/800-63-3/sp800-63-3.html

2. The technique of hashing uses a one-way encryption algorithm that makes it impossible to recover the password from the encrypted or 'hashed' original. Imagine dicing a potato into small cubes and then trying to reassemble it!

3. See http://news.bbc.co.uk/1/hi/uk/7449927.stm

4. See www.bbc.co.uk/news/technology-38415067

5. https://www.gov.uk/government/uploads/system/uploads/attachment_data/file/555795/ip-crime-report-2015-16.pdf

6. See www.bbc.co.uk/news/technology-38365859

7. See www.bbc.co.uk/news/business-30125728

5 CYBER THREATS

If you want to hit a country severely you hit its power and water supplies. Cyber technology can do this without shooting a single bullet.

Isaac Ben-Israel, Major General, Israeli Air Force

In this chapter, we shall examine the various types of threat that individuals and organisations face, including types of attacker, types of attack, the motivations for and the benefits of launching an attack, the risks involved in doing so and how attacks typically are conducted.

There are a number of terms associated with cyber threats that are worth exploring before we look into the types of threat in greater detail:

- **Threat source or sponsor** is the person or organisation that wishes to benefit from attacking an information asset. Threat sources often pay or otherwise pressurise threat actors to attack information assets on their behalf.

- **Threat actors or agents** are the individuals or groups of individuals who actually execute a cyber-attack.

- **Threat actions** describe the actual attacks. These are often not a single isolated event, but can consist of many discrete activities, involving surveillance, initial activities, testing and the final attacks.

- **Threat analysis** describes the process of understanding the level of threat – this is referred to in more detail in Chapter 6 – Risk management overview.

- **Threat vectors or attack vectors** are the tools, techniques and mechanisms by which an attacker conducts the attack on their target.

- **Threat consequences or impacts** are the results or impacts of a cyber-attack, which we dealt with in Chapter 4.

Whilst some attacks are more likely to take place than others, the level of impacts does not necessarily mirror the type of organisation affected or the likelihood that they will occur. Any individual or organisation can be attacked, and very probably has been.

Before we can begin to plan to put preventative measures in place or to develop the means to respond to cyber-attacks, we need to understand the kinds of people and organisations that will attempt them, together with their possible motivations for doing so. Once we have a clear understanding of this aspect of cyber security, we will be much better placed to deal with them.

Any attacker or criminal requires three distinct things in order to achieve their goal:

- **Motive** – there must be a reason for them undertaking a cyber-attack – even if it appears to be a rather futile one. Most cybercrime is motivated by money, but there are elements who attack systems for revenge; to establish their perceived superiority; to make a political statement; or simply to be a nuisance.

- **Means** – the attacker must possess a minimum level of skill in order to mount a successful attack. Often attackers with little or no skill will fail in their endeavours and will probably be identified and face justice, whilst those with sufficient motivation will persist, and further develop their skills over time.

- **Method** – a more experienced attacker will develop a plan for their attack. This may require an interim break-in, followed by extended periods of reconnaissance before the real attack takes place.

Some of these attackers will be individuals, operating entirely on their own; some will be groups of individuals, often organised into a loose community; whilst others will be highly organised criminal gangs. At the other end of the spectrum are the nation states, and whilst some will be using the attack for purely espionage purposes, others will have a far more sinister agenda.

TYPES OF ATTACKER

Attackers fall into a number of categories:

- script kiddies;
- hacktivists;
- lone wolves;
- investigative journalists;
- minor criminals;
- organised criminals;
- terrorists;
- insiders;
- security agencies.

Before we examine their motives, means and methods, it is worth examining an attacker's capabilities, as these will vary considerably.

Outside organisations

We shall begin with those attacker types who conduct cyber-attacks from outside conventional organisations.

Script kiddies

Script kiddies are beginners in the cyber security game. They need not be young, but are generally relatively inexperienced in computing and cyber security matters, and are on a learning curve. This will typically involve downloading free malware from internet resources and attacking 'soft' targets where there is less chance of causing damage or being caught. More experienced hackers tend to look down on script kiddies, despite that fact that this is where many of them may have started.

Hacktivists

Most hacktivists already have a cause to support. Some of these will be political; some religious; some may be concerned with the protection of civil liberties; some will be attacking a major corporation whom they feel has caused them some injustice; some will be trying to save the planet from destruction by humanity.

Whatever their cause, hacktivists will invariably target major websites, often defacing the organisation's 'landing' pages, or replacing them with their own versions of the 'truth'.

Since hacktivists rarely attack individuals, and are not usually motivated by theft, they present relatively little threat to us as individuals, unless, for example, the individual works in a laboratory that conducts experiments on live animals, or in some other similarly controversial area. To organisations however, they are a major nuisance, cause public embarrassment and occasionally cause the targeted organisation some financial loss, both of which are very much the hacktivists' primary objectives.

They normally take advantage of known vulnerabilities in website applications to conduct their attacks and, once identified, these are relatively easily corrected, but in the meantime, if they have enjoyed sufficient exposure, they feel that their point will have been made.

A small minority of hacktivists are just out to cause mischief, and are usually less concerned about making a particular point; rather they have found a vulnerability and deface a website just to show their prowess.

However, some hacktivist attacks have had a much higher profile, as in the example of the Anonymous attack on the Church of Scientology following its legal action against YouTube for publishing one of its propaganda videos.[1]

Lone wolves

So-called lone wolves are frequently newcomers to hacking. Although not restricted to the Hollywood vision of a brilliant teenager hunched over a computer in a darkened bedroom, they often begin as 'script kiddies', who learn their basic hacking skills from chatrooms and blogs on the internet, download malware and try their hand at attacking increasingly high profile websites.

Their motivation is usually to gain kudos from their peers, but may also be to cause a certain amount of mischief, and this type of lone wolf sometimes graduates from minor hacking into minor crime or hacktivism.

Another, more benign type of lone wolf is motivated purely by inquisitiveness, and is more reminiscent of the original hacking community, who simply wanted to find out how things worked and if possible to improve them. This type of hacker will often graduate to become a security specialist or penetration tester.

Investigative journalists

Investigative journalists are an interesting group. Whilst their intentions may be honour-able, they frequently resort to underhand methods to achieve their goals. Some such activity has been by hacking into the voice mailboxes of celebrities, politicians and members of the UK royal family – deemed 'illegal interception' – and attributed largely to journalists working for the News International group of papers during the mid-2000s.

It is not hard to imagine that a journalist willing to illegally access someone's voicemail would also be prepared to illegally access someone's computing device, email messages or internet browsing records, whether they achieved this themselves or by some form of proxy – that is paying a hacker to undertake the technical aspects.

Minor criminals

I have referred to this group as minor criminals simply because they represent a community who will usually target individuals and smaller businesses, rather than major corporations. Their motivation is generally either financial or information theft.

In the first instance, they will enjoy direct financial gain from someone's bank account or by abuse of their credit card; in the second, they may simply post copies of software, music or films on torrent websites so that others may download them free of charge. Naturally, this causes a financial loss to the copyright owner of the pirated material.

Minor criminals can drift either into major crime, especially if their expertise comes to the attention of the organised criminal fraternity, or can become respectable security specialists. Their choice is sometimes decided by how much money they can make, and whether or not they have been caught!

Organised criminals

We now move up another layer in the hierarchy of cybercrime to that of organised criminals. This group are almost exclusively motivated by financial gain, although instances have been reported in the media where known organised criminal gangs have undertaken cyber-attacks on behalf of terrorist groups or nation states in order to disguise their true identity.

Occasionally, the threat actors (as opposed to the threat sponsors) will be acting in their own interests, and will benefit in full from their activities. At other times, they will be acting on behalf of others, who will pay either a fixed fee or a cut of the 'take' for undertaking the cyber-attack.

Organised criminals will often purchase information such as lists of valid credit card names and numbers for use in mass financial scams, or will set the threat actor a specific task to obtain information of value, which can then be sold on to the highest bidder.

Terrorists

Terrorist groups tend to use cyber-attacks for a number of reasons. The first is to make or reinforce a political or religious point – defacement of western websites is quite typical of this variety. The second is the theft of money from organisations in order to further their beliefs and aims. The third, and far more dangerous, is to attack the infrastructure of their political or religious enemies.

Since the first two methods have already been covered, it is worth focusing on the third here.

All nations have some degree of critical infrastructure. As we saw in Chapter 3, the sectors include:

- communications;
- emergency services;
- energy;
- financial services;
- Food;
- government;
- health;
- transport;
- water;
- defence;
- civil nuclear;
- space;
- chemicals.

Of these, the communications and energy sectors are prime targets for terrorism, since a successful attack on either of these will cause enormous disruption to an enemy. All other sectors of course will be considered as useful targets, but the impact may not be felt with such immediacy.

There is a crossover here between cyber-attacks by terrorist organisations and those initiated by nation states. The term 'cyber warfare' is frequently used to describe cyber-attacks by one nation state on another, and although there remains no absolute proof of Russia's guilt, it is widely believed that the cyber-attacks on Estonia in 2007 were essentially considered to be an act of cyber warfare by Russia.[2]

Inside organisations

Having examined those attacker types that conduct cyber-attacks outside conventional organisations, let's now look at those who do so from within them.

Insiders

Until now, we have examined the threats from individuals and organisations who are physically located outside the organisation. However, one of the greatest threats comes from people already within the organisation itself. Many of the cyber incidents they cause are unintentional – often brought about by a lack of understanding of the risks involved when someone clicks on a malware link in an email. Others are more deliberate acts, in which an insider copies and subsequently steals corporate information that is of value to a competitor or a criminal organisation.

In terms of dealing with unintentional insider incidents, this can best be addressed by awareness and training, which we shall explore in much greater detail in Chapter 10.

In the case of deliberate insider activity, the active monitoring of user accounts, internet access and the use of intrusion detection software will identify some of this activity, but organisations can never be certain of completely combating insider cyber security attacks.

An insider who has been well trained and placed specifically within the organisation in order to cause loss or damage will probably be fully aware of the organisation's capabilities in identifying potential attackers, and will behave in a way that does not arouse suspicion.

Security agency surveillance

Security agencies should normally be viewed as being 'the good guys', unless of course you are one of 'the bad guys'. There is, however, a very active debate as to whether security agencies are operating completely within the law, since they have the ability to intercept our communications at many different points.

It is well known for example, that GCHQ monitors satellite and fibre-optic cable transmissions and that the resulting intelligence is shared with the NSA through their 'special' relationship. It is reasonable to assume that the NSA performs the same kinds of interception, and that they also hand over their results in a 'quid pro quo' arrangement.

However, let's for the moment look on the positive side, and remember that the key role of security agencies is to provide support to the police and the military and to protect the UK from cyber threats, terrorism, serious crime and espionage.

MOTIVES – WHAT DRIVES AN ATTACKER

Different types of attacker will have widely differing motives for conducting cyber-attacks. Although there may be other reasons, the following are the most prevalent.

Financial gain

Many, if not most, cyber-attackers are motivated by the prospect of 'easy' money, which will permit them to enjoy a more lavish lifestyle, or to fund further activities that go against the common good (such as crime and terrorism).

Financial gain generally breaks down into three distinct areas:

- ransom;
- theft;
- fraud.

Ransom

Ransomware attacks are very much on the increase. According to a report from Intel, the incidence of ransomware increased by 25 per cent in the first three months of 2016.[3] All the attacker has to do is gain access to a victim's computer – usually through some form of email scam in which the user either follows a link to a website containing malware or accidentally executes an application disguised within the email.

As an example, Fusob now accounts for a substantial proportion of the currently active ransomware. Fusob masquerades as a video player of pornographic films, detects whether the PC's language is of eastern European origin, and if not, locks the device. Purporting to originate from an official authority, it then demands a payment of between 100 and 200 US dollars.[4]

Theft

Theft breaks down into two slightly different areas. The first is one in which the target's banking or credit card credentials are stolen – a crime in itself – and the second is one in which these details are used to purchase goods or services, and the rightful owners of the money are parted unwillingly from it. The credentials may also be sold to other criminals as part of a larger undertaking.

Fraud

This is considered to be slightly different from theft, since fraud leads people to part willingly with their money, and usually delivers little or nothing in return. Cyber fraud often offers for sale expensive computer software (for example Adobe Photoshop) at a knockdown price. The software (if actually delivered) may be useless, impossible to register or may contain malware.

Remember the adage – if it sounds too good to be true, it very probably is.

Another example of this is CEO fraud in which someone with financial sign-off rights at the CEO's organisation is tricked into authorising funds to be transferred to the attacker who may use either phishing techniques to gain access to the CEO's email account, or may email an employee from an email domain name chosen to resemble the target company's true domain name.

Revenge or malicious damage

Some cyber-attacks are carried out in response to an action undertaken or perceived to have been undertaken by the victim. The action itself may have been fully justifiable, but the attacker perceives that they have suffered some injury, deprivation or harm from the action and decides that a cyber reprisal is appropriate. The results of revenge or malicious damage attacks can be quite devastating and have almost ruined many careers, since the statements made and accusations levied in the attack may well be believed, whether true or false.

Attacks of this type can lead the attacker into difficult waters, especially if libel actions ensue, or if the material they post is deemed defamatory, racist, homophobic or fits into any one of a number of proscribed categories. These attacks tend to be either one individual against another; one individual against an organisation; or a number of individuals against an organisation, as in the case of the Anonymous attacks on PayPal, Visa and MasterCard in 2010 in response to the blocking of payments to Wikileaks, known as Operation Payback.[5]

Although the cyber-attack was a success for Anonymous, it was less so for the attackers themselves, as they were identified, tried and convicted.

Espionage

Espionage has been included in this section because whatever its purpose, in the cyber security context it invariably involves some form of cyber-attack, and regardless of whose side the attackers are on, the 'other' side will see them as hostile. One must assume that the security services are extremely well versed in cyber espionage, and that identifying and tracking down criminals and terrorists is an activity that they undertake just as much as discovering the enemy's intentions and capabilities.

There is also a distinction between corporate or industrial espionage conducted in order to gain a commercial or other advantage over another organisation; legitimate surveillance conducted by the police and security services; and finally, espionage conducted by one nation state against another.

However, espionage is a difficult area for many people, since it cuts across our desire for privacy, and although we are generally confident that the security services have our best interests at heart, we do worry that our privacy is being invaded whether it actually is or not.

Cyber espionage generally falls into one of two categories – commercial or military/ nation state. In the case of the Lockheed Martin attack mentioned both in Chapter 3 and below, both of these appear to have been the case.

Intellectual property theft

The theft of IP covers many areas including, but not limited to, music, filmography, formulae, industrial processes, software, designs and development. Industrial espionage has been around for decades.

In the 1960s, the then Soviet Union obtained plans for the supersonic Anglo-French Concorde aircraft, and developed their own Tupolev Tu-144, which for many reasons was not an outstanding success.[6] The potential consequences for British Aerospace and Aerospatiale were of an economic nature, but did not amount to much of a blow in the long term. However, it was later suggested that the development team knew of the Soviets' intention to steal the designs, and allowed them to acquire blueprints with inbuilt design flaws.

In another example, from 2009, in an operation known as Night Dragon, purported to originate from China, attackers stole proprietary information from six American and European oil exploration companies, including Exxon Mobil, Royal Dutch Shell and BP. The attackers' targets were computerised topographical maps that located potential oil and gas reserves, and resulted in the loss of financing information for a number of oil and gas field bids and operations.

Organisations continue to suffer the loss of IP – partly from poor security, but also in part for their failure to adapt sufficiently quickly to new technology. The music industry especially failed to see the potential for music sales over the internet and insisted on sticking with its outdated model of CDs and cassette tapes until it was too late. They are now attempting to fight a rear-guard action against pirated music that is readily available using torrent sharing sites, and are now increasingly adopting the online model, since the problem is clearly not going to go away.

Investigative journalism

Another area that touches a raw nerve is that of investigative journalism. Recently, the press managed to convince the government that there was no need for additional regulation for investigative journalism, and that self-regulation would suffice.[7] This may be true, and as long as an investigation is genuinely 'in the public interest', there would be little or no objection other than from those who are under scrutiny.

However, the press in the UK is notorious for its loose interpretation of its own code of conduct, and frequently crosses the line, becoming invasive and causing great distress to innocent people. Hacking into a celebrity's voicemail may not be a difficult thing to do, but this often results in mere gossip rather than exposing genuine wrongdoing.

Whistle-blowing

Until recently, few people would have associated whistle-blowing with cyber security; then along came Edward Snowden and everything changed.[8]

In early 2013, Snowden, who had been working as a National Security Agency contractor, revealed to three carefully selected journalists that the NSA had been running mass-surveillance programmes against its own citizens. This included information stored by some of the USA's largest technology companies, and data intercepted from global telephone networks and the internet to compile information on millions of US subjects. Snowden also identified the UK's GCHQ as having collected, stored and analysed vast amounts of personal information from global email messages, telephone calls and other resources. Snowden described this as 'probably the most invasive intercept system in the world'.

Governments on both sides of the Atlantic began hasty (and possibly ill thought-out) changes to legislation to either make some of their activities legal, or conversely to wrap their more nefarious activities in such legal jargon that they appear to be legal, whilst providing sufficient leeway for 'interpretation'.

Snowden, now resident in Russia, was not alone in blowing the whistle on some of these operations – Bradley (now Chelsea) Manning also felt sufficiently strongly about some of the US activities and gave more than 700,000 classified or sensitive documents to Wikileaks,[9] which landed him in prison, and Julian Assange of Wikileaks is now a virtual prisoner in the Ecuadorian embassy in London.

Whistle-blowers must be completely committed to their cause, in the full knowledge that although what they expose may be morally or legally reprehensible, the state will probably find ways to present them as criminals and they will almost certainly be punished for doing what they and many other people believe is morally appropriate.

MEANS

Now we should understand how a hacker may go about attacking an individual or an organisation. A quick search on the internet for the term 'hacking tools' returned more than seven million results, so it should be no surprise that somewhere in there should be a software tool that will achieve almost any objective.

Many of these tools are freely downloadable, whilst others may demand some form of payment – either as a one-off fee or on a subscription basis. Hackers, and especially those who also possess good coding skills, are becoming increasingly commercially aware!

The low cost and high availability of these tools is just one side of the coin – the other is that the tools are becoming much simpler to use, so it is easy to see that almost anyone who has more than a little motivation can mount a cyber-attack, often with little concept of the damage they might cause (as in the case of script kiddies) or the depth of trouble they might eventually find themselves in. More experienced attackers will fully understand both the tools and the possible consequences, and will plan accordingly.

As an example, these are just a small selection of the commonly used tools both for penetration testing and also for hacking:

Kali Linux,[10] as the name suggests, is a specialised Linux distribution that can be downloaded for most computing platforms. It contains over 600 penetration testing tools that, amongst other things, are capable of cracking WiFi passwords, creating fake networks and testing for vulnerabilities.

John the Ripper[11] is a password cracking tool that uses a brute force attack method together with dictionaries of commonly used words. As with all such password cracking tools, the complexity of the password (mix of character types and length of password) will determine how long this takes.

Nmap[12] is a network scanning tool that allows the user to understand what host systems are available on the network, what services (application names and versions) those hosts are offering, what operating systems (and OS versions) they are running, and what type of packet filters/firewalls are in use.

Aircrack-NG[13] is a wireless network tool that includes the capability for capturing packets and exporting data to text files for further processing by third party tools; replay attacks, de-authentication, fake access points; checking WiFi cards and driver capabilities; and cracking Wired Equivalent Privacy (WEP) and Wireless Protected Access Pre-Shared Key (WPA-PSK) (Wireless Protected Access (WPA) 1 and 2) passwords.

Wireshark[14] is a network protocol analysis tool for both Unix and Windows networks. It is able to capture live packet data from a network interface; open files containing captured packet data; import packets from text files containing dumps of packet data;

display packets with very detailed protocol information; save captured packet data; export packets in a number of capture file formats; and many more features.

Nessus[15] is a vulnerability scanning tool that can assess systems, networks and applications for weaknesses; detect malware as well as potentially unwanted and unmanaged software; audit system configurations and content against standards; ensure that IT assets are compliant with policy and standards; and identify private information on systems or in documents. Nessus is available in both free and paid-for versions – updates to the free version are generally around six months behind the paid-for version.

Angry IP Scanner[16] is a network discovery tool that 'pings' each IP address on the network to check whether it responds. It can then resolve the hostname, determine the media access control (MAC) address and scan its ports. The amount of information gathered about each host can be extended with plugins.

Metasploit[17] allows a penetration tester (or attacker) the ability to search for security vulnerabilities within networks and systems and has an audit capability. Additionally, Metasploit permits testing of intrusion detection systems.

CYBER-ATTACK METHODS

In this section, we shall examine the approaches to conducting cyber-attacks and the methods employed by attackers to achieve their objectives.

Stages of an attack

Cyber-attacks can occur as seemingly random events – often these will be untargeted attacks, in which the attacker uses a scattergun approach to try and hit as many targets as possible. This type of attack may require some preliminary investigation work, but is more likely to result from the purchase of an email address list or a list of credit card users. The resources or tools required to undertake this type of attack will almost certainly be so-called 'commodity' resources that can be found or bought from sources on the internet.

Another type of attack is posed by more organised individuals or groups, and will usually be targeted directly at individuals, groups of individuals or organisations. Some of the resources or tools required to undertake this type of attack will almost certainly be the 'commodity' type referred to above, but in those cases where specialist attackers have been hired, the tools will often form a bespoke payload, and may be individually crafted or modified for that particular attack.

For a more complex cyber-attack, it would be unusual for the attacker to use just one tool to carry out the attack. It is much more likely that they would use a mixture of tools, each designed to carry out a portion of the overall plan, and these are often referred to as 'blended' attacks.

Whilst the stages of an attack will vary, a sophisticated cyber-attack will typically take a highly structured form, such as the model described by Lockheed Martin's 'Cyber Kill Chain'.[18] There are seven distinct stages:

1. **Reconnaissance**. In the first stage, the attacker will reconnoitre the target's networks and systems, looking for known vulnerabilities that can be exploited as a means of entry. This reconnaissance itself is like to be highly sophisticated, since it must achieve its aims without alerting an intrusion detection system.

2. **Weaponisation (preparation)**. Once the target has been surveyed and the detailed objectives are understood, the attacker will prepare the software tools required to achieve them. This may involve the modification of existing commodity tools, or in extreme cases the development of specialist bespoke tools.

   Attackers may also take this opportunity of elevating their network or system access status, at least until they have deployed and tested the payload.

3. **Delivery**. The attacker will now upload the tools onto the target system or systems, or to a targeted user, checking that they are hidden from both normal view and from detection by more sophisticated means. Delivery could be as simple as loading it onto a USB memory stick that will be found by or given to a user, attaching the malware to an email, placing it on a social media website or in a 'watering hole' website.

4. **Exploitation**. The attacker needs to be certain that the final attack will be successful, so a known vulnerability on the target system will be exploited in order to execute the malware. This might also be the action of a user clicking on a link or opening an email attachment.

5. **Installation**. Having gained access to the target system or systems, the attacker will now install the malware. Often the malware suite will contain additional code to ensure that it cannot be deliberately removed, and may also be time-stamped by the attacker so that it appears to blend in with other legitimate operating systems or application software.

6. **Command and control (C2)**. Having verified that the tools will work as expected, the actual attack can be executed, by possibly choosing the most appropriate moment, for example when many of the security support staff are not at work; or by staging a major diversion, which will draw attention away from the real attack.

   The attacker may use a channel over the internet, DNS or email protocols to achieve this.

7. **Actions on objectives.** Now the attacker can begin the real work, which may be to harvest user credential information, to escalate privileges so that they can gain access to systems currently out of reach, to exfiltrate other data, or simply to modify, delete data or destroy systems.

The theory of the Lockheed Martin Cyber Kill Chain is that if the defending organisation understands the type of attack, with the right tools and techniques they can stop it at any of the earlier stages and prevent the attacker from achieving their final objectives. However, this presupposes that the defending organisation can either be ahead of the attacker, or can at least keep pace with the attack.

In some extreme cases, there will be two separate attacks – the first to establish the exact details of the target, and the second to conduct the actual attack. The whole process can take many months, especially if there is a significant amount of bespoke software to be developed and tested.

A simpler approach would be used for commodity-type attacks, in which no further software development is required, and following the initial reconnaissance, the payload is deployed and the attack is executed very quickly, so as to take advantage of the element of surprise, which might be lost if the time interval is too great.

TYPES OF CYBER-ATTACK AND ATTACK VECTORS

There are numerous types of attack used to breach computers – there are far too many to list them all in this book, so here is a selection of the most common attack types.

Dark patterns

Whilst not actually a cyber-attack as such, dark patterns are an excellent starting point, since they show what can be achieved whilst remaining just on the right side of the law.

Dark patterns are perfectly legal (but usually unethical) methods used by website designers to tempt the unwary into making a choice or selection they might not normally make. Each has a link to an example from www.darkpatterns.org/ in the notes. There are many more such examples of these on their website. Examples of dark patterns include:

Bait and switch techniques – an example of which was included in a Windows 10 upgrade offer by Microsoft. When the user clicked the red 'x' button, expecting to reject the upgrade, the upgrade was actually initialised instead.[19]

Disguised adverts, in which clicking on what appears to be a legitimate link to a website the user wishes to visit, takes them instead to somewhere different, and this can be a malware site.[20]

Enforced subscriptions, in which the user finds they have committed themselves to an ongoing subscription rather than a one-off transaction. Often, the only way to get out of this is to call the organisation's helpline, which can involve a premium rate call.[21]

Friend spam, in which you register your email, Facebook or Twitter account with a website, which then publishes content or sends out bulk email, Facebook messages or Twitter messages using your account.[22]

Hidden costs are a common example of dark patterns. The user begins to make a purchase on a website, but as they progress to the payment, they find that additional charges, such as transaction fees, taxes and so on have been added. The charges may be legitimate, but have been deducted from the original advertised cost to make it appear more attractive.[23]

Misdirection techniques are used to increase revenues from websites. In the recent case of Ryanair, their website led customers to believe that it required some 'Passenger details', which they duly completed. It then added travel insurance to the total cost of the flights, and the only way to remove this was to select the 'No travel insurance' option carefully concealed in a drop-down menu described as 'Country of residence', which defaulted to United Kingdom.[24]

With **price comparison prevention** techniques, users are either not permitted to copy and paste details from a supplier's website, as a means of discouraging them from finding a better price, or the organisation refuses to allow its products to appear on price comparison websites, claiming that this gives the shopper a better deal.[25]

Road blocks are frequently used in order to prevent a user going further with a transaction until they have agreed to something. It frequently requires considerable effort to bypass this type of dark pattern.[26]

Basket extras can be items in a user's website shopping basket that have unexpectedly changed cost. You may be purchasing a subscription and find that the website has changed your choice to a three-year deal, when in fact a one-year subscription is actually better value for money. This type of dark pattern can also include additional items such as insurance in a user's website shopping basket without their knowledge.[27]

Application layer attacks

Application layer attacks take place when firewall ports are left open for an attacker to use as a means of entry. Unfortunately, if an organisation is to be able to conduct business, at least two ports (port 80 – Hypertext Transfer Protocol (HTTP) and port 443 – Hypertext Transfer Protocol Secure (HTTPS)) must always be open for general internet traffic, and a further two ports (port 25 – Simple Mail Transfer Protocol (SMTP) and port 445 – used by Microsoft services) for email traffic. It is through these and other ports that a cyber-attacker can target specific applications – for example a web server application – and take advantage of a known vulnerability.

Botnets

Botnets are a means by which cyber criminals can target a large number of potential victims, most of whom are almost certainly unwilling recipients. Botnets consist of a very large number of malware-infected computers, known as 'zombies', which deliver the payload, whether this is spam email or a DDoS attack. These computers will have been accessed at some time by the botnet owner, sometimes known as a 'herder', who will probably have gained access either by the user clicking on a link in a spam email, or by clicking on a link on a web page, either of which will have downloaded some form of malware onto the user's computer without their knowledge.

This malware will allow the botnet owner to take control of the computer when they require, using one or a group of command and control computers.

The botnet owner may not actually make use of the botnet himself, but may sell the service to people or organisations who wish to send spam email or mount DDoS attacks without having to create their own botnet.

It is important, however, to understand the difference between botnets, which are an aggressive means of conducting a cyber-attack, and distributed computing, where many computers are linked together in an organised endeavour in research.

Occasionally however, the law enforcement agencies manage to identify the botnet's command and control servers and are able to take down the entire botnet, as in the case of the 'GameOverZeus' botnet, which at its peak included over a million zombie computers and had been designed to be impossible to take down.[28]

Brute force attacks

Brute force attacks are those in which a cyber-attacker attempts to discover something – for example, a password – by testing every possible combination of characters until the correct password is revealed.

Brute force attacks can take extended periods of time to succeed, but will invariably find the correct result eventually. The development of faster distributed and parallel computing will reduce the time taken, but it is still a time-consuming activity, and it can often be more efficient to try and find a password by other means such as social engineering.

Buffer overflow attacks

This type of attack is a well-tried and trusted method of breaking an application by providing it with more input than its designer expected or planned for. For example, if an application suggests one uses a username of up to 20 alpha-numeric characters and the user inputs 21, the application might go into an unknown state unless the programmer had applied a check to discard the input if the total was greater than 20 characters. One method of deploying malware is to hide it within user input of this type.

Once an application has been broken in this way, it is quite conceivable that a cyber-attacker might be able to use the application's functions as if he were a bona-fide user.

Most recently written software usually takes account of buffer overflows, but occasionally a new one turns up and the cyber-attackers have a field day until a fix can be developed and installed.

Injection attacks

Another form of attack is the injection attack, in which the attacker either injects software code into a program, or otherwise inserts forbidden characters that might cause an application to terminate, leaving access clear for the attacker. An example of this in Structured Query Language (SQL) databases is to inject an '&' character in order to execute SQL commands.

Network protocol attacks

As mentioned in an earlier chapter, the protocols that underpin the internet are far from secure. These include the following protocols without which the internet does not work:

- User Datagram Protocol (UDP),[29] defined in Request for Comments (RFC) 768;
- Internet Protocol (IP),[30] originally defined in RFC 791;

- Transmission Control Protocol (TCP),[31] originally defined in RFC 793;
- Network Time Protocol (NTP),[32] originally defined in RFC 1305;
- Internet Protocol Version 6 (IPv6),[33] originally defined in RFC 2460;
- BGP[34] originally defined in RFC 1654.

There is no real need for the reader to understand exactly how these work or inter-relate – as with the earlier analogy of the motor car engine, we can still surf the internet without this knowledge, but suffice it to say that if attackers can subvert any of these (and some others), they can do considerable harm.

Rogue update attacks

Rogue update attacks are an extremely popular method of conducting a cyber-attack. They often take advantage of unsuspecting or inexperienced users by suggesting – often in an email or as a pop-up on a website – that some element of the user's computer is out of date and requires an urgent update. This may be either an operating system or commonly used application, and will inevitably end with the computer being infected with some form of malware or ransomware.

Email-borne attacks

Email is very commonly used as a vector for conducting cyber-attacks, since many usernames can be easily guessed by simple software that combines known first names with known surnames, placing a full stop between them, and adding '@' and a known email provider's domain name, such as 'john.smith@gmail.com'.

Software can generate such email address lists extremely quickly, and emails using these addresses can be delivered at little or no cost to the cyber-attacker, potentially reaching thousands of email users at a keystroke. The malware, ransomware or other message that these emails contain will invariably result in some successes, and spammers rely on people's susceptibility to great offers.

Following the Monty Python 'Spam' sketch[35] in 1970, this form of email was dubbed 'spam', and the name has stuck. Fortunately, an increasing number of Internet Service Providers are on the case very promptly, and can identify spam and delete it before it can reach its destination. However, this may, in some cases, require the end user to pay for a premium service. Alternatively, they could purchase the anti-spam service from an independent provider such as Message Labs or AVG.

Wireless network attacks

Cyber-attacks that use wireless connectivity can generally be in one of three areas:

- cyber-attacks on a WiFi (802.x) infrastructure;
- cyber-attacks on a Bluetooth infrastructure;
- cyber-attacks on a Global System for Mobile Communications (GSM)/third generation (3G)/fourth generation (4G) cellular mobile infrastructure.

WiFi attacks

WiFi attacks are extremely common, and can usually be conducted in one of two ways. The more difficult approach is for the attacker to intercept the signal of a wireless access point, to store the intercepted data, and to attempt to recover the access key by 'brute force' searching. Those access points that only have WEP or WPA encryption will be much easier to break into than those with WPA2.

The second (and often more straightforward) method is for the cyber-attacker to introduce his own access point with an SSID similar or identical to that of a genuine access point, for example in any public space offering 'free' WiFi. When an unsuspecting user tries to connect, and gives their access key, the attacker's computer will capture the data and he will be able to access the real network as if he were a genuine user. Further, if the attacker is even more skilled, he will allow the user's computer to make an onward connection to the real network, creating a 'man-in-the-middle' attack. He can now monitor the user's application login details, providing him with access to at least one system within the organisation, from which he may be able to access other systems, or even find he has administrative access.

Bluetooth attacks

Bluetooth attacks tend to be focused on end-user devices that have their Bluetooth wireless connection enabled, and which can be intercepted and accessed from the attacker's device. These generally lead less to full network access, and if the attacker is targeting a particular user, Bluetooth will be an excellent way of achieving his objectives.

Through Bluetooth, an attacker can gain access to the victim's address book, calendar, email and much more besides. An example of the misuse of Bluetooth is in the case of Dublin Airport, which uses a passenger's Bluetooth identity to track them as they pass through the airport.[36]

GSM/3G/4G attacks

Cyber-attacks against cellular mobile devices such as smartphones and tablet computers will mostly use either WiFi or Bluetooth as a mechanism for attacking the device, since the cellular networks use a significantly more complex key management and encryption mechanism to protect the device and its data. Attacks against the GSM (2G) encryption standards are demonstrable using a false base station (similar to a fake wireless access point, but rather more complicated), but are relatively rare unless the attacker is being sponsored by a nation state government or security organisation.

The attacker must also ensure that the target is in close proximity to the false base station in order to verify that their phone connects to this rather than to a genuine network base station.

Attacks on third and fourth generation mobile phones are much less easy to undertake, since the key management and encryption standards have been greatly enhanced so as to make interception and key recovery virtually impossible – at least for the time being.

Social media attacks

Attacks using social media methods are extremely common. These focus on two distinct areas:

- acquisition of personally identifiable information;
- tempting users to enter 'watering holes'.[37]

Acquisition of personally identifiable information (PII)

People using social media sites such as Facebook, Twitter and LinkedIn frequently provide vast quantities of information about themselves, which could be used by a cyber-attacker not only to gain access to the individual's social media account, but also to be able to enter their bank accounts and other websites.

Equally problematic is when people's friends, acquaintances and colleagues post information about an individual on social media, often being thoughtless about the possible consequences.

Many organisations now search for the social media accounts of prospective employees, as this allows them to screen possible recruits covertly.

An attacker looking to discover the names of company directors need only search the Company's House website for free.

Tempting users with a gift or possible prize (a watering hole)

Once a cyber-attacker identifies a potential target on a social media site, they have the opportunity to tempt them into accessing a website containing malware, known as a 'watering hole'. For example, some time ago, I received frequent requests through LinkedIn, offering me the opportunity to win an iPad. All of these were traced to malware sites, at least one of which would have resulted in additional personal information being provided as well as the planting of a virus on the computer.

Social engineering

Social engineering techniques are invariably a low-tech method for a cyber-attacker to acquire personally identifiable information or to gain unauthorised access to a computer.

Often this can begin with a simple phone call or email, and as with the watering hole example above, to tempt or invite the individual to part with information or to click on a link to a malware website.

Other examples of methods of social engineering include an engineer tracing a fault or needing to check the gas/electricity meter; for companies, a person posing as someone from the IT department, often via a telephone call; or 'contractor' attempting to talk their way past the reception desk. Much social engineering is performed by people skilled in 'sweet talking' the user, pretending to be trying to help (especially elderly or less technically aware users) and offering to make their computers more secure or to operate more quickly. Frequently these types of call result in the user's computer being infected with malware or ransomware.

Data aggregation

Data aggregation itself does not actually constitute a cyber-attack. It is simply a means of bringing together items of data or information concerning an individual or group of individuals in order to gain a more detailed picture of them with a view to some form of exploitation as discussed in earlier chapters.

However, when combined with the various methods of cyber-attack covered here, aggregating the resulting data becomes an extremely powerful tool in the hands of an attacker.

THE RISKS OF CONDUCTING A CYBER-ATTACK

There is an old saying, 'Thou shalt not be found out.' Much used in the past, the threat of being discovered applies just as much to cyber-attacks as it does to conventional behaviour. The impact of being identified as the originator of a cyber-attack varies from one type of attacker to another. Some will result in little more than public embarrassment for the miscreant; others could result in an extended holiday at Her Majesty's pleasure; whilst some could precipitate an international incident.

The likelihood of being identified will also vary, based on the attacker's technical abilities and their attention to detail. Inexperienced cyber criminals are more likely to make basic mistakes in their methods, whereas a more mature or experienced attacker or a state-sponsored group are almost certain to mount a highly professional, possibly multi-part attack, using methods described in the 'stages of an attack' section earlier in this chapter.

Although we will examine the principles of risk management in the following chapter, it is worth stating here that the impact or consequences that might befall a cyber-attacker, taken together with the likelihood of their being identified, combine to dictate the level of risk that the attacker faces, and that those individuals or organisations that undertake cyber-attacks must ensure they are equipped to handle them in a skilful manner, or to accept the consequences.

The cyber-attacker will ultimately balance the risks against the possible benefits of success in the cyber equivalent of a cost/benefit analysis, and make an informed choice either to proceed, or to leave well alone. Alternatively, of course, they may simply chance their arm!

At one extreme, an inexperienced hacker who defaces the website of a charitable organisation or posts unsavoury material might expect to find himself being 'flamed'[38] by his peers. At the opposite end of the scale, American government agencies whose networks and systems have been penetrated – however innocently – have been known to demand extradition of the alleged offender.

The message is that unless you are at the very top of your cyber game, don't mess with government or military organisations unless you are prepared to accept the consequences.

NOTES

1. See www.scmagazine.com/ddos-hack-attack-targets-church-of-scientology/article/104588/

2. See www.iar-gwu.org/node/65

3. See www.bbc.co.uk/news/technology-36459022

4. See https://www.cyber.nj.gov/threat-profiles/mobile-malware-variants/fusob

5. See https://www.theguardian.com/technology/2012/nov/22/anonymous-cyber-attacks-paypal-court

6. See www.aviastar.org/air/russia/tu-144.php

7. Following the News International phone hacking scandal, the Leveson inquiry recommended an independent body to oversee the press, but this was rejected by the government.

8. See www.telegraph.co.uk/culture/film/11185627/Edward-Snowden-the-true-story-behind-his-NSA-leaks.html

9. See www.telegraph.co.uk/news/worldnews/wikileaks/10210160/WikiLeaks-Q-and-A-who-is-Bradley-Manning-and-what-did-he-do.html

10. See https://www.kali.org/

11. See www.openwall.com/john/

12. See https://nmap.org/

13. See www.aircrack-ng.org

14. See https://www.wireshark.org/

15. See www.tenable.com/products/nessus-vulnerability-scanner

16. See http://angryip.org/about/

17. See https://www.metasploit.com

18. See www.lockheedmartin.com/us/what-we-do/aerospace-defense/cyber/cyber-kill-chain.html

19. See www.bbc.co.uk/news/technology-36367221

20. See http://darkpatterns.org/softpedia-com-july-2010/

21. See http://darkpatterns.org/audible/

22. See http://darkpatterns.org/wattpad-2010/

23. See http://darkpatterns.org/hotels-com-hidden-costs/

24. See http://darkpatterns.org/ryanair-hide-free-option-dont-insure-me/

25. See http://darkpatterns.org/www-tfl-gov-ukoyster-may-2010/

26. See http://darkpatterns.org/splunk-com-november-2013/

27. See http://darkpatterns.org/norton-online-store/

28. See http://motherboard.vice.com/read/how-the-fbi-took-down-the-botnet-designed-to-be-impossible-to-take-down

29. See https://www.ietf.org/rfc/rfc0768.txt

30. See https://www.ietf.org/rfc/rfc0791.txt

31. See https://www.ietf.org/rfc/rfc0793.txt

32. See https://www.ietf.org/rfc/rfc1305.txt

33. See https://www.ietf.org/rfc/rfc3513.txt

34. See https://www.ietf.org/rfc/rfc4271.txt

35. See https://www.youtube.com/watch?v=anwy2MPT5RE

36. See https://www.usatoday.com/story/travel/roadwarriorvoices/2015/11/17/is-your-airport-secretly-spying-on-you-yes-if-you-are-in-dublin/83302142/

37. In which cyber attackers set up websites that contain attack malware. These are often aimed at specific groups of users.

38. Flaming is the practice of exchanging insults or harsh criticisms of someone's comments made on the internet.

PART II
IMPROVING CYBER SECURITY

6   RISK MANAGEMENT OVERVIEW

The first step in the risk management process is to acknowledge the reality of risk. Denial is a common tactic that substitutes deliberate ignorance for thoughtful planning.

Charles Tremper, American author on law and risk management

In this chapter, we shall review the underlying principle of cyber security – that of risk management. This chapter is not a detailed review of the subject – you can find this in my previous book *Information Risk Management: A practitioner's guide*,[1] also published by BCS, The Chartered Institute for IT.

A GENERAL VIEW OF RISK

In Part I of this book, we looked at some of the impacts of cyber-attacks, the threats that can cause them and some of the possible motives behind an attack. Impacts or consequences are just two of the elements of risk management. The others are assets – the things we care about; vulnerabilities – those things that weaken our defences against cyber-attacks; and likelihood or probability – the chance that the threat will be successfully carried out.

We have already covered impacts in Chapter 4 and threats in Chapter 5, both in some detail, so let's consider the others.

Figure 6.1 shows the relationship between the various elements of risk, and is described in the following paragraphs.

Looking at the relationship between these elements, we can see that threats act on a vulnerability in an asset, which in turn leads to an impact. They also, when there is motivation, combine with the existence of a vulnerability to provide us with the likelihood

Figure 6.1 A general view of the risk environment

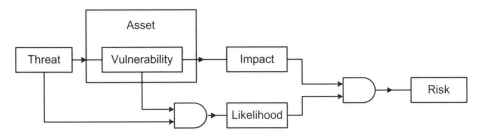

or probability of the threat being carried out. Following this, impacts and likelihood combine to produce risk.

However, there are two sides to the question of motivation – on one hand, there are attackers who have a strong motive for carrying out the attack, whilst on the other, there are script kiddies who happen upon an exploit and try it out to see what happens. When combined with a vulnerability, either situation can result in the likelihood being high.

Occasionally, people confuse 'threats' and 'risks'. They may say that there is the risk of rain when they actually mean there is the threat of rain. The risk is that if it does rain, we might get wet as a result. As we shall see later, the difference is subtle, but important when it comes to risk management.

It is also not unusual for people to confuse probability and likelihood. As we shall see later in this chapter, there is a considerable difference between them, probability being an objective assessment with some form of statistical underpinning, and likelihood being subjective, based on emotions and gut feel.

There are so-called 'inherent' risks in many areas of cyber security, the main one being the possibility that despite all efforts to secure the organisation, an attacker may still find a way of accessing a system and causing damage.

ASSETS

Assets in the wider sense can be almost anything, but in cyber security terms, assets can include not only the data – information we may be trying to protect – but also the complete technical infrastructure – hardware, software, data and information HVAC and premises. Last, but by no means least, are the staff who have the technical knowledge and skills to design and implement the appropriate security measures in place, to maintain them and to respond to incidents.

Although I have drawn the distinction between data and information, for the purposes of this book I have considered the terms to be interchangeable, since they are both assets that have value for their owners and must be equally protected, although the owner of the original data and the owner of the resulting information may be entirely different entities.

VULNERABILITIES

Vulnerabilities are things that reduce the effectiveness of securing assets and come in two distinct varieties. Intrinsic vulnerabilities are inherent in the very nature of an asset, such as the ease of erasing information from magnetic media (whether accidental or deliberate), whereas extrinsic vulnerabilities are those that are poorly applied, such as software that is out of date due to a lack of patching, or vulnerable due to poor coding practices.

Threats exploit vulnerabilities in order to cause an impact to an asset, as shown in Figure 6.1 above, whether it is copied or stolen (confidentiality), changed or damaged (integrity) or access to it is prevented (availability).

Vulnerabilities can exist without our knowledge. There may be security issues with an operating system or an application that a hacker has discovered, but is unknown to the software vendor – this type of vulnerability is called a zero-day vulnerability.

One of the biggest problems with this kind of vulnerability is that once it becomes known to the hacking community it will be ruthlessly exploited until a fix is developed – and more importantly, applied. Once the software vendor announces the fix, knowledge of the vulnerability becomes even greater, and will often result in increased attacks, and an added danger is that individuals and organisations will fail to apply the fix placing themselves at greater risk.

An interesting twist on the publication of known vulnerabilities is the situation in which attackers reverse engineer the vulnerabilities in order to design and build dedicated attack tools.

Other vulnerabilities are more obvious – the lack of antivirus software, which can allow malware to reach the target through email, or firewall protection, which can result in the same problems for internet access. Disaffected staff can either allow malware through the organisation's defences by reconfiguring them, or by bypassing them completely, introducing malware on a USB stick for example. Computers without passwords, with default passwords for operating system software and application software, and shared passwords present easy pickings for even the least experienced attacker.

As we shall see later in this chapter, and also in Chapters 7 to 11, removing or reducing vulnerabilities will go a considerable way towards improving cyber security.

LIKELIHOOD OR PROBABILITY

The chance that something will happen is called the likelihood. Sometimes the term probability is used instead, but it is useful to understand, for our purposes, that there is a considerable difference between the two.

Likelihood is a rather subjective term. If there are dark clouds in the sky, it may rain – but it may not. All we can say is that there is the likelihood of rain, and we may think that the chance of rain may be greater or lesser, depending on the amount of cloud. It is not an especially scientific method of predicting the weather, but provides us with a general guide as to whether or not we should take an umbrella.

Probability on the other hand is much more objective in nature. Probability relies on data – usually statistical data – that will underpin our judgement, and is often expressed in percentage terms. Again, it may be incorrect or expressed as having a margin of error, but at the very least, probability has a rather more scientific basis. Sometimes you may hear of likelihood being referred to as a qualitative assessment, whereas probability is sometimes referred to as a quantitative assessment.

QUALITATIVE AND QUANTITATIVE ASSESSMENTS

The problem we face in risk management is deciding which of the two types of measure to use – a subjective assessment of likelihood or an objective assessment of probability. In fact, one commonly used technique is to combine the two – for example, to use ranges of numerical values to improve the subjective nature of both impact and likelihood as shown in Tables 6.1 and 6.2.

Table 6.1 Typical impact scales

Level of impact	Operational	Financial	Legal and regulatory	Reputational
Very low	Partial loss of a single service	Loss of less than £25K	Warning from regulatory body	Minor negative publicity
Low	Total loss of a single service	Loss between £25K and £250K	Penalties up to £10K	Local negative publicity
Medium	Partial loss of multiple services	Loss between £250K and £1M	Penalties between £10K and £50K	National negative publicity
High	Total loss of multiple services	Loss between £1M and £25M	Penalties between £50K and £500K	EU-wide negative publicity
Very high	Total loss of all services	Loss exceeds £25M	Penalties exceed £500K	Worldwide negative publicity

Although we have provided boundaries for the levels, there will be a degree of uncertainty about the upper and lower limits of each, but in general the ranges should be sufficient to provide a fairly accurate assessment. Clearly these ranges will differ from one scenario to another, but set a common frame of reference when there are a substantial number of assessments to be carried out.

THE RISK MANAGEMENT PROCESS

The generic process for managing risk is illustrated in Figure 6.2. Since we are only taking a brief look at risk management, we will focus on context establishment, risk assessment and risk treatment and omit the communication and consultation, and monitoring and review stages. A more detailed explanation of all of these stages is given in *Information Risk Management: A practitioner's guide.*[2]

Table 6.2 Typical likelihood scales

Level of likelihood	Hacking, malware and social engineering	Environmental	Errors, failures, misuse and physical
Very unlikely	The event is likely to occur once a week	The event is likely to occur once a decade	The event is likely to occur once a month
Unlikely	The event is likely to occur once a day	The event is likely to occur once a year	The event is likely to occur once a week
Possible	The event is likely to occur several times a day	The event is likely to occur once a month	The event is likely to occur once a day
Likely	The event is likely to occur several times an hour	The event is likely to occur weekly	The event is likely to occur several times a day
Very likely	The event is likely to occur at any time	The event is likely to occur at any time	The event is likely to occur at any time

Figure 6.2 The overall risk management process

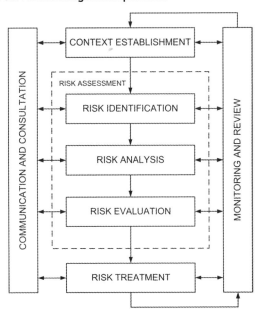

Context establishment

If we look at just the basic components of risk as described above, we can certainly make some form of assessment, but unless this is placed within the context in which the organisation operates, any judgement will have been taken in isolation.

The first stage of the risk management process then is to understand the context in which the organisation operates – financial, commercial and political – so that the later steps take these into account when making decisions regarding how to treat the risks.

Risk assessment

This second stage of the risk management process is broken down into three distinct areas: risk identification, risk analysis and risk evaluation.

Risk identification

Risk management begins by identifying the assets, deciding what value they have to the organisation, and therefore what the impact will be if they were damaged or lost. All assets require a single clearly identified owner who will have overall responsibility for the asset, even if the asset is shared between a number of departments in an organisation.

Some organisations mistakenly allocate ownership of information assets to the IT department, but this (unless it is an IT-specific asset) is a mistake, since the IT department can easily become the unwitting owner of many assets over which they have little or no influence, despite the assets being held on the IT department's systems, since only the genuine owner of the asset will be able to estimate its value to the organisation.

Once we have established the assets, their ownership and their value to the organisation, we can move on to understand what might threaten these assets and what (if any) vulnerabilities the assets have, which provides us with a basis for deciding on the likelihood or probability.

There is an ongoing debate about which aspects of risk identification come in which order. Some people feel that it is easier to identify the impacts if they understand the threats first; others feel that threat assessment can come later. Whichever approach you favour, it is important that you assess:

- the impact of the loss or degradation of assets;
- the vulnerabilities that might contribute to this;
- the threats those assets face;
- the likelihood or probability that the threats will exploit the vulnerabilities and result in an impact.

When assessing the threats, we can make use of a number of models – one of these is referred to by the initial letters D.R.E.A.D. and asks five questions:

- **D**amage – how bad would an attack be?
- **R**eproducibility – how easy is it to reproduce the attack?

- **E**xploitability – how much work is required to launch the attack?
- **A**ffected users – how many people will be impacted?
- **D**iscoverability – how easy it is to discover the threat?

Although rather subjective, the answer to each question is allocated a value (say between 1 for 'low' and 3 for 'high'), and the sum of the five elements delivers the relative threat level.

Impact and likelihood are the two key outputs of this part of the process, and there are two methods of deciding the level of them:

- qualitative impact and likelihood assessment;
- quantitative impact and likelihood assessment.

In the case of the qualitative assessment, the outputs are measured in general subjective terms, such as low, medium and high, whereas in quantitative assessment, objective numerical data is used – for example, financial values for impact and percentages for likelihood.

Each method has its own merits – qualitative assessment can be carried out quite quickly and does not require detailed research or investigation, whereas quantitative assessment can be time-consuming but will usually deliver more accurate results.

It is for the organisation to decide whether such a high degree of accuracy adds value to the assessment exercise – if the resulting risk is very high, the problem will require urgent attention, regardless of whether the risk comes out at 90 per cent or 95 per cent.

As already mentioned, there is, however, a halfway house in which qualitative and quantitative assessments are combined in a 'semi-quantitative' assessment. In these, boundaries are set for the values – for example for impact assessments, 'low' might indicate a financial value between zero and one million pounds; 'medium' might indicate a financial value between one million and ten million pounds, and 'high' might indicate a financial value above ten million pounds.

Similarly, for likelihood assessments, 'low' might indicate a likelihood between zero and 35 per cent; 'medium' might indicate a likelihood between 35 per cent and 70 per cent, and 'high' might indicate a likelihood above 70 per cent.

This provides a more meaningful assessment of risk, especially when presenting a business case to the board for approval.

Risk analysis

Once we have conducted the initial risk identification, we then take the impact and likelihood and combine them in the form of a risk matrix as shown in Figure 6.3, which will allow us to compare the risk levels.

The risk matrix is simply a pictorial representation of the relative levels of all the risks we have identified, and which will allow us to understand the order in which we wish to treat them, based on some form of priority.

Risk matrices most commonly consist of three, four or five ranges of values. Three is often considered to be too few to be meaningful, whilst five allows the possibility of too many results being in the middle. Four is sometimes thought to be a better choice, since the assessor must choose some value either side of the middle ground.

In conjunction with others, the risk assessor will allocate a risk category to each part of the matrix, in order to assist prioritisation. Alternatively, values can be assigned to each cell in the matrix, which enables grouping of risks. A typical example of a risk matrix is shown in Figure 6.3.

Risks measuring 1 to 5 might be graded as trivial; 6 to 10 might be minor; 11 to 15 might be moderate; 16 to 21 might be major; and 21 to 25 might be critical.

Figure 6.3 A typical risk matrix

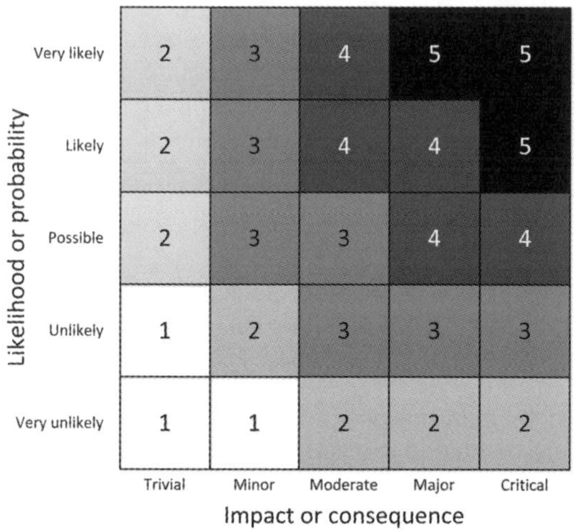

Likelihood or probability	Trivial	Minor	Moderate	Major	Critical
Very likely	2	3	4	5	5
Likely	2	3	4	4	5
Possible	2	3	3	4	4
Unlikely	1	2	3	3	3
Very unlikely	1	1	2	2	2

Impact or consequence

Risk evaluation

Finally, we can decide how we are going to deal with the various risks, usually recording the results in a risk register. There are four ways in which we can deal with or treat them, as shown in Figure 6.4.

- **Risk avoidance or termination**

    In this method of risk treatment, we either stop doing whatever it is that has caused or might cause the risk, or if it is a planned activity, we simply avoid doing it. Whilst this will usually result in the risk being completely eliminated, it may cause the organisation other problems, for example if an organisation was planning to build a data centre and the risk assessment indicated a high likelihood of flooding in the proposed location, the decision would almost certainly be to avoid the risk by abandoning that location and building elsewhere. However, this might prove problematic, since alternative sites might be difficult to locate, be excessively costly or have other limiting factors. This would result in the organisation reviewing all these risks against one another.

Figure 6.4 Strategic risk management options

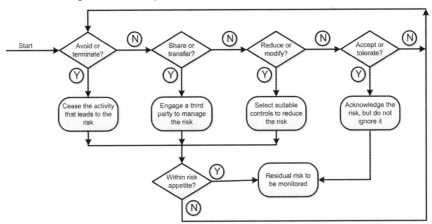

- **Risk sharing or transfer**

  If we find that we cannot avoid the risk, an organisation may decide to share it with a third party. This is usually in the form of insurance, but it is important to remember that even though the organisation may let someone else share or take the risk, they still own the responsibility for it.

  However, some insurance companies will refuse to insure certain types of risk, particularly when the full possible impact is unknown, and in such cases, the organisation must find an alternative method of dealing with it.

- **Risk reduction or modification**

  Some people refer to this as risk treatment, although it is actually just one form of risk treatment. In this option, we do something that will reduce either the impact of the risk or its likelihood, which in turn may require that we reduce either the threat or the vulnerability where this is possible.

  It is often the case that threats cannot be reduced – one cannot, for example, remove the threat of a criminal attempting to hack into an organisation's website, but it may in such cases be possible to reduce the likelihood by applying strict firewall rules or other countermeasures.

- **Risk acceptance or tolerance**

  The final option is to accept or tolerate the risk, especially if it has either a very low impact or likelihood. This is not to be confused with ignoring risk – never a sensible option – but is undertaken knowingly and objectively, and is reviewed at intervals or when a component of the risk changes, such as the asset value, the threat level or the vulnerability.

  Risk acceptance is based largely on the organisation's attitude to risk, known as its risk appetite. Some organisations have a very low risk appetite – for example pharmaceutical companies, who understand that the impact of failure to keep details of their products secure can mean enormous financial loss if they are stolen, or that patients could die if the manufacturing process is tampered with.

On the other hand, organisations like petrochemical companies will have a much higher risk appetite, investing vast sums of money in test drilling for oil reserves, knowing that some attempts will produce no useful results.

- **Residual risk**

  Whilst some forms of risk treatment will completely remove the risk, others will inevitably leave behind an amount of so-called 'residual' risk. This residual risk is either not possible to treat, or, more frequently, too expensive when compared to the cost of the likely impact. Residual risk must be accepted by the organisation, and will require monitoring and regular reviews to ensure that it does not grow and become a treatable risk.

Risk treatment

Risk treatment is also sometimes referred to as risk mitigation, which is generally taken to mean a reduction in the exposure to risk (the impact or consequence) and/or the likelihood of its occurrence.

Once we have decided the most appropriate method of treating risks, we move to the final stage of the risk management process – risk treatment and the use of controls or countermeasures to carry out our decisions.

There are four distinct types of controls:

- detective controls, which allow us to know or be made aware when something has happened or is actually happening;
- directive controls, which invoke some form of procedure that must be followed;
- preventative controls, which stop something from happening;
- corrective controls, which fix a problem after it has happened.

Directive and preventative controls are proactive in nature, since they are carried out before an attack has occurred in order to reduce its impact or the likelihood of it occurring.

Detective and corrective controls are reactive in nature, since they take effect once an attack has actually happened.

The four types of control are implemented in one of three ways:

- Procedural controls, which dictate what actions must be taken in a particular situation. An example of a procedural control would be one in which users are required to change their system access passwords at regular intervals. Such controls might include the vetting of staff by the HR department.
- Physical controls, which prevent some form of physical activity from taking place, such as fitting locks on computer room doors to prevent unauthorised entry.
- Technical controls, which change the way in which some form of hardware or software operates, such as configuring firewall rules in a network.

Sometimes, the risk treatment options – avoid/terminate, transfer/share, reduce/modify and accept/tolerate – are referred to as strategic risk treatment controls; the four types of control – detective, directive, preventative and corrective can be referred to as tactical risk treatment options; and finally, the three methods of implementing the controls – procedural, physical and technical are sometimes referred to as operational controls.

Although it is not strictly speaking an information risk topic, for many years, and for a variety of purposes, organisations have linked the risk management process with a system known as the Plan–Do–Check–Act (PDCA) cycle, otherwise known as the Deming cycle,[3] illustrated in Figure 6.5.

Figure 6.5 The Plan–Do–Check–Act cycle

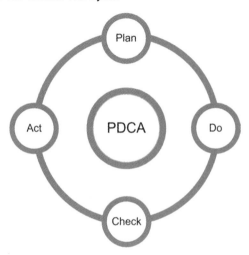

The PDCA cycle has been widely adopted as a basic reference framework in the cyber security, information security, information risk management and business continuity management disciplines as well as many others.

The four stages are described as follows:

Plan

In this stage, we establish the objectives and the processes necessary to deliver the required results. In the cyber security context, this equates to understanding the organisation and its context.

Do

The next stage of the process implements the plan, initially as a means of testing that the plan has been successful. In the cyber security context, this equates to implementation of the information risk management framework.

Check

In this stage, we examine the results we have achieved by either measurement or observation. In the cyber security context, this equates to testing, monitoring and review of the framework.

Act

In the final stage, we put the validated plans into action when an incident occurs and bring lessons learnt from incidents into revisions of the plan. In the cyber security context, this equates to continual improvement of the framework.

Although the descriptions above relate to the wider area of risk management, in cyber security terms, any of these methods can be used to treat risk, since cyber threats can be used equally easily against poor procedures, a lack of good physical security and poor technical security.

We will examine the kinds of controls best suited to cyber security in Chapters 7 to 11.

NOTES

1. *Information Risk Management: A practitioner's guide*, 2014.

2. Ibid

3. See http://whatis.techtarget.com/definition/PDCA-plan-do-check-act

7 BUSINESS CONTINUITY AND DISASTER RECOVERY

Just because the river is quiet does not mean the crocodiles have left.

Malay proverb

In this chapter, we will briefly examine the concepts of business continuity, which looks at the business as a whole, and disaster recovery (DR), which looks at just the IT infrastructure, and which usually forms a component part of an organisation's business continuity (BC) programme.

Although business continuity covers a much broader area than just cyber security, it is important to understand the underlying principles since it is a means of preparing for possible cyber security incidents. Likewise, disaster recovery again is not all about cyber security, but can play a major part in recovering from cyber security incidents.

Both business continuity and disaster recovery have a proactive and a reactive element to their contribution to cyber security; the proactive side attempts to reduce the likelihood that a threat or hazard may cause a disruption, and the reactive side takes care of the recovery if one does occur.

Generally speaking, the longer a disruption lasts, the greater the impact on the organisation, so it helps to clarify the type of disruption, its duration and impact, and how an organisation manages the situation. Table 7.1 provides an example of this and the failure types are covered in more detail below.

Table 7.1 Incident durations and recovery methods

Timescale	Seconds	Minutes	Hours	Days	Weeks	Months
Failure type	Glitch	Event	Incident	Crisis	Disaster	Catastrophe
Recovery by	Equipment	Equipment	Operations	Management	Board	Government
Recovery mode	Automatic	Automatic	Process	Improvisation	Ad hoc	Rebuild
Action	Proactive	Proactive	Proactive	Reactive	Reactive	Reactive

Type of disruption & Duration

Glitches

These are extremely short occurrences, usually lasting just a few seconds at the most and are generally caused by brief interruptions in power or loss of radio or network signal. Activities usually return to normal following most glitches as equipment self-corrects automatically.

Events

Events normally last no more than a few minutes. As with glitches, the equipment they affect is frequently automatically self-correcting, but may on occasion require a degree of manual intervention.

Incidents

Incidents are usually viewed as lasting no more than a few hours. Unlike glitches and events, they require operational resolution, normally involving manual intervention that follows some form of process.

The methods of dealing with glitches, events and incidents are mostly proactive in nature.

Crises

Crises can often last for several days. Although organisations may have plans, processes and procedures to deal with them, and although operational staff will carry out any remedial actions, some degree of improvisation may be required. Crises almost invariably require a higher layer of management to take control of the situation, make decisions and communicate with senior management and the media.

Disasters

Disasters frequently last for weeks. As with crises, operational staff will carry out remedial actions, although at this stage, a degree of ad hoc action may be necessary and although a higher management layer will control activities, the senior management layer will take overall charge of the situation.

Catastrophes

Catastrophes are the most serious level, often lasting for months, or in some cases for years. Their scale tends to affect many communities, and so although individual organisations may be operating their own recovery plans, it is likely that local, regional or even national government will oversee the situation and that a complete rebuilding of the infrastructure may be required.

Despite any proactive planning or activities to lessen their impact or likelihood, crises, disasters and catastrophes all require significant reactive activity, and each will demand an increasing amount of incident management capability.

It is important for organisations to understand that the more time spent in proactive work, the less time will generally be required in reactive work following a cyber-attack.

Business continuity and disaster recovery share the same fundamental Plan–Do–Check–Act cycle as discussed in Chapter 6, in which during the 'Plan' stage we carry out the risk assessment (risk identification, risk analysis and risk evaluation); in the 'Do' stage, we implement the risk treatment options and assemble the plans; in the 'Check' stage, we verify that the plans are fit for purpose by testing and exercising; and finally in the 'Act' stage, we put the plans into practice when a disruptive incident occurs.

BUSINESS CONTINUITY

Putting business continuity into practice is strongly linked to the process of risk management described in Chapter 6, in which we identify the organisation's assets, owners and impacts; assess the likelihood of risks happening; and combine the two to provide a perceived level of risk. From this, we are able to propose strategic, tactical and operational controls, one of the main components of which will be the business continuity plan (BCP) itself.

The plan should include the actions that will cause it to be triggered; who (or which departments) will be responsible for what actions; how they will be contacted; what actions they will take; how, where and when they will communicate with senior management and other stakeholders; and finally, how they will determine when business has resumed to a pre-determined level of normality.

The plan itself may not always contain detailed instructions, as these may change at intervals, but they should be referred to in the plan.

Although cyber security covers only a part of the overall business continuity process, there are certain aspects, especially with regard to the ongoing availability of information and resources, that are very much an integral part of cyber security.

The most obvious of these is that of disaster recovery of information and communications technology (ICT) systems, in which the systems that are likely to be impacted require some form of duplication in order to permit short-term or even immediate recovery.

Business continuity is often referred to as a journey rather than a destination. It looks at the organisation as a whole as opposed to just the information technology aspects. However, that said, the generic business continuity process applies extremely well to cyber security, and can be used to help an organisation to place itself in a very strong position.

The Business Continuity Institute (BCI) describes business continuity as 'The capability of the organisation to continue delivery of its products or services at acceptable redefined levels following a disruptive incident.' It provides excellent guidance on the entire process, and its latest *Good Practice Guidelines* (2013 version)[1] can be purchased for around £24 for a downloaded version or £30 for a printed copy. BCI members enjoy a £10 discount on the printed version, whilst the download version is free of charge to them.

Over several years, the BCI has developed a business continuity management life cycle, having six distinct areas. It is basically a variation on the theme of risk management:

1. Business continuity policy and programme management, in which the overall organisation's business strategy is used to develop the programme of work, each component of which is then managed as a project.

2. Embedding business continuity into the organisation's culture, which includes training, education and awareness, and is covered in Chapter 10 of this book.

3. Analysis, which is all about understanding the organisation, its priorities and objectives, its assets, the potential impacts, the threats or hazards and the vulnerabilities it faces. From this a risk assessment can be undertaken, and the key metrics such as the recovery time objective (RTO),[2] the maximum acceptable outage (MAO)[3] and the maximum tolerable data loss (MTDL)[4] can be derived.

4. Determining the business continuity management strategy and designing the approach to deliver this can now take place, based on the metrics arrived at in the analysis stage, and decisions can be made regarding what proactive measures should be put in place; how response to an incident will be organised; and how the organisation will recover to normal operational levels or to a new, revised level of normality.

5. Implementing the business continuity response will require the efforts of people in various parts of the organisation to put in place the proactive and reactive measures agreed in the previous stage.

6. Validation, which includes exercising, maintaining and reviewing, is a separate activity to embedding the business continuity culture into the organisation, since it deals with the inclusion of people who may already have been involved in the previous stages, and who need no introduction to the subject; rather they need to be able to exercise the various response and recovery plans, validate them and fine-tune them where necessary.

The general timeline for business continuity is illustrated in Figure 7.1. If the organisation is well organised, all six stages of the life cycle should have been completed before an incident occurs.

Figure 7.1 Business continuity timeline

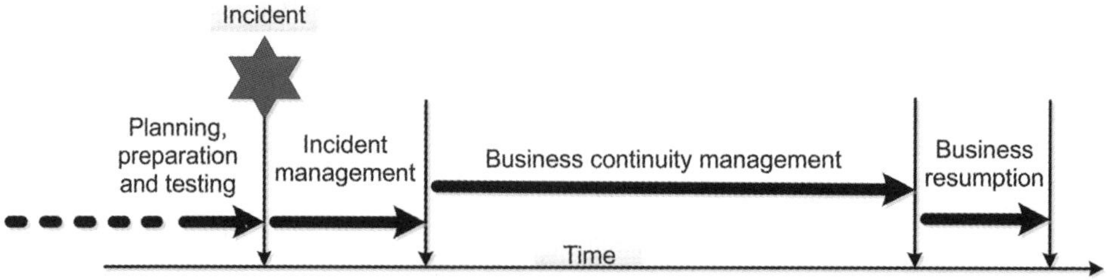

The first actions will be to respond to the incident itself, bringing together the incident management team, gaining an understanding of the situation and agreeing which aspects of the plan are to be implemented. At this time, it will also be important to consider preparing some form of statement that can be given to the media, customers and suppliers so that their expectations are managed.

Next, the processes and procedures that have been developed (which may include disaster recovery mechanisms) will be brought into action, and depending upon the nature of the situation as seen in Table 7.1 above, may be in progress for some time. If this is the case, follow-up media statements will be required.

Finally, once the situation has been resolved, business can be returned to normal, or if the impacts have been considerable, to a new level of normality.

The international standard ISO 22301:2012 – *Societal security – Business continuity management systems – Requirements* covers all aspects of business continuity.

DISASTER RECOVERY

One of the main features of a business continuity plan is in providing the availability determined by the analysis stage of the business continuity process. Disaster recovery is perhaps a misnomer, since it implies that systems, applications and services have failed catastrophically and need to be brought back online. Whilst this might be the case for some services, it is not true for all, since an element of proactive work can (and usually should) be carried out, and it may be the case that just one component in the service has failed, but that this requires a disaster recovery process to be invoked.

As with any business continuity work, there are both proactive and reactive sides to disaster recovery, and since there are no 'one size fits all' solutions, we'll discuss some of the options in general terms.

Standby systems

Conventionally, there are three basic types of standby system – cold, warm and hot – although there are variants within these. Most well-designed standby operations will ensure that there is an effective physical separation between the 'active' and 'standby' systems, since the loss of a data centre or computer room containing both systems would clearly result in no recovery capability.

Traditionally, organisations work on the basis that a minimum separation of 30 km is sufficient to guarantee that a major incident affecting one data centre will not affect the other.

Systems, as we refer to them here, can mean any system that is involved in providing the organisation's service and can include web servers at the front end of the operation as well as back-end servers and support systems and essential parts of the interconnecting networks.

Cold standby systems frequently make use of hardware platforms that are shared by a number of organisations. They may have power applied, and may also have an OS loaded, but they are unlikely to have much, if any, user application software installed, since each organisation's requirements will be subtly different. There will also be no data loaded.

This is the least effective method of restoration, since it may take a significant amount of time and effort to load the operating system (if not already done), to load and configure the user applications and to restore the data from backup media. It will, however, invariably be the lowest cost solution for those organisations who are able to tolerate a longer RTO.

Another disadvantage of cold standby systems is that if they are shared with other organisations, there may be a conflict of resources if more than one organisation declares an incident at, or around, the same time. An example of this was the situation on 11 September 2001, when the attacks on the World Trade Center in New York took place. Most organisations had disaster recovery plans, but a number of them relied on the same providers, which completely overwhelmed their capabilities.

Warm standby systems will generally be pre-loaded with operating systems, some or all user applications, and also data up to a certain backup point. This means that the main task is to bring the data fully up to date, and therefore much reduce the restoration time required.

Warm standby systems are invariably costlier to provide then cold standby, and it is common practice for organisations to use one warm standby system to provide restoration capability for a number of similar systems where this provides an economy of scale. Additionally, those organisations who regularly update their application software may make use of their warm standby systems as training, development and testing platforms before a new or updated application is taken into live service.

Hot standby systems come in several flavours, but increasingly, and especially where no outage time can be tolerated at all, high availability systems are becoming the norm. A basic hot standby system will be as similar as possible in design to a warm standby system, except that the data will be fully up to date, requiring a real-time connection between the active and standby systems.

Two slightly different methods of synchronising the systems are in common use – the first (and faster) method is known as asynchronous working, in which the active system simply transmits data to the standby, but continues processing without waiting for confirmation that the data has been written to disk. The second, slightly slower (but more reliable) method is known as synchronous working, in which the active system transmits data to the standby and waits for confirmation that the data has been written to disk before it continues processing.

In the first method, there is always the possibility that some data will not be received by the standby system, and in cases where nothing less than 100 per cent reliability is required (for example in financial transactions) this will not be sufficiently robust.

In the second method, there will always be a slight time lag between transactions, since this method will provide 100 per cent reliability at the expense of speed. It will also be costlier to implement, since very fast transmission circuits will be required – usually point-to-point optical fibre.

Networks and communications

Whilst the emphasis tends to be on the recovery of key systems, organisations should not overlook the networks and communications technology that support them. Wherever possible, key elements of the communications network should be duplicated so that the failure of one does not cause a total loss of connectivity. Many organisations now use two different transmission providers to ensure that if one has a major network failure, the other should still be able to provide service. This will of course depend on whether one is acting as a carrier for the other, in which case a failure of the main provider's network could result in the other losing service as well.

Larger organisations make use of load balancing systems to ensure that in peak demands on their websites they are able to spread the load across a number of servers, and many also duplicate their firewall infrastructure as added insurance.

Separacy is also a wise consideration – the scenario in which a road repair takes out an organisation's communications is all too familiar, and by providing diverse communications cables on routes separated by 30 m or more and using entry points on opposite sides of a building, the likelihood of failure is much reduced.

Naturally, all this costs money, but when compared with the potential losses that would be incurred in the event of a total infrastructure failure, it is a vital form of insurance – and one that can reduce the cost of revenue loss insurance premiums.

Power

Power is at the heart of everything. Without it, the systems and networks cannot run, and business would grind very quickly to a halt.

Those organisations that suffer regular power outages will probably already have invested in a standby generator or at least an uninterruptible power supply (UPS) system that will continue to deliver sufficient power for a defined period of time.

More frequently nowadays, the two are combined, so that a UPS system will continue to deliver power and remove any power spikes from the supply, after which the standby generator will cut in and deliver power as long as the fuel supply lasts.

The international standard ISO/IEC 27031:2011 – *Information technology – Security techniques – Guidelines for information and communication technology readiness for business continuity* covers many aspects of disaster recovery.

Fire prevention and smoke detection

Whilst this may not immediately appear to be a cyber security issue, access to a fire prevention system could affect an organisation's ability to deliver service. No computer room or data centre would be complete without having smoke detection systems and fire prevention facilities. Systems such as Very Early Smoke Detection Apparatus (VESDA) can identify the release of smoke (and therefore the possibility of fire) before it takes hold and causes real problems.

The system works by sucking air from the area through pipes and sampling the quality of air passing through a laser detection chamber. If the quality falls below acceptable levels, a response can be triggered, and this is often as a result of detection by more than one detector. The extinguishing chemical, normally nowadays an inert gas called Inergen, is discharged to the affected area.

An interesting example of a problem in this area was highlighted in September 2016, when ING tested the system in their data centre in Bucharest. The gas discharge produced sound levels in excess of 130 decibels, which caused excessive vibrations and head crashes in disk drives. The entire data centre was out of action for an extended period of time, resulting in no access by ING's customers.

NOTES

1. See www.thebci.org/index.php/resources/the-good-practice-guidelines

2. The RTO is the duration of time within which business processes must be restored after a disruptive incident in order to avoid unacceptable consequences to the business.

3. The MAO is the time a system can be unavailable before its loss will compromise the organisation's business objectives.

4. The MTDL is the maximum loss of data or information (whether electronic and otherwise) that an organisation can tolerate.

8   BASIC CYBER SECURITY STEPS

If you think technology can solve your problems, you don't understand the problems and you don't understand the technology.
Bruce Schneier, American cryptographer and information security author

In this chapter, we examine steps that can be taken both by individuals and corporate users to improve their cyber security. It provides details of the general steps that can be taken by any user – technical or non-technical–and then covers those steps that are of a rather more technical nature. Finally, the chapter includes a section on mobile working.

As discussed earlier, the response to cyber issues comes in two distinct areas. The first area is that of proactive response, in which we try to either lessen the likelihood of the event happening, or if we cannot do this, lessen its impact.

The other area is reactive response, which will include the disaster recovery capabilities described in the previous chapter, as well as the hands-on work of changing system configurations to apply corrective controls once a cyber security incident has been detected. Either method should reduce the risk, but we may have to accept that there may be some residual loss or damage.

When we leave our house, we take care to lock the doors and windows. This might not prevent a burglar from gaining entry, but it does make his job more difficult. Unless the burglar is specifically targeting us, there is a definite chance that he will go elsewhere and try to enter someone else's property.

It is very much the same with cyber security. If a determined attacker is sufficiently well motivated, skilled and equipped, he will almost certainly eventually succeed in gaining access to our data. However, financial constraints might make it difficult or impossible to repel him, so the emphasis should not therefore be to make 100 per cent sure he is unable to achieve this, since this is an unrealistic expectation. Rather we should try to make the attacker's job so difficult that he goes elsewhere.

We shall deal with personal cyber security steps first, since these, for the most part, will apply both to individuals as well as to people within organisations, and we shall examine the additional steps that larger organisations can take to implement good security in Chapter 9.

GENERAL SECURITY ADVICE

The steps outlined below apply equally to individual home users, SME users and users within larger organisations.

Implementing controls

In Chapter 6, we looked briefly at the process of risk management. This provided us with some high-level options:

- risk avoidance or termination, in which we stop doing whatever it is that gives rise to the risk;
- risk sharing or transfer, in which we share the risk with a third party, often an insurance company;
- risk modification or reduction, in which we find some way of reducing either the likelihood or the impact of the attack;
- risk acceptance or tolerance, in which we accept that some things cannot be readily fixed and that we must accept the consequences.

Most of the actions we can take in the world of cyber security tend to be in the third of these – that of risk modification or reduction, and it is this area that we shall focus on most.

At the next level, there are four general directions we can take. Three of these are pro-active in nature:

- detective, in which we put something in place to detect that an attack is in progress, such as IDSs or antivirus software (which will also react to malware it has detected);
- preventative, in which we put additional facilities in place in an attempt to stop an attack from being successful, such as firewalls;
- directive, in which we set out policies, processes and procedures that people must follow in order to reduce the risk, such as password policies.

The fourth direction is reactive in nature:

- corrective, in which we try to fix something that has happened as the result of an attack, such as removing infected files and blocking unnecessary ports.

Finally, we reach the point at which we can examine the actual actions known as controls or countermeasures that we can take. There are three options, which we shall examine in greater depth:

- physical controls, such as access control systems, which prevent intruders gaining access to equipment or its environment in order to launch a cyber-attack or otherwise cause damage;
- technical controls, such as firewalls, which directly address the security of systems and software that hold our information;
- procedural controls, which tell people both what not to do and also what they must do before, during or following an attack, and, as mentioned earlier, may include vetting of staff by the HR department.

A number of documents providing sound cyber security advice are available, and would be especially valuable to SMEs:

The NCSC publishes a number of cyber security-related advice documents, including the UK government's '10 Steps to Cyber Security', 'Common Cyber Attacks: Reducing the Impact' and '10 Steps: Board Level Responsibility'.[1]

For those looking for more specific detail, there are more than 200 additional documents published, dealing with all aspects of cyber security.[2]

It is worth making a brief examination of the SANS Institute Sliding Scale for Cyber Security,[3] which provides general guidance starting from a proactive position and potentially moving to a highly reactive one.

At the proactive level, the scheme begins with security designed and planned in to the organisation's information architecture, based on the business objectives. This is often the most difficult to achieve, since the security aspects of many systems' hardware and software are outside our control. This represents both preventative and directive action.

It continues proactively, with passive defence, in which additional technology is added to the underlying infrastructure to provide protection against cyber-attacks without the need for human intervention. This represents both preventative and detective action.

From this point, we move into the reactive sphere, beginning with active defence, in which security teams respond to events that cannot be completely controlled by passive defence means. This may include gaining a full understanding of the target, the method of attack, and even, if possible, the identity of the attacker. This represents corrective action.

An example of this might be the case in which an organisation finds itself under a massive DDoS attack. One of the defence mechanisms taken in conjunction with the ISP is to move the company's internet presence to a different connection and IP address, and the ISP then points the DDoS attack into a 'sink' or black hole.

Next, we move into the area of intelligence, in which we use the attacker's identity to discover more detail about them, their motivations, means and methods, which may enable us to prevent further similar attacks. This part of the process will require tools to capture information about the attacker, and also a means of analysing this information to produce viable intelligence.

However, this could be outside the scope of most organisations, and this sort of investigation could well be undertaken by an outside company offering specialist InfoSec skills assisting the attacked company to restore their service. There are a number of models that enable this work; one such is the Diamond Model of Intrusion Analysis;[4] however, it is rather detailed and falls outside the scope of this book, so a link is provided in the notes for you to explore if you wish to do so.

Finally, we arrive at the reactive point of offence – fighting back. This course of action is not recommended, since it could be fraught with danger, and could constitute a cyber-attack in its own right. Individuals and businesses should be discouraged from any form of retaliation – it's much more sensible to respond by alerting the appropriate authorities where possible, and leaving offensive retaliation to security services and where applicable, military agencies.

Physical security

It would appear at first sight that since we're dealing with cyber security, physical security actions might not feature strongly. Whilst there is an element of truth in this, we should not overlook the fact that if an attacker can gain physical access to a key computer system, he can probably achieve anything he wishes just by connecting a USB stick with key-logger software, or inserting a CD or DVD loaded with malware or the data of a fake website.

Restricting physical access to business-critical systems should always be the first step in any proactive activities. Not only does this mean keeping the bad guys out of the computer room, but also everyday users unless they have a very specific requirement to be there. Access to controlled areas should be the exception rather than the rule, and all permissions for access should be subject to a formal procedure, and should be reviewed at regular intervals.

It is good practice to ensure that that any visitor to a computer or network equipment room should be accompanied by a trusted member of staff, preferably one of the organisation's system administrators. It should also be noted that cleaners are not exempt from this policy.

Some simple steps that will make a difference include:

- Locking electronic devices (smartphones, tablet computers and laptops) somewhere secure when you have to leave them.

- Never leaving them unattended in a public place, and keeping them hidden from view when travelling, especially in crowded places like railway stations and airports.

- If you're concerned about your computer camera being accessed by someone, a very simple solution is to place a sticky note over the top of it.

- If you use a lockable steel security cable to secure a device, make sure that it is fastened to something that cannot easily be removed, and make sure you keep the key with you when you leave.

Individual user steps whilst surfing the web

- Users should resist the temptation to install or download unknown or unsolicited applications or programs unless they are confident that they are secure and free from malware. In a corporate environment, no privileged user should use an administrative account for downloading unauthorised software. Their day-to-day user account should not have the level of privilege required to do so.

- When visiting a new website, users should avoid clicking on links to other pages unless they are sure they are valid. Some websites shorten the URL, so the final address is hidden. Let the mouse pointer hover over the link before you click to show the link's real address.

- Cookies are essential to many internet activities such as online shopping, but many are irritating and some are harmful by invading our privacy. Users should periodically edit the cookie list and clean out any that are not needed.

- The Onion Router (TOR) is a browser system that protects users by routing internet traffic through a network of relays run by volunteers all across the globe. It prevents one's internet activities from being observed and prevents the sites we visit from identifying our physical location. TOR should not be used in a corporate environment, since it is well known for subverting end-user security controls, such as anti-malware products.

- Online forms frequently ask for information they really don't require. If you think the question is unnecessary or intrusive, give an answer such as 'not relevant'. If you don't think they really need your telephone number for example, type in something like 01234 000000.

- Users should always delete browser history on public computers. This prevents the next user discovering personal information they may have inadvertently left behind. It's also a good idea to periodically delete it on home computers as well, since it can eat up valuable disk space.

- Users should delete temporary internet files on home computers occasionally, and every time after using a public computer, for example in a library or internet café. This is invariably achieved by accessing the security tab in the browser's preferences, since different browsers will store them in different locations. They take up considerable space on the hard disk, and rarely serve any useful purpose. As with browser history, they can also be used to track one's web surfing experiences.

- Internet passwords should be treated in exactly the same way as ordinary system passwords. See the section on user passwords later in this chapter.

Social engineering

One method by which attackers will attempt to break into a network or system is to use his social engineering skills to talk their way around the organisation's security defences.

- Never provide cold callers with your credentials.

- If you receive spam text messages on your mobile phone, report these to your network provider. Use the number 7726, which spells SPAM on the keyboard of non-smartphones.

- Unless you are confident of the originator of a text message that includes 'Text STOP to unsubscribe' or similar, never do so, since this may be simply a ruse to discover if there is a real person behind the number as opposed to a system of some kind.

- Resist the temptation to reply 'Go away' or words to that effect.

Email

Once an attacker has acquired (or guessed) your email address, they may send offers of apparently attractive goods or services to tempt you into clicking on a link, which is almost certainly going to cause you problems. At best, it will connect you to a website that offers fake goods; at worst, it will download malware onto your device that will be used to extract further information such as banking details, passwords and so on.

- If an email looks suspicious, delete it without opening it. To do this, in most email applications you can usually right-click on the message and consign it to the waste bin with no risk at all.

- Never respond to emails that invite you to enter your credentials such as bank account number and PIN or password. Banks and credit card companies will never ask you to do this, and even if the email appears to be from your own bank, it may well be a scam. It is a sensible idea to check any such emails against one that is known to be legitimate. However, spammers are becoming increasingly professional, and it is often difficult to discern spam from the real thing. If in doubt, allow the mouse to hover over the URL, and check that this has not been obfuscated.

- Phishing attacks often originate from respectable-looking emails purporting to originate from a reputable financial institution requesting that the user verifies their online identity. These are invariably scams, and will take the unsuspecting user to a fake website that is to all intents and purposes an identical copy of the real one. It is essential not to respond to these, and it can be helpful to notify the real institution whose genuine website is being abused.

- Spam email is a blight. Fortunately, many email providers now have highly tuned filters that detect and delete spam without the user even being aware of it. If spam email does make it through their filter, it may (with luck) wind up in a spam email folder in your mail application, making it simple to identify and delete. Do so. Do not be tempted to reply, since this will merely let the originator know that they have found a working email address, and you may end up receiving even more.

- Consider using encrypted email to send sensitive information over the internet. We deal with this in greater detail in the section about encryption later on. For organisations with their own email servers there is the option of turning on 'opportunistic encryption' described in RFC 7435: 'Opportunistic Security: Some Protection Most of the Time'.[5]

Backup and restore

It is incredibly easy to accidentally delete something important, but it is just as easy to make sure you don't.

- It is not recommended that you back up your files to the same hard disk drive that the operating system is installed on, so buy a reliable backup disk drive and make use of the inbuilt software in Microsoft Windows and Apple Mac operating systems.

- As an alternative to a hard disk drive you may consider backing up data to a DVD, Blu-ray or memory stick, but always encrypt the data on your backup device.
- Always store the media used for backups in a secure location to prevent unauthorised access to your data. A fireproof safe is an ideal storage solution, but keep it separate from your computer.

Pirated software

The best advice for pirated material, including films, music and software is just don't download it! You don't know that the material is malware-free, and in any case, much of it is actually illegal, since it usually represents the theft of intellectual property.

- For a business, legal liability where pirated or illicit material is found on one of its computers lies with the business owner, and not with the user of the computer.
- If you discover pirated material, the copyright owner may be interested in hearing about it, and in the case of software, the Federation Against Software Theft (FAST) may take an active interest.[6]

Personal information

Keeping your personal information secure is one of the main objectives of cyber security.

- If the information is extremely sensitive, consider whether you should be keeping it on a device in the first place. If the answer is 'yes', then consider encrypting it.
- Be extremely careful what information you share, and with whom you share it. Consider where the information might be stored, and where it might end up if the person or organisation to whom you are giving it is not as careful about security as you are.

File sharing

Many people and organisations now make use of cloud-based services to share information with friends, family and colleagues. All this is absolutely fine, provided that you have legitimate reasons for sharing information and it does not infringe someone else's copyright. However, there is increasing use of file sharing mechanisms to distribute material illegally.

Corporate staff who access personal cloud-based file sharing services from the workplace pose an additional threat of the possible exfiltration of corporate data/information.

Films, audio recordings, books and other material is hosted or 'seeded' by individual sharers. The user acquiring the information obtains a 'torrent' file from a file sharing service and runs this within file sharing download software. The software links to the individual seed computers and downloads small portions of the file, linking them all together.

- Only share information with family, friends and colleagues if it is not someone else's copyright or unless you have their express permission to do so.

- If you use a file sharing service (such as Dropbox, Amazon Cloud or Microsoft OneDrive), consider encrypting the information, especially if it is in any way sensitive.

Social networks

The use of social networks has increased dramatically in recent years. Facebook, Twitter, Flickr, LinkedIn and Instagram are just a few examples of the most widely used social networking sites. Whilst the idea behind these is to share information between friends, family and colleagues, there are significant dangers in making use of them.

First, you may not know who is reading them if you have not correctly set your access preferences (which may be difficult to identify). Many organisations now examine the social networking site pages of job applicants before deciding whether to invite them for interview.

Second, you do not necessarily know what other people may be posting about you – that embarrassing photograph taken on a recent night out may have been purely in jest, but could reveal some aspect of your character that you would prefer to keep to yourself.

Third, you do not necessarily know the impact of something you have posted about someone else.

- Be careful what you post on any social media networking site. It might come back to bite you later on!

- Be very careful about who you accept as a 'friend'.

- Always ensure your information sharing preferences are set to the most appropriate level.

'Free' USB sticks

Anyone attending a conference these days will probably receive a free USB memory stick containing the presentations and usually some form of advertising or marketing material provided by organisers and sponsors. Most of this is harmless, but there exists the possibility that the memory stick may also contain malware, and it is sound practice to run this through a virus scanner on a stand-alone computer before attempting to make further use of it.

It is well worth remembering the phrase 'There is no such thing as a free lunch'!

A scam sometimes used by the hacking community is to load malware onto a USB memory stick – often a high capacity one – and leave it where their target will be likely to find it. Once plugged into the target's computer, the malware will install itself without the user's knowledge, and (if the attacker has done his job well) will then delete itself from the memory stick leaving no trace. The malware can then commence its task.

114

- Always test a 'free' USB memory stick on a stand-alone computer before plugging it into any other.
- Never use a memory stick you find lying around – it may well be a trap.

Banking applications

Banks are increasingly trying to persuade us to use their online banking applications, both from fixed computers and from mobile phones and tablets. The reason is simple – it saves them money.

Fortunately, the applications they provide and their web interfaces have been thoroughly tested and appear very robust. However, back in 2014 it was a very different story, with vulnerabilities found especially in the mobile applications, but this does not mean we should not be vigilant.

- Remember to keep your banking details secure.
- Log out of the banking application when you have finished your transactions.
- If using a public computer, clear the cookies, browser history and temporary internet files.
- Be aware of people 'shoulder surfing', who may be able to see what you are typing on the screen.

TECHNICAL SECURITY ADVICE

There are many activities covered by technical security, so I have tried to break these down into a few distinct areas.

Device locking

Physical locks are fine, provided that no-one can access your device without the need to remove it.

- The device should be equipped with a password, and a password protected screensaver should cut in at a suitable interval once the device is unattended.

Further protection can be provided by setting the device to delete its data after a number of incorrect password attempts, but this must take into consideration the need for all the data to be backed up.

Encryption

One relatively simple step to prevent unauthorised access to information on a computer, CD/DVD or USB memory stick is to use encryption. There are two distinct methods of achieving this:

- File encryption – in cases where one or two files are of a confidential nature, it is easy to encrypt the individual files, and provide the encryption key securely to those who should have access.

- Drive encryption – in cases where there are multiple files that require protection, or where access to the computer's operating system or applications could constitute a significant threat, the entire drive can be encrypted. When the user switches on the machine, a boot-level password is required to be entered before the computer will even commence starting.

Operating systems and applications

Every computer has a specific operating system, whether it be Linux, Windows or Mac OS X, or indeed a proprietary operating system used by more specialised computer hardware. New or replacement operating systems should only ever be purchased or acquired through a reputable supplier – normally Microsoft and Apple for their operating systems, and a variety of trusted suppliers for Linux.

Once installed, it is essential to ensure that these operating systems are kept up to date, and the suppliers will usually provide a free online updating system to allow this to happen – provided of course that the facility has been enabled.

The same is true for key applications – for example, computers that run Microsoft Office applications can receive updates at the same time as the Windows operating system updates, and Microsoft Office applications that run on Mac OS X can check automatically for updates.

Regular updates contain not only fixes for problems, but also from time to time introduce new features. In these cases, larger organisations should always test an updated operating system or application in a sterile environment before introducing it to the user community to ensure that it does not cause any conflict with existing corporate services.

Antivirus software should be installed – especially on Windows PCs, which are the most prone to virus attacks, but also on Apple Mac computers, which although considerably less susceptible, are still at risk from malware. Some security specialists claim that antivirus software will only catch around 5 per cent of viruses, but it is always wise to have it installed, since failure to do so could still result in a successful attack. It is also essential to install regular antivirus updates – most antivirus software will do this automatically – and to perform regular scans of the computer in case a virus was already present on the machine before the antivirus software was brought completely up to date.

- Ensure that operating systems and key applications are kept fully up to date.

- Enable automatic updates if at all possible.

- Keep antivirus threat databases updated. Even though this doesn't guarantee 100 per cent protection, a good antivirus system will catch the main viruses.

User Account Control (UAC)

In recent years, Microsoft Windows introduced the concept of User Account Control or UAC. This facility prevents users with non-administrative privileges from installing software.

- If several people share the use of a single computer, make sure that all their user accounts are non-administrative, and retain just one master administrative account that is only ever used when required.

- Even if you are the only user of a computer, it is essential to allocate a non-administrative account and to use this instead of the master administrative account, since unauthorised access to this account will enable the user to take complete control of the computer.

- Similar constraints apply to Apple Mac computers, in which non-administrative users are automatically unable to install software, and additionally, the system can be set to prevent an administrative user from installing software that does not originate from the Mac App Store or from an accredited developer.

Firewalls

If the computer has a built-in firewall capability (for example in Windows versions 7, 8 and 10), this should always be enabled, as it is usually quite reliable. There is no need to buy third party firewall software or enable the firewall that comes with many antivirus products, since doing so can cause compatibility issues. The firewall can be configured (using an administrative user account) to prevent or allow access by certain applications, providing an additional layer of security.

Windows 10 offers built-in firewall software called Defender, although it requires enabling.[7]

Antivirus software

Although it is claimed that most antivirus software only traps a small proportion of malware, this small proportion may be sufficient to cause damage or allow malware to infect the user's computer.

Install a reputable antivirus package, such as Norton, AVG, McAfee or Kaspersky. Many of these are free. An antivirus option is built into Windows 10's Defender firewall software.

- Most antivirus packages offer features in addition to antivirus such as protection when surfing the internet, for example, URL checking.

- Enable automatic updating, which will ensure that the latest virus profiles are available.

- Enable the software to conduct regular scans of the computer, so ensuring that any malware that was present before a new virus was identified can be removed.

Java

Although it is an occasionally useful application, Java is known to suffer from a number of vulnerabilities, and unless it is essential that it is used on the computer, it is best turned off, so cutting off another means of attack. It can always be turned back on temporarily or reinstalled if required.

Application software updates

Reputable software companies will always provide updates, not only when they have developed new features, but also when they have identified and fixed vulnerabilities in the software.

- If a known application, such as Microsoft Office or Adobe Acrobat flags up that an update is available, it is always best to allow the update to take place.

- Better still, if the operating system permits automatic updates to take place, this is worth enabling, as it means that your applications are up to date without the need for you to make a decision.

Miscellaneous user activities

User-related activities are often the cause of many of the cyber security issues we face, including misuse – and occasionally abuse – of networks, systems and services. A certain amount of personal discipline is essential, and we shall cover training and awareness in greater detail in Chapter 10.

Keeping users on the straight and narrow is also a management responsibility, and this involves the monitoring of user behaviour and occasionally some form of remedial (possibly disciplinary) action in order to resolve matters.

There are a number of general guidelines that both individual and company users can and should follow.

User passwords

Passwords are like toothbrushes – they should be changed regularly and never shared. Most people (myself included) struggle to keep track of passwords. Whenever you access a new service on the internet, shop for goods or register for information, you are obliged to select a username and password. There is a great deal of common sense in this – it helps the supplier to identify individual users; it (in theory at least) keeps your transactions separate from those of others; and it provides you as a user with a degree of confidence that the website you are using is relatively secure.

Unfortunately, this means that we have multiple usernames and passwords, and we have difficulty remembering them all, so we write them down somewhere, which never a good idea since the piece of paper is likely either to be found by someone who should not know your passwords or to be lost forever in the recycling bin.

The great temptation is to use the same username and password for as many logins as possible, but this is the first step on a slippery slope, since if an attacker finds one instance of it, he will have the opportunity to use it elsewhere.

An attacker will often be able to guess your username, since many websites invite you to use your email address for this, so if you do find yourself in the unfortunate position of having multiple passwords, there are a number of ways in which you can make your life simpler whilst retaining a measure of security.

As mentioned previously and in Appendix A of this book, there are new guidelines regarding passwords in draft by NIST, and although not formally published at the time of writing, are worth investigating.[8]

- Avoid all passwords that include all or part of your name, the names of family members (especially your mother's maiden name) and pets. These are usually extremely easy to guess or discover.

- If you must use simple passwords, use those that can't be easily guessed, such as fictitious' words, like 'gunzleswiped'.[9]

- Where possible, use a mixture of upper and lower case letters, numbers and other symbols.

- Longer passwords are always more secure than shorter ones.

- Do not write passwords down where other people can find them. If you find complex passwords difficult to memorise, or if you have a large number of them, use a password management tool such as KeePass[10] for Microsoft Windows or mSecure[11] for Mac OS X. That way, you will only have to remember the one password to access that. There are many such tools available.

Screen locking

When moving away from your computer in a location where others could obtain access to it, it is always advisable to engage the screensaver, suitably protected by a password. On corporate user computers, this should be set to happen automatically after a pre-determined period of time.

- Configure a screensaver with password protection to cut in after no more than five minutes of inactivity.

- If possible, configure a shortcut to enable the screensaver – a single keystroke or mouse movement are both ideal.

- Never leave a computer unattended in a public place unless the password-protected screensaver has been enabled and the computer is physically secured.

Least privilege

When configuring new users of a system, always follow the rule of least privilege, meaning that they only have the level of access they actually require, as opposed to being made a system administrator. All too often when people buy a new computer, they set their own account as the system administrator. Instead, they should set up the computer using administrative privileges, and then create their own user account without them.

If that account's username and password are obtained by someone else, they can only then access a limited set of functions on the system itself, and not be able to make system changes.

As mentioned earlier in the book, organisations with systems administrators must ensure that they have two accounts, one with administrative privileges and one for day-to-day email and office work. It should be a security policy rule that no-one should ever undertake day-to-day activities with an account that has elevated or administrative privileges.

- Never configure a guest user on a computer to have administrative privileges.

- Always ensure that guest user accounts have password protection turned on.

- Always set up the main user of a computer with a non-administrative account.

- Use the administration account user for essential systems changes only.

Surfing the internet

There is so much information available on the internet that it's difficult to do anything these days without downloading photographs or documents. When visiting websites, and downloading from them, users should take care to ensure that they are reaching a legitimate website. There are proactive preventative steps the user or the organisation can take by putting controls into place to reduce the likelihood of a successful attack, and also simple steps that users themselves can take to avoid risks when surfing the web. The latter were covered earlier in the chapter so we will focus on the proactive preventative steps here:

- Internet browsers are able to block pop-up windows that can contain malware or scripts linking to websites that contain malware. Microsoft Internet Explorer, Mozilla Firefox, Apple Safari and Google Chrome all have this capability using freely available add-in software, such as AdBlock.

- The 'protected' mode on browsers allows a high degree of anonymous web surfing. It isn't guaranteed to be 100 per cent effective, but using it should hide your computer's identity from most prying eyes.

- Parental control can be set in both Microsoft Windows and Apple Mac operating systems to safeguard underage web surfers. In Windows, they are located within the Control Panel application and in Mac they can be found under Preferences.

- Adware and spyware are aggravating intrusions that we experience when we surf the internet. Much of this can be disabled within the internet browser, by disabling pop-up windows for example. However, this will only solve part of the problem, so the use of an 'add-ins or extensions' such as Adblock Plus[12] to the browser can block some adware and spyware, and there are commercial adware blockers available to download. Be cautious though – some of these 'free' applications can actually install adware and spyware instead of removing it.

Encryption of stored and shared information

Encryption is a method of maintaining confidentiality and integrity by scrambling information, usually referred to as 'plain text', so that is cannot be read or changed by unauthorised persons.

In order to encrypt information, a 'key' – invariably a very large number – is used in conjunction with software known as an encryption algorithm to change the plain text to 'cipher text'. The cipher text can only be decrypted by using the correct key in conjunction with the same algorithm.

There are two different flavours of encryption used to ensure confidentiality:

- Symmetric encryption, in which sender and recipient of information share an identical key. Symmetric encryption keys are more at risk of being discovered, since more than one person has access to them. For this reason, they must be changed at intervals, for example daily, or even changed each time they are used.

- Asymmetric encryption, also known as public key encryption, in which both sender and recipient each have two keys, one of which is published publicly, and the other of which is kept private. The recipient's public key is used by the sender to encrypt the information, and the recipient's private key is used by them to decrypt the information.

Symmetric and asymmetric encryption methods are normally used for the encryption of information being transmitted to others, which can be achieved by using an application such as Pretty Good Privacy (PGP),[13] which not only encrypts the information you wish to send, but also allows digital signing of messages, which provides an increased level of trust for the recipient. PGP can also be used to encrypt hard disk drives, but this application of it is less common.

To ensure integrity, a one-way encryption method is adopted, in which a key is used in conjunction with a so-called 'hashing' algorithm that scrambles the plain text in such a way that it cannot be reversed.

Uses of this type of encryption include:

- Hard disk drive encryption in which either the entire hard disk drive or selected files are encrypted. Microsoft Windows (but not all versions) uses an application called BitLocker, whilst Apple Mac OS X has FileVault built into the operating system to achieve this. There are also a number of third party and open source drive encryption products such as PGPDisk and SecureDoc.

The storage of passwords, where the user enters their password, which is then hashed, and the resulting hash value is compared with a previously stored value. Storage of information in the cloud also demands that the information should be encrypted, since this is invariably stored in locations over which users have no control.

Encryption as a technical policy was discussed earlier in the chapter.

MOBILE WORKING

It is always tempting to use 'free' WiFi whenever we have the opportunity, but this brings its own set of threats, such as an attacker who intercepts the data being transmitted between the device and the access point, and if sufficient data can be captured, attempts to recover the encryption key in use (if indeed there is one) and uses the recovered key to gain access to the user's information.

Earlier in the book we heard about the company that provided free WiFi in London's Docklands, but potentially at a terrible cost. This example is extreme, but when we sign up for a free WiFi service, we really have no idea what is happening to our data, since once it has passed through the wireless access point, it is normally completely unencrypted.

Out and about

The recommendations for using free WiFi, especially in unknown locations, include:

- Not using the service for anything that involves a financial transaction where your bank or credit card details are passed.

- Not using any service that does not have an encryption key. Most bars and restaurants who provide free WiFi for example will always make use of an encryption key, since this prevents 'drive-by' users who are not spending money there.

- Avoiding those free WiFi services that use an insecure key such as WEP or WPA. WPA2 (the next generation) is much more secure and resistant to key recovery. Ensure you select WPA2-Personal (aka WPA2-PSK) with Advanced Encryption Standard (AES) encryption.

- For Corporate network users, if a WiFi hot spot must be used, then this should always be done by using a virtual private network (VPN) back to the corporate network. Additionally, corporate machines should always be configured to prevent a feature known as split tunneling, so that when a VPN is in use all traffic is passed over that VPN.

WiFi in the home and the workplace

Most home broadband services nowadays provide the user with a router that contains a wireless access point as well as Ethernet ports, and this is in many ways a much more convenient method of connecting, since we can move around the house without the need to cable up in every room.

There are some basic rules that should be observed when setting up wireless networks in the home and the office:

- Begin by changing the SSID name of the router. Preferably avoid calling it something that would identify your property.

- After setting up the router or wireless access points, change the administration username (if possible), and definitely change the password. See the earlier discussion on user passwords for recommendations.

- Always enable WPA2-Personal with AES encryption.

- Use a long and complex key, which prevents outsiders from making free use of your wireless network, since you never know what they'll be doing. The router supplier will probably print the default key on the side of the router, and you'll need to use this in order to set it up, but it's essential to change it afterwards.

- If the router supports remote administration, turn this off. If you ever need to use it, you can turn it on locally until you have done what you need to do.

- Again, if your router supports Universal Plug 'n' Play, turn it off, as it is a totally insecure protocol.

- Unless you need to use WiFi Protected Setup (WPS) in order to connect to a wireless printer, you should consider turning this off, since it provides an additional vulnerability.

Bluetooth

The history of Bluetooth vulnerabilities is legendary. There is little that an individual can do to make their Bluetooth devices more secure. In some cases, there are no user settings apart from 'on' or 'off'. Here are a few suggestions that should reduce the likelihood of Bluetooth problems:

- Ensure that the Bluetooth device (for example, a smartphone) is password protected.

- Refuse all connection requests from devices you don't recognise.

- If you lose a Bluetooth device (for example a headset), remove it from the list of paired devices so that it can no longer be used to connect to yours.

- Switch Bluetooth-enabled devices off when you're not actually using them.

Location services

This feature applies to mobile devices that make use of GPS to make use of their location, for example when using a mapping application to plot a route between two points. Many smartphone and tablet applications turn on location services automatically when you install them, meaning that they can track your movements. This may be essential as in the example given above, but there is no justification why a smartphone game should require it at all.

- Think carefully about each application on your smartphone or tablet, and make an informed choice about whether location services will enhance your experience, or whether they are simply giving away information to someone about where you are.

- Turn off location services in the general settings menu on all applications that you think should not be making use of them. If the application does require it, it will ask for them to be turned on, and it is your decision as to whether or not you do so.

NOTES

1. See https://www.ncsc.gov.uk/guidance/10-steps-cyber-security

2. See https://www.ncsc.gov.uk/index/guidance

3. See https://www.sans.org/reading-room/whitepapers/analyst/sliding-scale-cyber-security-36240

4. See https://www.threatconnect.com/wp-content/uploads/ThreatConnect-The-Diamond-Model-of-Intrusion-Analysis.pdf

5. See https://tools.ietf.org/html/rfc7435 and https://en.wikipedia.org/wiki/Opportunistic_encryption

6. See www.fast.org

7. See www.pcadvisor.co.uk/how-to/windows/how-turn-on-defender-in-windows-10-3466684/

8. See https://nakedsecurity.sophos.com/2016/08/18/nists-new-password-rules-what-you-need-to-know/

9. 'Gunzleswiped', meaning 'caught' is an example of Gobblefunk – Roald Dahl's own invented language. 'Unwinese' would be a highly appropriate alternative.

10. See http://keepass.info/

11. See https://www.msecure.com/

12. See https://adblockplus.org/

13. See http://openpgp.org

9 ORGANISATIONAL SECURITY STEPS

If you're not doing scans and penetration tests, then just know that someone else is. And they don't work for you.

George Grachis, American author on security and compliance

In this chapter, we cover the security policies that organisations should take in order not only to protect their users from being attacked, but ultimately to protect the organisation itself. The chapter covers directive policies, which are aimed at informing users what they may or may not do; administrative policies, which detail how the organisation should prepare for and, if necessary, respond to cyber security incidents; communal policies including business continuity and disaster recovery; and finally, technical policies, which go into greater detail about technical issues.

Whilst all of the personal, physical and technical controls described in Chapter 8 will be sufficient for individuals and small businesses, larger organisations will need to undertake more significant activities in order to maintain good security. However, before we examine these areas, there are two key points that organisations should consider in far greater detail:

- **Understand your data** – It is absolutely vital that organisations understand the nature of the information over which they have control. This will not only be their own data, but may also be information for which they are deemed to be data processors in the sense of the data protection legislation, or which they are simply storing, as in the case of a cloud provider.

- **Protect the data, not just the perimeter** – Many organisations concentrate on preventing unauthorised access from outside the network without realising that an equally dangerous threat comes from insiders. Whilst it is essential to protect the organisation's network perimeter, it is vital to ensure that access to information from within is equally well protected, principally by the use of strictly enforced access permissions.

SECURITY POLICIES OVERVIEW

Organisations should produce and maintain an overall security policy, which will set the scene for other policies that may be required. In general, security policies need not be lengthy documents, since they do not require a great level of detail – this can be incorporated in lower-level documents such as processes, procedures and work instructions.

For ease of use and clarity, a security policy should generally contain no more than eight sections:

- an overview, stating what aspect of the organisation's operations the policy is intended to address;
- the actual purpose of the policy;
- the scope of the policy – both what is within scope and what is not;
- the policy statements themselves – usually the largest part of the policy document;
- requirements for compliance – including, if appropriate, the penalties for failing to observe the policy, whether these are required by the organisation, the sector regulator, national legislation, national or international standards, or whether they are simply good practice;
- any related standards, policies and procedures;
- definitions of terms used within the policy;
- revision history.

The overall security policy would normally contain policy statements along the lines of:

- The organisation's information must be protected in line with all relevant legislation, sector regulations, business policies and international standards, in particular those relating to data protection, human rights and freedom of information.
- Each of the organisation's information assets will have a nominated information owner who will accept responsibility for defining the appropriate uses of that asset and ensuring that appropriate security measures are in place to protect it.
- The organisation's information will only be made available to those who have a legitimate business need.
- All the organisation's information will be classified according to an appropriate level of privacy and sensitivity.
- The integrity of the organisation's information assets must be maintained at all times.
- Individuals who have been granted access to information have the responsibility to handle it in an appropriate manner and according to its classification.
- The organisation's information must be protected against unauthorised access.
- Compliance with the organisation's information security policies will be enforced.

Organisational security steps fall broadly into four areas:

- **directive policies** that state 'thou shalt' or 'thou shalt not';
- **administrative policies**, that is those that are underpinned by an administrative function;
- **communal policies** in which large parts of the organisation must work together;
- **technical policies** that require specific hardware, software or both.

The following policies and operational controls are likely to be implemented by SMEs and within medium to large organisations.

DIRECTIVE POLICIES

Directive policies are concerned with individual behaviours and tell individuals either what they should do or should not do. As with all policies there should be some mention not only of the consequences of failing to adhere to them, but also of the penalties for failing to do so.

Acceptable use

Acceptable use policies are those to which all users of the organisation's network and services, whether temporary staff, contractors or permanent members of staff, should adhere.

Acceptable use will normally include such areas as personal access (browsing, shopping, etc.) to the internet and email. It may also cover use of organisational facilities when posting on blogs and social media.

Information retention

This policy determines the duration for which information can be stored, and how it should be disposed of when the end of the retention period is reached. This policy will have strong links with the Information Classification Policy and any data protection legislation requirements.

Data and information retention

The organisation's data and information retention policy will link closely with its Information Classification Policy and where appropriate must take into account the requirements of data protection, human rights and freedom of information legislation, since this will impact on the amount of time for which personal information may be stored, for example, as required by Principle 5 of the Data Protection Act.[1]

Information classification

The organisation is likely to possess many different types of information, including publicly available information; information that should be restricted to staff generally; and information that should be available only to very specific members of staff.

The information classification policy should define these levels, avoiding generic terms such as 'confidential' or 'restricted', since these can have different meanings, not only between the public and private sectors, but also between similar organisations.

For each type of information, the policy will dictate how and where the information is stored (and in some cases where it may not be stored); its retention period; how it is labelled; the extent to which it may be shared; how and where it must be backed up; how it is transported; and finally, how it is destroyed when no longer required.

Peer-to-peer (P2P) networking

One of the simplest methods for distributing malware is by concealing it inside files being shared on peer-to-peer (P2P) networks. Unless it is a business imperative, organisations should enforce a policy forbidding the use of P2P networking, including P2P on company computers used at home and on individuals' personal computers used on the organisation's network.

ADMINISTRATIVE POLICIES

Administrative policies deal more with the steps that individuals or groups of individuals take in order to protect the wider organisation. These policies will determine the capabilities of all users within the organisation as opposed to the dos and don'ts of individual users.

Access control

This determines how applications and information are accessed, and can be achieved in a number of ways, including role-based, time of day or date, level of privilege, and whether access is read only or read and write.

An access control policy can quite reasonably include the requirement for different methods of authentication, such as single sign-on, digital certificates, biometrics and token-based authentication.

Change control

Uncontrolled changes are a frequent cause of problems in systems and services. The change control policy will describe the process for making changes to the systems and their supporting network, including the operating system and applications. This may involve detailed analysis of the proposals prior to any attempt at implementation, and will usually include functionality and load testing prior to roll out.

Hand in hand with the change control function is that of change management, which includes informing users of impending changes and having a back-out process that would be invoked should the change fail for any reason.

Termination of access

When employees leave the organisation, it is vital that their access permissions are terminated. If an employee transfers to a new department or to a new role within the existing department, then existing permissions should still be terminated (as opposed to being modified), and then reinstated at levels appropriate to the new role.

Viruses and malware

Viruses and other malware can infect systems without warning, and must be dealt with in a formalised manner rather than an ad hoc approach that may do more harm than good. The policy will define who will address the problem and the procedure they will follow to identify, isolate if possible, and remove or quarantine the virus.

Passwords

Password management is a key aspect of information security policy, and one that is frequently overlooked.

Users are notoriously bad at password management. They will (when they can get away with it) use passwords they find easy to remember, such as their mother's maiden name, their birthday or the name of their pet, all of which are relatively simple for an attacker to guess or discover. Users should be warned of the dangers of this practice, and advised how to create strong passwords.

In the past, the general advice has always been to recommend a minimum password length; to use a complex combination of letters, numbers and other symbols; and to force the user to change their password at intervals.

The USA's National Institute of Standards and Technology has recently changed its view on passwords, and has published a draft of a new standard – SP 800 63-3,[2] which deals with digital identity. The draft currently makes three recommendations of things that organisations should do, and four that they should avoid.

Things that organisations should do:

- Since users are only human, instead of placing the burden on the user, place the burden on the verifier. It is much easier to write one piece of software than it is to force hundreds or thousands of users to conform to a set of rules, and this is also less stressful on the users.

- Size matters – by all means check for password length, and encourage users to make use of longer passwords.

- Check the passwords the users enter against a dictionary list of known poor or bad passwords, and require the users to try again if the test proves positive.

Things that organisations should avoid:

- Complex rules for composition, such as a combination of upper and lower case letters, numbers and other keyboard symbols. These are almost impossible for users to remember (especially if they are required to have different passwords for each application), and may only result in users writing them down.

- Password hints can help the users remember their passwords, but they can also provide clues to an attacker. Since the originator of a targeted attack may well have undertaken considerable research into their target, such clues could easily betray the user's credentials.

- Credentials chosen from lists are similarly of dubious value. Such choices as mother's maiden name, town of birth, name of first school and so on are just as likely to be known to a serious attacker as the hints described above.

- Expiration of passwords after a finite period of time does little to improve password security, and only serves to complicate matters for the user. Users should have the option to change their password if they feel that it may have been compromised, but forcing them to do it without good cause only adds to their burden.

The policy should also include a statement regarding the changing of default passwords, especially those that allow root access to systems and network devices such as firewalls and routers.

Occasionally, passwords are embedded within applications, especially in cases where one application must connect and exchange data with another without human intervention. The use of embedded passwords should be avoided wherever possible, since they may be widely known and therefore represent a potential avenue of attack, but if they must be used, they should be changed from the manufacturer's default.

No password is immune from a 'brute force' search in which an attacker's computer tries every combination of characters until it eventually finds the right one. Using long passwords will make this much more complicated, and the attacker may simply give up and move on to another, possibly easier, target.

Users also have a habit of using the same password on multiple systems. Attackers know this, and if they discover one of a user's passwords, it will normally allow them to access other systems as well. Users should have a different password for each system to which they require access.

If users must have multiple passwords and have difficulty in remembering them all, a password management tool may well be an appropriate solution as discussed in Chapter 8; alternatively, single sign-on is a method that can be used to alleviate multiple password issues.

Users should also be discouraged from reusing passwords, and where available, some access control systems, such as Microsoft's Active Directory, can be configured to forbid reuse within a certain period of time.

As mentioned previously and in Appendix A of this book, there are new guidelines regarding passwords in draft by NIST, and, although not formally published at the time of writing, they are worth investigating.[3]

Removable media

Removable media, including USB memory sticks, DVDs and external disk drives can all be not only a source of malware if they have been infected on another system outside the organisation, but also a means of users removing information from the organisation without authority.

Although not obviously seen as removable media, there are many USB devices that can easily act as removeable media and become a source of malware, including so-called smartphones, tablet computers and even e-cigarettes.

System hardware can be easily configured to prevent the use of removable media unless the user has a very specific, authorised need.

Shared network resources

Shared network drives are an extremely useful resource, allowing staff to move large volume files around the organisation. However, they suffer from one serious failure and that is that there is usually no audit trail of who copied files onto the hard drive and who subsequently copied them off.

Additionally, some forms of malware such as worms can infect multiple shared drives within a network.

If files are to be shared between users within the organisation, or with users outside the organisation, then a collaborative system such as Microsoft SharePoint should be considered, since this allows the organisation to select who can make use of the system to share files, and retain an audit trail of who has done what and when.

Segregation of duties

It is all too easy for organisations to allocate people who understand IT to wide-ranging roles, and in some situations, this is a mistake, since it can provide administration-level users with the capability to create and allocate high-level user accounts for people who do not or should not have them.

This can lead, for example, to a member of staff being able both to order goods and authorise their purchase, which can lead to fraudulent activities. The correct method of addressing this is to ensure that a particular type of user account cannot carry out both functions – in other words, to completely segregate the duties and access permissions of two account types.

Backups and restoral

Organisations should always operate a policy that demands that information is backed up; including the backup intervals (which may differ for different information elements); the backup method (for example, full or incremental); the media upon which backups are stored; whether backup media is kept on the organisation's premises (but not the same location as that of the data being backed up) or at a third party location; the maximum time allowed for recovering the data including transport from third party sites; and how often backup media is tested for reliable restoral.

Most large organisations will have a backup policy, but as with all policies, this should be regularly reviewed to ensure that the correct systems are being backed up to some form of removable (encrypted) media, which is then stored off-site in a secure location. However, that is only half the story, since many organisations have discovered to their cost that after a period of time, some backup tapes or disks cannot be read, and so it is essential to perform a test restoral of data at intervals as a sanity check.

As an alternative to conventional backups, some organisations rely on the use of cloud services to maintain a long-term store of data, and whilst this might be a cost-effective solution, it does require careful planning and management, since it is often very easy to delete files stored in the cloud, which rather defeats the object of the exercise.

Another increasingly popular alternative is where the move to virtualisation has occurred and storage area networks (SAN) are becoming widely used, configured with a second SAN for backup. The SAN can be updated daily or by regular snapshots during the day. However, additional backups to other media would normally be recommended.

Antivirus software

Some organisations have begun to move away from antivirus software, having been put off by stories in the media about its lack of effectiveness, especially when new malware appears but has not yet been addressed by the antivirus software author. These are called 'zero-day' vulnerabilities, since once they become known, the author has no time at all in which to provide a fix.

However, even if antivirus software does not identify and trap every vulnerability, it will prevent known vulnerabilities from causing problems by neutralising or quarantining the offending virus, so it is still very much worthwhile maintaining an antivirus capability, and ensuring that it is kept fully up to date.

Software updates

Many of the key applications upon which organisations rely – for example, Microsoft Windows, Internet Explorer and Office; Adobe Acrobat Reader, Mozilla Firefox or Google Chrome – are all targets in which attackers find vulnerabilities. The authors of this software will invariably produce updates to fix known vulnerabilities at regular intervals, and it is essential that organisations keep these operating systems and applications fully up to date with the latest patches. Failure to do this can result in an attacker taking advantage of the gap between the vulnerability becoming known and the organisation applying the patch to fix it.

Where possible and practicable, automatic updating should be applied, since this does not require further manual input from support staff, and reduces the 'patch gap' to a minimum.

Additionally, any software update that will result in a major change to the operating system or applications should have a back-out plan so that the organisation can revert quickly and easily to the original version.

Remote access/guest/third party access

Whether or not an organisation makes use of VPNs for network access, it will be necessary to define how staff and third party contractors are able to access the network and its systems. This policy will also link closely with other policies such as access control, security awareness and passwords.

Wireless/mobile devices

This type of policy will set out the organisation's requirements for implementing wireless access points around its premises; how the wireless infrastructure devices must be configured and secured, including the encryption method; whether the SSID is broadcast; and which bands and channels are to be used.

When considering devices that make use of Bluetooth for communications, it should only be enabled when it is actually required and then turned off. Once initially configured for use, the organisation should ensure that the device's visibility is set to 'Hidden' so that it cannot be scanned by other Bluetooth devices. If device pairing is mandated, all devices must be configured to 'Unauthorised', which then requires authorisation for each connection request. Applications that are unsigned or sent from unknown sources should be rejected.

For mobile devices supplied by the organisation, there will also need to be a section of the policy that regulates when and where these may be used over wireless networks that are not owned or provided by the organisation, for example public wireless or third party networks.

This policy will also include a definition of what information may be stored on the device; what applications may be loaded onto it; whether it may be used to gain access to the wider internet; and whether information stored on the device is or becomes the intellectual property of the organisation.

Bring your own device (BYOD)

This policy will overlap to a certain extent with the mobile device policy described above, but in this case, the device – such as a laptop computer, tablet computer or smartphone – will be the personal property of the staff member as opposed to being owned by the organisation.

The policy may include statements regarding use by friends or members of the user's family, and may also require separate login procedures for access to the organisation's network and, where necessary, hard disk drive encryption.

Peripherals

By default, many operating systems install auxiliary services that are not critical to the operation of the system and which provide avenues of attack. When configuring users' computers, system administrators can disable and remove unnecessary services and peripherals such as USB ports, SD card slots and CD/DVD drives, which, once they are removed, cannot be enabled or used. This policy may form part of a more general procurement policy on the organisation's IT infrastructure.

Isolation of compromised systems

Organisations that have detected that a system has been compromised would be well advised to isolate it quickly from the network in order to prevent possible malware from spreading to other systems on the network. Once removed, it would be useful to perform a forensic analysis on the system, using a specialist organisation if the relevant skills are not available internally, and finally to restore the systems to normal operation using trusted media.

Browser add-ins and extensions

Attacks on internet browsers, add-ins and extensions are becoming increasingly prevalent, and it is critical that attackers should not be able to use vulnerabilities in software such as Microsoft's Internet Explorer or Adobe's Acrobat Reader or Adobe Flash to gain access to systems. Organisations should make use of the vendor's automatic update or software distribution facilities to install patches as soon as they become available.

AutoRun

AutoRun is a facility provided on Microsoft Windows that permits a command file on media such as a USB memory stick, CD or DVD to execute when it is inserted into the computer. This is an extremely simple way for an attacker to gain access to a system, since the user may be totally unaware that the media is infected and may not notice the program is running.

Turning off AutoRun will probably be a minor inconvenience both to users and to system administrators.

It is interesting to note that Apple's OS X operating system does not support this kind of facility.

Adobe Acrobat Reader

Adobe's Portable Document Format (PDF) has become the de facto standard format for sharing information. Almost any file, presentation or document can be exported or converted into PDF format, and will look identical on any type of computer, smartphone or tablet that has Acrobat Reader software loaded. However, an increasing number of cyber-attacks are being conducted by inserting malware into PDF documents, which are then transferred to the device.

Organisations can protect their machines from such attacks hidden inside PDF files by hardening Acrobat Reader, by downloading the advice from the NSA.[4]

Outsourcing

Organisations may find it economically advantageous to outsource certain aspects of their operations. This is becoming increasingly so in the case of the organisation's ICT infrastructure, and outsource service providers may offer to provide not only data storage, but also the operating system hardware and software and the application software required for the organisation's operations.

In some cases, this will be provided at a dedicated third party site, as is frequently used in DR arrangements; or may be provided in a more virtual environment such as cloud services.

In either case, it will be vital that the organisation has a clear policy regarding the selection of suppliers for this type of service, which will form the basis of a service level agreement (SLA), and should also include an exit policy should the organisation decide to move away from a supplier, especially with regard to ownership of indexing to the organisation's information and subsequent destruction of any the organisation's information remaining in the cloud.

COMMUNAL POLICIES

Communal policies are those that may have an impact not only on individuals within the organisation, but also on the wider context of the business and the environment in which it exists.

Contingency planning

Contingency planning determines how data or access to systems is made available to users during the prescribed hours of operation. The policy will cover what measures are to be put in place to ensure that access is available in the event of failure of either the systems themselves or the means of accessing them such as a web server and the associated supporting network.

A contingency planning policy will often link directly to a business continuity or to a disaster recovery policy.

Incident response

The organisation's incident response policy will detail how incidents are reported, investigated and how they are resolved. In the event that certain predefined failure thresholds are exceeded, additional measures such as business continuity and disaster recovery plans may need to be invoked.

An incident may also require communication regarding the incident to be made available to staff, customers, third party suppliers, the public at large and, if the organisation is part of a highly regulated sector (such as energy, finance or transport), the incident may also require notification to the sector regulator.

As with business continuity and disaster recovery plans, incident response plans should be reviewed at regular intervals or when any major aspect of the organisation's business changes, and also tested at regular intervals.

User awareness and training

Since many of the cyber security issues we experience are caused by users, making them aware of the risks they face – including the major threats, vulnerabilities and potential impacts – is a highly important step to achieving better cyber security.

Awareness is the first step, and introduces users gradually to the things they need to know and understand, so that security becomes second nature to them, and they cease to foster bad security habits and move towards a position where they are fully committed to good security practice. This is then supplemented with training for those people who are more actively involved in day-to-day security operations, and who require specialist training courses in order to properly fulfil their role.

User awareness and training are covered in greater detail in Chapter 10.

TECHNICAL POLICIES

Technical policies are those of a purely technical nature. They may be necessary either in order to allow other policies previously described to operate successfully, or may stand on their own.

Spam email filtering

Spam email is the bane of most people's lives. It can range from the simply annoying to the positively alarming. Nowadays, most email service providers check email passing through their systems and filter out those that have been previously flagged as spam.

However, this may not remove all spam email, as new spam messages will always arise, and some filters may either never add them to their blacklist, or it may take time for the spam to be reported. Organisations can make use of their own spam filters such as SpamAssassin,[5] which will remove unwanted email from entering users' inboxes and junk mail folders.

Alternatively, organisations may outsource email scanning to a specialist organisation such as Message Labs. It is also vitally important to instruct users as part of the organisation's awareness programme how to identify spam and junk mail even if it originates from a known and normally trusted source.

Audit trails

These allow an organisation to follow a sequence of events in cases where security incidents have occurred and, where necessary, to be able to show that a user has or has not carried out a particular action. Such evidence might be required in cases where legal proceedings take place, in which case the audit trail must also be forensically robust.

Firewalls

Firewall policies will determine the way in which firewalls are deployed and configured to form an integral part of the network, especially with regard to the rules that must be applied and subsequently maintained.

Firewalls should be used to block all incoming connections from the internet to services that the organisation does not wish to be available. By default, all incoming connections should be denied, and only allowed for those services that the organisation explicitly wishes to offer to the outside world.

Good practice also calls for the IP address of the incoming session to be a valid public IP address and not an IP address associated with the business itself. For example, if the business has a block of 32 public IP addresses these must be filtered out.

In addition to firewalls, it may be an advantage to partition the organisation's network into separate areas by splitting them according to their function, such as research and development, operations and finance, making it more difficult for an attacker to reach a particular service (see the later item on VPNs).

It is also common practice for organisations to create another barrier between the external and internal networks by introducing a so-called demilitarised zone or DMZ.

Good practice also requires that any outgoing connection from the organisation to the internet originates from a specific proxy server or service located on a DMZ and not within the main network.

Firewalls come in various shapes and sizes. Many require specialised hardware on which to operate, and require well-trained staff to configure and maintain them. The decision on which type of firewall to use and how it should be configured is best left to specialist advice, since it must not only provide protection for the business against unwanted intrusion, but also meet the business needs as regards what can and cannot be transmitted through it.

Other firewalls come built in to desktop operating systems – these are much simpler and require little, if any, configuration. On user computers, these should always be enabled, and the user's access should prevent them from changing this by providing them with a non-administrative account.

Encryption

The information encryption policy will go hand in hand with the information classification policy, in that it will define, for certain levels of information classification (for example, secret or top secret), how sensitive information will be encrypted and how the encryption keys will be managed and exchanged.

For example, information classified at a certain level could be exchanged between two people using a straightforward encryption mechanism such as PGP, with each owning their own encryption keys, whilst other information might require the use of a full-blown public key management system, with encryption keys centrally managed and distributed.

The policy should additionally make the distinction between information in transit (for example, within emails) and information at rest – that is stored on hard drives or other media, especially if stored in the cloud.

For information at rest, encrypting the hard drive of a mobile user's computer is relatively straightforward, and means that the device cannot be used without the user's password to decrypt the data, making the information useless to anyone who steals it.

On Apple Mac computers, turning on the free built-in FileVault software[6] will encrypt the entire hard drive, whilst for Windows users there are two options. The first, for Professional or Enterprise versions of Windows, is to enable the inbuilt BitLocker software.[7] The second, for other versions of Windows, is to download and install the free VeraCrypt encryption software.[8]

Business data that is being stored in the cloud should always be encrypted, since it is always uncertain in which country or countries the cloud storage is located, and those countries' jurisdictions may not place a high level of protection on data, even to the extent of intercepting and analysing it themselves.

Sensitive information that is being moved to another location – whether by some form of media like a memory stick or by email – should always be encrypted, so that, again, anyone who is able to intercept the transmission or steal the media will be unable to access the information.

The key lengths used in symmetric encryption algorithms such as Data Encryption Standard (DES), 3DES and AES are typically 56, 112, 128 or 256 bits in length, whereas the keys used in asymmetric or public key cryptography (typically 2048 bits in length) are used in the initial set-up of an encrypted session that determines the actual fixed encryption key that will be used by the symmetric algorithm during the session. These keys are not typically used for the main encryption work because they require too much computation resource.

Secure Socket Shell (SSH) and Transport Layer Security (TLS) keys

Secure Socket Shell (SSH), is a network protocol that provides administrators with a secure method of access to remote systems. It provides a means of strong authentication and encrypted communication between two systems over an insecure network, especially the internet. It is widely used by network administrators for the remote management of systems and applications, enabling them to log on to another system, execute commands and move files between systems.

The Transport Layer Security (TLS) protocol provides both confidentiality and integrity between two communicating applications exchanging information such as that between a user's web browser and an internet banking or e-commerce application. TLS is also used in VPN connections, instant messaging services and Voice-Over IP (VoIP) applications.

Both SSH and TLS make use of encryption keys (as described above) to secure the transfers, and are typically 256 bits in length

Abuse of SSH and TLS keys is not uncommon. In order to reduce the likelihood of insiders taking advantage of these when they leave the organisation, which renders critical network infrastructure open to malicious access, it is recommended that organisations rotate SSH and TLS keys at intervals.

Digital certificates

Digital certificates are widely used to provide authentication of websites, particularly when conducting financial transactions. Digital certificates can be purchased from accredited certification authorities (CAs) both for personal use and by organisations. However, it is important to remember to renew the certificate (normally annually), since failure to do so renders the certificate useless, and users whose web browser detects this will receive a notification that the certificate has expired. This may result in their deciding not to continue with the online transaction.

Email attachments

As an integral part of their awareness training, employees should be instructed that they should not open email attachments unless they are expecting them. Additionally, users should be forbidden to execute software that has been downloaded from the internet unless it has been scanned for viruses and tested for security vulnerabilities. Users who visit a compromised website can unintentionally introduce malware.

Organisations should configure email servers to block or remove emails that contain those file attachments that are commonly used to spread malware, such as .vbs, .bat, .exe, .pif, .zip and .scr files.

Network security

Network security policies are very wide-ranging, taking into account how the organisation's networks can be secured against intrusion using a combination of firewalls, intrusion detection software, antivirus software, operating system and application patching and password protection.

These should include fixed and wireless local area networks (LANs), VPNs, wide area networks (WANs) and SANs.

Virtual private networks (VPNs)

The use of virtual private networks is commonplace, especially in larger organisations, and a policy will be required that sets out how and where these are deployed; who may make use of them (for example, for remote access by staff, guests and third party contractors); and how they are configured and secured.

The use of VPNs should be part of the organisation's strategy that includes network segregation and firewall deployment.

Physical access

This will define how access to the physical areas of the organisation is controlled, and may include perimeter fencing and gates with movement detection and/or CCTV systems, electronically controlled gates and physical security guards.

Within the organisation's sites, physical access control will normally be governed by electronic door access systems, whether by personal identification number (PIN), wireless proximity card or a combination of both. The supporting system will dictate the levels and locations of access available to individual members of staff, visitors and contractors.

Internally, infrared movement detection and CCTV systems are also frequently used, especially in highly sensitive areas.

Intrusion detection systems (IDS)

As with many security tools, intrusion detection systems are just one weapon in the security manager's armoury. As the name suggests, their purpose is to try to identify when unauthorised intrusion to a network or computer system is being attempted, and they are available in a variety of forms:

- Host intrusion detection systems (HIDS) are installed on individual computer systems, and monitor that system's configuration only. If an HIDS perceives an abnormal change in a system configuration, it will send an alert message to a console for a security operator to examine.

- Network intrusion detection systems (NIDS) are installed on internal networks and subnetworks in order to detect abnormal network traffic such as attacks on firewalls. They will also report to a console if they detect an attack, but additionally can take some form of action, such as to change firewall rules.

- Under certain circumstances it may be necessary to undertake such work using forensic techniques and to retain hard drives and data for possible use in legal proceedings.

NOTES

1. See www.legislation.gov.uk/ukpga/1998/29/contents

2. See https://pages.nist.gov/800-63-3/

3. See https://nakedsecurity.sophos.com/2016/08/18/nists-new-password-rules-what-you-need-to-know/

4. See https://www.scribd.com/document/280616716/Recommendations-for-Configuring-Adobe-Acrobat-Reader-XI-in-a-Windows-Environment

5. See http://spamassassin.apache.org/

6. See https://support.apple.com/en-gb/HT204837

7. See https://support.microsoft.com/en-us/instantanswers/e7d75dd2-29c2-16ac-f03d-20cfdf54202f/turn-on-device-encryption

8. See https://veracrypt.codeplex.com/wikipage?title=Downloads

10 AWARENESS AND TRAINING

Human beings, who are almost unique in having the ability to learn from the experience of others, are also remarkable for their apparent disinclination to do so.

Douglas Adams, *Last Chance to See*[1]

In this chapter, we cover steps that an organisation can take to ensure that users are better prepared to make use of cyberspace, and to understand not only the issues they may encounter in doing so, but also their responsibilities to the organisation itself.

For the most part, one of the greatest security liabilities in any organisation is caused by the user. They may not act deliberately, but often they will unintentionally perform acts of cyber vandalism that will cause untold problems for the IT and security support staff. Their actions (or inactions) may be that they behave inappropriately and release information or allow information to be released, but this may often be due to the fact that they have not been properly trained by the organisation to react appropriately to information security events.

Some – but not all – of this can be corrected by educating and training the users in good security practice, making them aware of the risks that they will face when using both their own and the organisation's systems.

The 'not all' referred to above covers two different aspects of human behaviour – first, when the user simply forgets or ignores their training, and second, when they are carrying out some act in a very deliberate manner, either to cause loss of the organisation's information (selling it to a competitor for example) or to cause damage or loss as an act of revenge.

However, making users aware of the threats, vulnerabilities and impacts that they may face is an essential precursor to training.

There is little that the organisation can do to ensure that users never make a mistake, although some organisations as a means of reducing the likelihood levy a fine on staff who leave sensitive documents or their computer unattended.

Preventing or reducing the likelihood of information theft or damage to systems and information can be achieved to a certain extent by implementing very strict access control mechanisms and introducing monitoring software that looks for anomalies in user behaviour and flags up an early warning if something out of character is detected. Banks and credit card companies adopt a similar approach as a means of early detection of fraud, and will often contact a customer immediately if they appear to be making purchases that do not match previous spending patterns.

Although it may appear obvious, it is worth stating that awareness and training are two different but inter-related concepts. Awareness provides users with the information they need in order to avoid making mistakes, whilst training equips them with the skills they require to deal effectively with challenging situations when they arise.

This chapter focuses mainly on changing people's behaviour, so that the instances of people-related cyber-attacks can be reduced.

AWARENESS

Awareness of cyber security issues permits both individuals and an organisation's users to act as a first – or indeed a last – line of defence in combating cyber-attacks. It is never a one-off activity, and should be considered to be an integral part of personal development, whilst remaining a rather less formal activity than training.

An awareness programme allows people to understand the threats they face whenever they use a computer, the techniques used by social engineers to achieve their goals, the vulnerabilities faced by them or by their organisation, and finally the potential impacts of their actions or inactions.

This doesn't imply that it is necessary to turn everybody into cyber security experts, but that a basic level of understanding is required, similar to that in driving a car – we need to know how to operate the vehicle, the rules of the road and the dangers we face, but we do not need to understand how the engine management system works.

As with any process, there are a number of discrete steps in an awareness programme:

- Plan and design the programme:
  - select the most appropriate topics for awareness, such as email etiquette, correct handling of information assets or password security, for example;
  - make a business case to justify any expenditure;
  - develop a means of communicating with the users.

- Deliver and manage the programme:
  - develop the materials and content;
  - implement the awareness campaign.
- Evaluate and modify the programme as necessary:
  - evaluate the campaign's effectiveness;
  - improve and update the material with new information.

Like many other aspects of working life, awareness is a journey, not a destination, since new people will join the organisation and need to be included in the programme, and new threats and vulnerabilities will arise.

The campaign should also focus on continuous reinforcement though such things as poster campaigns and pop-ups when people access the internet or log on.

The general trend of user engagement in the programme should be along the lines of:

- initial contact with the user community – letting them know that something will be happening in which they will need to become involved and providing a general idea of what the programme will be all about, so that their expectations can be managed;

- further understanding of the programme, so that they appreciate what the implications will be for them;

- timely engagement, so that they begin to understand that there is a new way of working;

- acceptance by users, in which the user community begin to work in the new way;

- full commitment to new ways of working, so that they do not revert to their old ways;

- evangelism, in which they encourage others to follow their example.

Possible obstacles to a successful awareness programme

It is easy to assume that once an awareness programme is underway that all will go to plan, and organisations will only need to react and respond to problems when they arise. However, if forewarned about some of the possible issues, organisations should have a contingency plan in place so that faster reaction is possible.

Some of the issues that organisations may face include:

- Initial lack of understanding. When the awareness programme is initiated, it is vital that the communication that goes out to the audience involved explains not just what the organisation expects to achieve, but also why it is undertaking the work. This will greatly aid acceptance of the programme.

- The introduction of new technology which complicates a programme that is already underway. Such changes in the IT infrastructure in an organisation can either enhance the ability to deliver the message or can complicate it; but as long as people from that part of the organisation are involved in the awareness programme, the team should be aware of the possibility before it arises and be able to include it in their programme or work around the problem.

- One size never fits all. Every organisation is different, and there are no standard methods of operating an awareness programme, and even within one organisation the different types of audience may have different requirements. Also, there will be a considerable difference in both the size and the scope of an awareness programme between one for a large organisation and one for an SME.

- Trying to deliver too much information. Many users in an organisation will be non-technical, and so the focus of the programme must take into account that the more technical aspects of cyber security could overwhelm them. It is essential to keep the focus on what the audience need to know and not try to extend the delivery of information to be too technical. Less is more.

- Ongoing management of the programme can become a challenge. If this becomes the case then the probability exists that the programme will flounder due to lack of support from those areas of the organisation that are involved in its delivery, and therefore senior management commitment must be assured.

- Follow-up failure. These can and will cause problems for the programme, since it is vital that the team understand how well the message has been received, understood and acted upon by the target audience. Regular monitoring and reviews are essential to delivering a quality programme.

- Inappropriate targeting of the subject matter. This can have a negative effect on the programme, since groups within the organisation may be receiving some awareness information that has little or no impact on their role, whilst others are not receiving information that would be essential to their daily activities.

- Ingrained behaviours. These are a constant challenge in this kind of programme. Some people will always challenge the programme saying, 'We've always done it this way and it has always worked, so why should we change?' Any organisation running an awareness programme must expect this kind of response and must develop sound arguments against it.

- Some people will take the view that security is the responsibility of the IT department. It is essential that they are disabused of this notion at an early stage and throughout the ongoing campaign. Cyber security is everybody's problem, and is not restricted to one department.

Programme planning and design

The process commences with the establishment of a small team who will develop and run the programme. Some of them will naturally have a degree of expertise in information security, whilst others may represent those parts of the organisation that might suffer serious impacts in the event of a cyber-attack. It may also be beneficial to involve the internal audit function, who may be able to offer constructive advice, since a programme such as this may well be audited at a later stage, and it's always good to have audit on your side.

The team's initial task will be to define the exact goals and objectives of the programme, and this will include whether the target audience is to be the whole organisation or just a small part as a pilot project. This latter option may be a much more beneficial approach, since it should be able to achieve its objectives on a small and therefore less costly scale than targeting the whole organisation, before widening the programme to include everyone.

In the initial part of the programme, the target audience might also be limited to one particular type of user, such as:

- employees working full-time in the organisation's premises. These are frequently the kind of users who will benefit the most from receiving cyber security awareness training;

- home-based users, who will have similar, but slightly more complex needs. Due to the different requirements for connecting into the organisation's network, these users may require a slightly higher level of understanding of the issues at stake;

- third party users, such as contractors, outsourced staff and suppliers who require connections into the organisation's networks in order to undertake their work;

- system administrators and IT support staff, who will already have at least a general appreciation of the issues;

- management-level users, who may be responsible for in-house employees or home-based users, and who need to understand how cyber security issues will affect their departments;

- senior executive users, who will be responsible for making many of the business decisions that would be impacted by a successful cyber-attack.

Alternatively, the organisation may decide to target a cross section of users from different groups so that the overall organisational benefits can be seen, rather than solely those for a particular community.

Some topics will have greater relevance to particular target groups, such as the issues of social engineering, which may possibly be more relevant to staff who have regular contact with customers and suppliers than to those who do not. This does not imply that those who do not have as much external contact should not be included in that aspect of awareness, but that they might gain less from it.

Next in the development of the programme, the team must clearly identify the topics that will be covered. It is pointless trying to cover all aspects of cyber awareness, since this will simply overwhelm the audience; instead the programme should focus initially on a very tightly defined subset such as usernames and passwords, spam email or social engineering. The campaign can be widened at a later stage once the results of the earlier work have been examined and the techniques used have been refined where appropriate.

The methods of communicating the message to the user community will vary considerably, and may well consist of some or all of the following:

- posters, which can be placed where staff can easily engage with the message, such as meeting rooms and other shared areas. Some posters might have a humorous focus in order to lighten the message, whilst others could be somewhat darker;

- newsletters, which can be delivered by desk-drop in office buildings, or by email for offices and home workers alike;

- give-away items such as coasters, coffee mugs, key fobs and mouse mats, which continue to reinforce the general message for as long as they are used;

- screensavers, which might display a variety of messages, and which could be changed either at regular intervals, or when a new message must be given out;

- intranet websites that provide helpful advice, examples of good and bad cyber security behaviour and links to additional informative material and training;

- fact sheets and leaflets, which may be particularly relevant to a group within the organisation, to the whole organisation or to its business sector;

- presentations at team meetings, in which a guest speaker talks for a few minutes on a hot topic and takes questions about the whole awareness programme, keeping the presentation 'short and sweet';

- computer-based training (CBT), which delivers a more detailed level of knowledge, and may be a mandatory requirement for the certain users' work. This might include data protection legislation for example.

Once this part of the work is complete, the team may well have to approach the senior management team or board of directors to obtain funding approval, since it is unrealistic to expect that the work can be undertaken at no cost.

As with all business cases, the approach should focus on the likely impacts that will occur if the work does not proceed, as well as the benefits that will accrue when it does. This is another reason for keeping the initial part of the campaign to a reduced volume of information, since the costs will be lower and the board will find it easier to give approval. Success at this early stage will then make it much easier to obtain board approval for further expenditure when the campaign moves on to cover more aspects of cyber security awareness.

The costs can be more easily identified if they are broken down into manageable areas, for example:

- the hourly costs of staff who are engaged in delivering the awareness campaign as well as those who will be on the receiving end;

- development costs, including development and maintenance of any intranet websites or the production of materials such as posters and newsletters;

- promotional costs, such as give-away items including branded pens, coffee mugs, key fobs, mouse mats and the like;

- training costs, where external trainers are brought in to deliver all or part of the awareness campaign.

Some of these will be one-off costs, whilst others will be recurring, and the board will expect that these will be clearly identified.

It should also be possible to attempt to quantify the potential impacts, since the directors of organisations will need to be certain that the programme will deliver value for money.

Potential impacts can include not only the direct financial losses anticipated if a particular incident occurs, such as the loss of sales revenue and the expenditure that would be incurred in responding to and recovering from the incident, but also the indirect losses such as share value, brand and the organisation's reputation, although these can be rather more subjective in nature.

Delivery and management of the programme

Although we have called this an awareness campaign, it actually goes further than this, because awareness is only the first stage in which the target audience are made aware of what they should know and when they are likely to need the information. This may be delivered in a variety of ways, for example by printed material, email, electronic newsletters and intranet portals for those organisations having more sophisticated resources.

The campaign then moves up a level so that the target audience gain an understanding of why they need to be involved and how best they can participate. This may include raising awareness topics at team meetings and delivering specific presentations on the subject matter.

Evaluation and modification of the programme

Finally, the campaign is ready to see results from the earlier work and to evaluate its effectiveness, and as the campaign develops and widens its scope, the organisation will expect to see the benefits in reduced or zero instances of successful cyber-attacks.

The team must ensure that the entire exercise has been carefully documented, and that they can demonstrate the resulting benefits at the end of the pilot project so that more of the organisation and greater areas of cyber security awareness can be addressed.

Once presented back to the board, success should breed success, and the team should be better placed to move on to raising awareness for the wider organisation or in more topic areas. The presentation should focus on both the financial and non-financial benefits, the value to the business itself and also to its external stakeholders, including suppliers and customers and the sector regulator if applicable, and should be completely honest about both the overall costs and the potential impacts of not progressing with a full rollout.

Once the board have given their commitment for this, the pilot user group should be given acknowledgement for their involvement, as this will not only reinforce the importance of the programme, but will encourage others to become actively involved.

TRAINING

As mentioned earlier in this chapter, awareness and training are two entirely different, but interconnected concepts. Whilst awareness places cyber security issues firmly in the minds of the user community in an organisation, training will deliver very specific and often highly targeted information to those individuals or groups who have a specific requirement for it.

Training, and especially highly technical training, can be costly, but as with awareness, has a direct payback in terms of reducing the number of incidents and the potential financial impact on the organisation.

Cyber security training falls into two distinct categories:

- Generic training, in which the underlying concepts of cyber security are explained, and which give a sound appreciation of the issues. This may be required by those managers who are responsible for specialist security design and operational staff.

- Specialised cyber security training, in which very specific skills are taught to a limited audience such as those security staff who manage the organisation's security infrastructure.

Appendix D lists a number of resources that provide cyber security training, and suggests appropriate topics.

A few final points to consider

In the case of product or technology-specific training, it should be taken into account that technology changes at an alarming rate, and the need for updated courses will undoubtedly become necessary as time progresses. The requirement for ongoing budget allocations for this should be factored into the cost estimates when preparing business cases.

One method of reducing training costs is by identifying those staff who already possess training skills, and who can pass on their knowledge to others. This 'train the trainer' approach can work well when budgets are limited.

The business cases for both generic and specialised cyber security training will need to be developed and presented on a case-by-case basis, and should be presented in a similar manner to those for the awareness programme. However, instead of being focused solely on benefits to the organisation as a whole by targeting all users within the organisation, these business cases should also focus on benefits to the organisation by addressing the specific training needs of individual specialists.

NOTE

1. *Last Chance to See* was first published when Douglas was still with us and was both a BBC radio documentary and a book. More recently, his co-producer Mark Carwardine joined Stephen Fry in making a BBC TV documentary version.

11 INFORMATION SHARING

The guardians of your company's cyber security should be encouraged to network within the industry to swap information on the latest hacker tricks and most effective defences.

Nina Easton, American journalist and author

In this chapter, we will take a look at one of the methods of reducing our cyber security risks – sharing information about threats and vulnerabilities.

It's worth bearing in mind that knowledge of vulnerabilities may lead an attacker to be able to mount a successful attack, but it's only by careful sharing of information that security can be improved. This dichotomy can lead to tensions in the cyber security world, and the occasional holding back of information regarding some vulnerabilities.

The organisations described below all have excellent websites, so rather than repeating their content, a brief description of their activities has been provided with links to the appropriate web pages.

The most important aspects of information sharing are:

- The whole concept of information sharing is based on trust.[1] This can exist at a personal level, with one individual trusting another, or can be between groups of people within organisations who share a common interest in the subject.

- Information to be shared requires some form of information classification. Many information sharing initiatives now make use of the so-called 'Traffic Light Protocol' (TLP)[2] for classifying how information that is to be shared must be handled.

- The information must be accurate. It is pointless in sharing information that has not been verified, since it can consume time and resources unnecessarily.

- Advice to others must be timely. There is no value in keeping information back from those who would make good use of it, since an attacker may also become aware of it and take advantage of the time lag to initiate a successful attack.

- Sharing must be done with care. The circle of interested parties with whom the information is shared must be trusted to handle it in an agreed manner, and not to allow it to fall into the wrong hands. There should be mechanisms built into the process to prevent onward distribution to people or organisations outside the sharing group.

- It should be possible to anonymise the source of the information. On occasions, revealing the identity of the organisation that raised the issue could prove detrimental, and a means of passing on the information without attribution is essential.

- It should be possible to share information with other critical infrastructure sectors. Frequently in cyber security, there are issues that will affect many, if not all critical infrastructure sectors, and a means of passing information between them in a controlled manner is essential.

TRUST

Trust between members of an information sharing community is an absolute prerequisite. But what do we mean by 'trust'? The Oxford dictionary definition is that trust is 'the firm belief in the reliability, truth or ability of someone or something'. In the context of cyber security, the implication of this is that we must trust not only the information we receive, but that in order to do so we must first and foremost trust the source of the information, whether this be an individual or an organisation.

Where information is shared on a face-to-face basis, it is often conducted under the so-called 'Chatham House Rule'[3] named after the Royal Institute of International Affairs at Chatham House in London, which states:

> When a meeting, or part thereof, is held under the Chatham House Rule, participants are free to use the information received, but neither the identity nor the affiliation of the speaker(s), nor that of any other participant, may be revealed.

A note adds:

> The world-famous Chatham House Rule may be invoked at meetings to encourage openness and the sharing of information.

As far as the classification of information to be shared is concerned, trust works on two levels. First, the originator must ensure that the information has been correctly classified, and must be confident that the recipients will handle the information in line with that classification. Second, recipients must have sufficient trust in the integrity of the originator so that they can have the same level of confidence in the accuracy and reliability of the information.

One final aspect of trust is the ability to have an independent party, trusted by all members of an information sharing community, who can act as a moderator, and can also perform the role of go-between in certain situations as we shall see later. This individual is sometimes known as the Trust Master.

INFORMATION CLASSIFICATION

Information to be shared must be classified according to its sensitivity, and whatever method is used, it must be possible for it to be used by both public and private sectors without the need to cross-reference their information classification schemes.

As mentioned previously, the Traffic Light Protocol is used by many information sharing initiatives and classifies information as one of four colours:

- RED – Personal for named recipients only – in the context of a face-to-face meeting for example, distribution of RED information is limited to those present at the meeting, and in most circumstances, will be passed verbally or in person.

- AMBER – Limited distribution – recipients may share AMBER information with others within their organisation, but only on a 'need-to-know' basis. The originator may be expected to specify the intended limits of that sharing.

- GREEN – Community-wide – information in this category can be circulated widely within a particular community or organisation. However, the information may not be published or posted on the internet, nor released outside the community.

- WHITE – Unlimited – subject to standard copyright rules, WHITE information may be distributed freely and without restriction.

This method of information classification is widely used in information sharing communities around the world since it is very simple to understand and implement, and additionally can be readily understood in other sectors or countries.

Most of the time, the originator of the information to be shared will determine its classification colour, but on occasion, Trust Masters may decide to raise it if they feel that it is set too low.

PROTECTION OF SHARED INFORMATION

When information is being shared, the originator may consider it necessary to restrict its onward distribution, or to ensure that the information can be revoked or deleted in situations where it is no longer valid, or when its level of sensitivity has changed.

This can be achieved by the use of a technique sometimes known as 'information rights management', which works by encrypting the information – for example, a text document – and allowing it to be opened by the recipients provided they can identify themselves to the central sharing resource.

Further, the document can be provided with additional protection choices, so that it can never be copied, including the copying of selected parts of the document and thereby preventing it being pasted into an unprotected document; or printed, preventing its onward distribution in physical or scanned form.

If the document is forwarded to another recipient, it will be necessary for them in turn to have access rights on the central sharing resource, and if the originator decides to remove the original document, any remaining copies will not be able to be opened since the original document's metadata that enables decryption will also be deleted.

As with information classification, originators must ensure that the information has been appropriately protected, and again, recipients must have sufficient trust in the integrity of the originator so that they can have the same level of confidence in the accuracy and reliability of the information.

It makes good business sense in organisations that have a requirement for very strict confidentiality to run all incoming or outgoing emails through a scanning system that is able to detect and isolate any message containing particular words or phrases, or which can direct encrypted messages to a central verification point prior to their release.

ANONYMISATION OF SHARED INFORMATION

Situations will inevitably arise when a participating organisation does not wish to be identified as having been the victim of an attack (possibly even more so for a successful attack) or other cyber security situation in which they have become embroiled. The reasons for this are generally connected with commercial interests, and organisations may be reluctant for a competitor who is part of the same information sharing community to know whom the incident affected, since this might place that organisation at a competitive disadvantage or have a negative effect on their share price or public reputation. At the same time however, they might still wish details of the exploit to be made available to the wider community.

In face-to-face situations, such an organisation might well approach the Trust Master and request that they raise the matter without identifying the originator. The Trust Master will take great pains to ensure that this request for anonymity is respected, ensuring that even having omitted the originator's identity, the information passed on contains no clues or additional metadata that might reveal, infer, suggest or identify the originator in any way.

In the context of a centralised information sharing system, the Trust Master's role must be performed by the system itself in conjunction with the originator of the information being shared. There are two general courses of action:

- The originator can select an 'anonymise' option on the system's preferences when setting up the specific information to be shared. This will remove any reference as to who originally submitted the information. However, should the information include other documents, for example, word processed documents, spreadsheets or presentations, the originator will be responsible for completely anonymising these.

- The originator can select an 'anonymise via the Trust Master' option instead. In this situation, the originator openly sends the information to the Trust Master, who then submits it to the community as if it had come from the Trust Master alone.

Here, the application of trust works slightly differently. Originators must again ensure that nothing in the information being shared can reveal their identity, nor could their identity be inferred from the content detail. They must also have trust in both the information sharing system and the Trust Master that their identity will not be revealed. No additional trust is required here by the recipient.

Organisations, or groups of communities, who wish to provide their own centralised systems for information sharing may later wish to interconnect these so that they can widen the scope of their operations, since some cyber security situational submissions will inevitably be of significant interest to other sectors, and sharing information with them would be highly beneficial if not essential, and this can often avoid possible duplication of effort.

> In order to supplement the ISO/IEC 27001 standard, the ISO produced an additional standard, ISO/IEC 27010:2015, that covers the secure exchange of information between centralised systems.[4]

Contact – and therefore trust – may already have been established between these different groups, communities or sectors, in which case information might be freely shared between them, following the same rules as those for sharing within a sector.

Alternatively, if no previous contact has been established and therefore no degree of trust exists, the Trust Masters in those sectors wishing to share information can act, as intermediaries and initiate a limited degree of information sharing – possibly one-way only in the first instance – and subsequently encourage bilateral information sharing as an increasing level of trust develops.

Finally, once trust is fully established between the sectors, the Trust Masters may set preferences in the information sharing system that allow individual sector users to share information – either on a one-to-one basis with a peer in another sector, or more widely to a whole sector.

Originators of information should have the same degree of trust in users within a different sector as they do for users within their own sector. The information should be classified, protected and anonymised in exactly the same way.

From the recipient's point of view, the only thing that matters is that they have trust in the originators of the information and therefore in the information itself.

ROUTES TO INFORMATION SHARING

There are four major routes to sharing information regarding cyber security issues, each of which has its own unique characteristics:

- warning, advice and reporting points (WARPs);[5]
- the Cyber Security Information Sharing Partnership (CiSP);
- computer emergency response teams (CERTs) and computer security incident response teams (CSIRTs);
- security information exchanges (SIEs) and information sharing and analysis centres (ISACs).

Additionally, an excellent Good Practice Guide to Network Security Information Exchanges has been written by European Union Agency for Network and Information Security (ENISA).[6]

Warning, advice and reporting points (WARPs)

WARPs are a UK initiative that began in 2002 under the auspices of the National Infrastructure Security Coordination Centre (NISCC), which is now known as CPNI. WARPs allow their members to receive and share up-to-date cyber threat information and best practice. WARPs are now provided by CERT-UK's CiSP.

Members of current WARPs tend to be regional government, emergency services or military organisations.

Cyber Security Information Sharing Partnership (CiSP)

The CiSP[7] is an initiative set up jointly between UK industry and government in order to share cyber security threat and vulnerability information. The objective is to increase situational awareness of cyber threats with a consequent reduction of impact on UK businesses.

CiSP membership can only be given to UK registered companies responsible for the administration of an electronic communications network in the UK, or organisations that are sponsored by either a government department, an existing CiSP member or a trade body or association.

CiSP members are able to exchange cyber threat information in real time, on a secure environment, operating within a framework that protects confidentiality. Information shared includes alerts and advisories, weekly and monthly summaries and trend analysis reporting.

Computer emergency response teams (CERTs) and computer security incident response teams (CSIRTs)

CERTs have been in existence for some years now – originally begun by the US Carnegie Mellon University, the practice of collecting, analysing and distributing security advisories has been a major influence on all sectors worldwide. CERTs and CSIRTs carry out the same function, and the mnemonics are used interchangeably.

Many countries now operate a CERT/CSIRT, and even some larger multinational organisations whose enterprises cross traditional national and continental boundaries may do likewise.

In the UK, CERT-UK[8] has four main responsibilities that flow from the UK's Cyber Security Strategy:

- national cyber security incident management;
- support to critical national infrastructure companies to handle cyber security incidents;
- promoting cyber security situational awareness across industry, academia and the public sector;

- providing the single international point of contact for coordination and collaboration between national CERTs.

Subscription to a CERT or CSIRT is possible for almost any individual or organisation wishing to receive updates. However, sometimes the volume and frequency of these can be overwhelming.

As an example, CERT-UK provides three main work streams:

- **Alerts** – In the exceptional event of a critical national cyber security incident, CERT-UK will issue an alert and appropriate guidance.

- **Advisories** – CERT-UK issues advisories that address cyber security issues being detected across government, industry or academia or that offer best practice updates.

- **Best practice guides** – Through CiSP, CERT-UK provides regular advice and guidance on a range of cyber issues, with the aims of sharing information and encouraging best practice amongst its partners.

Security information exchanges (SIEs) and information sharing and analysis centres (ISACs)

Whereas CERTs and CSIRTs concentrate both on information collection and response to incidents, SIEs and ISACs provide solely a means of exchanging information about threats, vulnerabilities and incidents. SIEs tend to provide raw data about incidents, whereas ISACs tend to provide a deeper analysis and suggestions for response.

SIEs and ISACs generally comprise both public and private sector organisations that form part of a critical national infrastructure, together with their lead government department and any other organisation having a legitimate interest in the security aspects of that particular sector such as the sector regulator.

In the UK, a number of SIEs are managed by CPNI.[9]

In the UK, CPNI considers that there are 13 areas of national infrastructure, which were discussed in greater detail in Chapter 3 of this book. Other countries adopt a similar approach, and in the USA for example, their ISACs broadly cover the same areas. Their website notes that there are some cross-sector themes such as technology wherein there may be infrastructure that supports the delivery of essential services across a number of sectors.

NOTES

1. For a detailed view on this topic, please see Sutton, D. (2015) Trusted information sharing for cyber security situational awareness. *Elektrotechnik und Informationstechnik.* Vol. 132, 2, pp. 113–116, Vienna: Springer. DOI 10.1007/s00502-015-0288-3. ISSN 0932-383X.

2. The Traffic Light Protocol was originally developed by the UK CPNI.

3. See www.chathamhouse.org/about/chatham-house-rule#

4. See ISO/IEC 27010:2015 – *Information technology – Security techniques – Information security management for inter-sector and inter-organisational communications.*

5. See https://www.warp.gov.uk/

6. See https://www.enisa.europa.eu/publications/good-practice-guide/at_download/fullReport

7. See https://www.cert.gov.uk/cisp/

8. See https://www.cert.gov.uk

9. See www.cpni.gov.uk/about/cni/

PART III
APPENDICES

APPENDIX A
STANDARDS

The nice thing about standards is that you have so many to choose from. Furthermore, if you do not like any of them, you can just wait for next year's model.

Andrew S. Tanenbaum, *Computer Networks*, Second edition 1989, p. 254

Standards and specifications are directives telling you what should be done, whilst guidelines and recommendations are informative, and tell you how you should go about it.

There are also so-called 'good practice' guides and documents, which, rather than being issued by a standards body, originate from an organisation that has a legitimate claim to be the main source of knowledge on matters pertaining to it. An example of this is the Information Security Forum's Standard of Good Practice, which we shall examine briefly later in this appendix.[1]

Regardless of their name or definition, standards, specifications, guidelines and recommendations are costly to produce and tend to be developed and distributed by large international organisations, which usually make a charge for them, or by government departments, which usually subsidise them to a greater or lesser degree.

Some standards bodies produce their output for local consumption only, whereas the larger ones tend to produce output intended for more widespread use. An example of the former category is the Standards Australia, whose output is generally just used within that country and sometimes in New Zealand. An example of the second category is BSI,[2] which has been at the forefront of standards development since 1901, and much of their output is utilised worldwide, often being turned into truly international standards.

There are a number of countries that produce their own standards of all kinds, but the principle ones for cyber security are the USA and the UK. However, many of these standards go on to become international standards, so we will deal primarily with those.

The standards body responsible for publishing them is ISO,[3] based in Geneva. Development of new standards can take many years, and involves representatives from all over the world who meet both in person and through collaborative file sharing to define and agree the detail.

The best-known series of information security standards is the ISO/IEC 27000 series (IEC[4] is also based in Geneva) and many of the so-called ISO standards are produced in consultation with them.

There are also some excellent British Standards and guideline documents as well as many American Federal Information Processing Standards (FIPSs). Finally, and possibly still of interest, are the Internet Engineering Task Force (IETF) RFCs and the International Telecommunication Union (ITU) standards.

At the time of writing, there are more than 40 published ISO standards in the information security area, with several more in the development pipeline. If you would like to see the details of any of them, the best place to look is either the ISO website, or the BSI website as the index of ISO standards is shown there. If you wish to purchase them, you will probably find that the BSI online route is less costly, especially if you become a member of BSI, in which case many of the standards are available at a discounted price.

The security standard considered to be the primary one is ISO/IEC 27001:2013, and it is to this standard that organisations can be accredited.

One thing to beware of is that the ISO standards portfolio is growing rapidly, and by the time you read this book, many more will have been produced. However, we have made best efforts to ensure that the list is up to date at the time of writing. Where appropriate, a brief description of the standard has been included.

CYBER SECURITY STANDARDS

There are more standards in this area than you could shake a stick at, so below are some of the most relevant ones.

BS 10012:2009 – *Specification for a personal information management system*

The title of this standard is slightly confusing – it would appear to refer to management of information for individual people, whereas it actually refers to organisational management of people's personal information.

Its main theme is to highlight the organisation's responsibilities with regard to data protection and is a useful introduction to the full Data Protection Act 1998.

PAS 555:2013 – *Cyber security risk – Governance and management – Specification*

For organisations wishing to achieve a reasonable standard of cyber security without the need for full ISO/IEC 27001 certification, PAS 555 is an excellent beginning. It does, however, only provide high-level statements as opposed to providing the level of detail that one would find in the full ISO standard. This might appeal to many SMEs.

ISO/IEC 27000 SERIES STANDARDS

ISO/IEC 27000:2016 – *Information technology – Security techniques – Information security management systems – Overview and vocabulary*

Apart from providing definitions of commonly used terms, this standard describes how an information security management system (ISMS) should work, and goes on to mention some of the standards listed below.

ISO/IEC 27001:2013 – *Information technology – Security techniques – Information security management systems – Requirements*

Although it covers areas beyond pure cyber security, this is the main standard, and it is against this that organisations can be accredited. Sections 4 to 10 describe the mandatory elements of the standard, and the abbreviated list of controls in its Annex A are described in much greater detail in ISO/IEC 27002:2013.

ISO/IEC 27002:2013 – *Information technology – Security techniques – Code of practice for information security controls*

This standard provides detailed descriptions of the controls listed in Annex A of ISO/IEC 27001:2013.

ISO/IEC 27003:2017 – *Information technology – Security techniques – Information security management systems implementation guidance*

This standard provides guidance on planning and information security management system aligned to ISO/IEC 27001.

ISO/IEC 27004:2009 – *Information technology – Security techniques – Information security management measurements*

This standard covers the types of metrics and measurements that can be applied to an ISO/IEC 27001 programme.

ISO/IEC 27005:2011 – *Information technology – Security techniques – Information security risk management*

This is the main standard used when conducting an information risk management programme, and can form a major input to an ISO/IEC 27001 programme. A somewhat older standard, ISO 31000:2009, *Risk management – Principles and guidelines*, provides principles and generic guidelines on risk management.

ISO/IEC 27006:2015 – *Information technology – Security techniques – Requirements for bodies providing audit and certification of information security management systems*

Although this standard is less relevant to individual organisations looking to attain ISO/IEC 27001 certification, it does illustrate the guidance for those bodies that provide the certification.

ISO/IEC 27007:2011 – *Information technology – Security techniques – Guidelines for information security management systems auditing*

As with the previous example, this standard is somewhat less relevant to organisations wishing to develop an ISMS programme, but has been included for completeness.

ISO/IEC 27008:2011 – *Information technology – Security techniques – Guidelines for auditors on information security controls*

This standard provides a slightly different aspect of the ISMS audit function – this time dealing with guidance on specific controls.

ISO/IEC 27010:2015 – *Information security management systems – Information security management for inter-sector and inter-organizational communications*

This standard was developed with the express intention of exchanging information securely between organisations, especially when concerned with sharing information on security issues, as discussed in Chapter 11.

ISO/IEC 27011:2008 – *Information technology – Security techniques – Information security management guidelines for telecommunications organisations based on ISO/IEC 27002*

The standard is for telecommunications organisations and will enable them to meet baseline ISMS requirements of confidentiality, integrity, availability and any other relevant security properties of telecommunications services.

ISO/IEC 27013:2015 – *Information technology – Security techniques – Guidance on the implementation of ISO/IEC 27001 and ISO/IEC 20000-1*

This standard provides guidance on what organisations need to do in order to build a management system that integrates ISO/IEC 27001 and also ISO/IEC 20000, which is concerned with service management.

ISO/IEC 27014:2013 – *Information technology – Security techniques – Governance of information security*

This standard allows organisations to make decisions about information security issues in support of the strategic organisational objectives.

ISO/IEC 27015:2012 – *BS ISO/IEC TR 27015:2012 ED1 – Information security management systems – Information security management guidelines for financial services*

This standard is important for any organisation planning to offer financial services covered by an ISMS. It may also be useful to consumers of such services.

ISO/IEC 27016:2014 – *Information technology – Security techniques – Information security management – Organisational economics*

This standard will be useful when making information security investment decisions, as well as for those who have to prepare the business cases for information security investment.

ISO/IEC 27017:2015 – *Information technology – Security techniques – Code of practice for information security controls based on ISO/IEC 27002 for cloud services*

This standard will be useful to organisations wishing to become providers or users of cloud services, both by identifying their responsibilities to ensure certification of related security controls, and as a checklist to ensure that potential providers of the cloud service have the necessary security policies, practices and controls in place.

ISO/IEC 27018:2014 – *Information technology – Security techniques – Code of practice for protection of personally identifiable information (PII) in public clouds acting as PII processors*

This standard is applicable to all types and sizes of organisations, including public and private companies, government entities and not-for-profit organisations, which provide information processing services as PII processors via cloud computing under contract to other organisations.

ISO/IEC 27019:2013 – *Information technology – Security techniques – Information security management guidelines based on ISO/IEC 27002 for process control systems specific to the energy utility industry*

This standard is important for any organisation in the energy utility sector planning to operate an ISMS. It may also be useful to related organisations such as utility plant suppliers, systems integrators and auditors.

ISO/IEC 27023:2015 – *Information technology – Security techniques – Mapping the revised editions of ISO/IEC 27001 and ISO/IEC 27002*

This standard simply does what it says in the title. The earlier (2005) versions of ISO/IEC 27001 and 27002 differed in many ways from the 2013 versions, and this standard provides clarification.

ISO/IEC 27031:2011 – *Information technology – Security techniques – Guidelines for information and communication technology readiness for business continuity*

This standard provides guidelines for preparation of information and communications technology systems in meeting business continuity requirements. It relates to ISO 22301, which falls largely outside the scope of this book, since that standard covers all aspects of business continuity.

ISO/IEC 27032:2012 – *Information technology – Security techniques – Guidelines for cybersecurity*

This standard will be of much greater value to those organisations who are investing in protection against cyber security problems. It provides a detailed framework for identifying cyber security issues, and a high-level set of controls for dealing with them.

ISO/IEC 27033-1:2015 – *Information technology – Security techniques – Network security – Overview and concepts*

The first of five standards relating to network security, this standard deals with the main issues that organisations are likely to face.

ISO/IEC 27033-2:2012 – *Information technology – Security techniques – Guidelines for the design and implementation of network security*

This standard takes matters to the next level and defines the network security requirements that are likely to be needed, and provides a checklist.

ISO/IEC 27033-3:2010 – *Information technology – Security techniques – Network security – Reference networking scenarios – Threats, design techniques and control issues*

This standard deals with security network design principles, and examines the threats and possible controls associated with them.

ISO/IEC 27033-4:2014 – *Information technology – Security techniques – Network security – Securing communications between networks using security gateways*

This standard provides guidance on securing communications between networks using security gateways and firewalls, and introduces the concept of intrusion detection systems.

ISO/IEC 27033-5:2013 – *Information technology – Security techniques – Network security – Securing communications across networks using Virtual Private Networks (VPNs)*

The final part of this standard deals with securing network interconnections and how to connect remote users by providing VPNs.

ISO/IEC 27034-1:2011 – *Information technology – Security techniques – Application security – Overview and concepts*

This standard sets the scene for the secure development of applications, and in particular deals with the application security management process.

ISO/IEC 27034-2:2015 – *Information technology – Security techniques – Application security – Organisation normative framework*

This standard follows on from ISO/IEC 27034-1, and provides more detailed guidance on the implementation of application security, including a detailed description of the application security life cycle reference model.

ISO/IEC 27035:2011 – *Information technology – Security techniques – Information security incident management*

This standard deals with the management of cyber security incidents.

ISO/IEC 27036-1:2014 – *Information technology – Security techniques – Information security for supplier relationships – Overview and concepts*

This series of three standards examines the security requirements for the relationship between organisations and their suppliers.

ISO/IEC 27036-2:2014 *– Information technology – Security techniques – Information security for supplier relationships – Requirements*

This standard goes into greater detail regarding the technical security requirements that must be agreed and managed between an organisation and its suppliers.

ISO/IEC 27036-3:2013 *– Information technology – Security techniques – Information security for supplier relationships – Guidelines for information and communication technology supply chain security*

Frequently, supply chains are multi-layered and global, and this third standard in the series provides guidance on managing the complex risk environment.

ISO/IEC 27036-4:2016 *– Information technology – Security techniques – Information security for supplier relationships – Part 4: Guidelines for security of cloud services*

This standard provides cloud service customers and cloud service providers with guidance on:

(a) gaining visibility into the information security risks associated with the use of cloud services and managing those risks effectively, and

(b) responding to risks specific to the acquisition or provision of cloud services that can have an information security impact on organizations using these services.

ISO/IEC 27037:2012 *– Information technology – Security techniques – Guidelines for identification, collection, acquisition and preservation of digital evidence*

When cyber incidents occur, it may be necessary to preserve evidence of the fact, and this standard provides guidelines for the forensic preservation of evidence.

ISO/IEC 27038:2014 *– Information technology – Security techniques – Specification for digital redaction*

When organisations are required to anonymise information within a document or to redact it completely, this standard provides guidelines on the process and techniques, and may be useful in information sharing situations.

ISO/IEC 27039:2015 *– Information technology – Security techniques – Selection, deployment and operations of intrusion detection and prevention systems (IDPS)*

Intrusion detection and prevention systems can provide an analysis of host and network traffic and/or audit trails for attack signatures or specific patterns that usually indicate malicious or suspicious intent. This standard provides guidelines for effective IDPS selection, deployment and operation, as well as fundamental knowledge about IDPS.

ISO/IEC 27040:2015 *– Information technology – Security techniques – Storage security*

This standard applies to all data owners, IT managers and security officers from small enterprises to global organisations, as well as manufacturers of general and specialised data storage products, and is particularly relevant to data destruction services.

ISO/IEC 27041:2015 – *Information technology – Security techniques – Guidance on assuring suitability and adequacy of incident investigative method*

This standard contains an assurance model with details of how to validate the methods used for investigations and shows how internal and external resources can be used to carry out assurance.

ISO/IEC 27042:2015 – *Information technology – Security techniques – Guidelines for the analysis and interpretation of digital evidence*

This standard provides a detailed framework for investigation, giving guidance on how to structure and prioritise investigative stages in order to produce analysis and reports that can be used to improve security in the future.

ISO/IEC 27043:2015 – *Information technology – Security techniques – Incident investigation principles and processes*

This standard is intended to aid in digital investigations, with the aim that a suitably skilled investigator should obtain the same result as another similarly skilled investigator, working under similar conditions.

OTHER RELEVANT ISO STANDARDS

ISO/IEC 17788:2014 – *Information technology – Cloud computing – Overview and vocabulary.*

ISO/IEC 17789:2014 – *Information technology – Cloud computing – Reference architecture*

These two standards should appeal to all kinds of cloud customers – from small enterprises to global organisations – and all kinds of cloud providers and partner organisations such as software developers and auditors.

ISO/IEC 24762:2008 – *Information technology – Security techniques – Guidelines for information and communications technology disaster recovery services*

This standard takes us into the area of disaster recovery, and is aimed at aiding the operation of an ISMS by providing guidance on the provision of information and communications technology disaster recovery services as part of business continuity management.

ISO/IEC 29100:2011 – *Information technology – Security techniques – Privacy framework*

This standard provides a high-level framework for the protection of personally identifiable information within IT systems.

ISO/IEC 29101:2013 – *Information technology – Security techniques – Privacy architecture framework*

The guidance in this standard is applicable to entities involved in specifying, procuring, architecting, designing, testing, maintaining, administering and operating IT systems that process PII. It focuses primarily on IT systems that are designed to interact with PII principals.

ISO/IEC 29147:2014 – *Information technology – Security techniques – Vulnerability disclosure*

This standard provides guidelines for vendors to be included in their business processes when receiving information about potential vulnerabilities and distributing vulnerability resolution information.

ISO/IEC 29190:2015 – *Information technology – Security techniques – Privacy capability assessment model*

This standard provides guidance for organisations in producing an overall 'score' against a simple capability assessment model; a set of metrics indicating assessment against key performance indicators; and the detailed outputs from privacy process management audits and management practices.

ISO/IEC 30111:2013 – *Information technology – Security techniques – Vulnerability handling processes*

This standard describes processes for vendors to handle reports of potential vulnerabilities in products and online services.

BUSINESS CONTINUITY STANDARDS

Since cyber security forms an integral part of business continuity, the following standards have been included for completeness.

The first real attempt at producing a business continuity standard in the UK was the introduction of the BSI's PAS 56 in 2003. Intended as an interim standard it was eventually replaced by BS 25999 Part 1 – *Business continuity management – Code of practice* in 2006 and BS 25999 Part 2 – *Business continuity management – Specification* in 2007. Both of these have now been superseded by the international standard ISO 22301 in 2014.

As with many BSI and ISO standards areas, there are a number of standards and good practice guides for business continuity. The following is a list of the most relevant, and includes standards relating to incident and crisis management, both of which may be required as part of a business continuity programme.

ISO 22301:2014 – *Societal security – Business continuity management systems – Requirements*

This is now the definitive business continuity standard, replacing BS 25999 Parts 1 and 2 in 2014.

ISO 22313:2014 – *Societal security – Business continuity management systems – Guidance*

This standard is the guidance document that supports the requirements of ISO 22301. It describes good practice guidelines and recommendations that organisations may adopt to ensure their Business Continuity Management (BCM) programme aligns with internationally recognised best practices.

ISO 22318:2015 – *Societal security – Business continuity management systems – Guidelines for supply chain continuity*

As the title suggests, this standard examines strategies and methods of managing supply chain disruptions.

ISO 22322:2015 – *Societal security – Emergency management – Guidelines for public warning*

This standard describes the processes for monitoring threats and hazards that might cause harm to the public at large, and how to communicate these.

PD 25111:2010 – *Business continuity management – Guidance on human aspects of business continuity*

This standard provides guidelines for the planning of strategies for human resource management both during and following a business-disruptive incident, taking into account not only staff, but also their families.

PD 25666:2010 – *Business continuity management – Guidance on exercising and testing for continuity and contingency programmes*

Exercising and testing is a key aspect of business continuity programmes, and PD 25666 delivers practical advice on how best to accomplish this, the aims and objectives of exercises, how to present a business case and developing staff competence through training.

BS 11200:2014 – *Crisis management – Guidance and good practice*

Crisis management requires a forward-looking, systematic approach that creates structures, trains people to work within them and is evaluated and developed in a continuous, purposeful and rigorous way.

BS BIP 2142:2012 – *The route map to business continuity management. Meeting the requirements of ISO 22301*

John Sharp, the author of this document, has taken ISO 22301 as a starting point, examined every aspect of its requirements, and explained in BIP 2142 how best these can be achieved. However, he has taken this document much further by adding sections that are not specifically covered by ISO 22301, and also by providing useful templates for the BC practitioner.

BS BIP 2143:2012 – *Business continuity exercises and tests. Delivering successful exercise programmes with ISO 22301*

This document covers the aspect of business continuity exercises and tests, expanding on the requirements of PD 25666 and explaining how best these can be achieved.

BS BIP 2151:2012 – *Auditing business continuity management plans. Assess and improve your performance against ISO 22301*

This document is probably better suited to larger enterprises, where internal audit is widely used and a strict compliance regime is in operation.

BS BIP 2185:2012 – *Business continuity communications. Successful incident communication planning with ISO 22301*

The business continuity plan itself is only part of the story. Communication with all stakeholders during a business-disruptive incident is essential both in making the plan work and in preserving the organisation's credibility with the media.

BS BIP 2214:2011 – *A practical approach to business impact analysis. Understanding the organisation through business continuity management*

BIP 2214 is one of the most useful documents in the whole of the BSI collection, and will guide the reader step by step through the entire business impact analysis (BIA) process.

BS BIP 2217:2011 – *Business continuity management for small and medium sized enterprises. How to survive a major disaster or failure*

This document takes the BCM approach from the perspective of the SME as opposed to that of the larger corporate organisation, at which many other standards and guides are directed.

PAS 77:2006 – *IT Service Continuity Management – Code of Practice.*

By investigating, developing and implementing preventative and recovery options beforehand, an organisation can minimise and manage interruptions to services that threaten the continuity of the business.

> British standards can be obtained in PDF or hard copy formats from the BSI online shop: www.bsigroup.com/Shop or by contacting BSI Customer Services for hard-copies only: Tel: +44 (0) 20 8996 9001, Email: cservices@bsigroup.com

NATIONAL INSTITUTE OF STANDARDS AND TECHNOLOGY (NIST) STANDARDS

There are many NIST standards and FIPSs relating to information security, but these are probably of greatest interest:

NIST SP 800-53A – *Guide for Assessing the Security Controls in Federal Information Systems and Organizations*

NIST SP 800-83 – *Guide to Malware Incident Prevention and Handling*

NIST SP 800-100 – *Information Security Handbook: A Guide for Managers*

NIST SP 800-153 – *Guidelines for Securing Wireless Local Area Networks (WLANs)*

These can all be downloaded free of charge from: http://csrc.nist.gov/publications/PubsSPs.html

NIST Cyber Security Framework (2014). *Framework for Improving Critical Infrastructure Cybersecurity.*[5]

NOTES

1. See https://www.securityforum.org/tool/the-isf-standardrmation-security/

2. See www.bsigroup.com/en-GB/standards/

3. See www.iso.org/iso/home.html

4. See www.iec.ch/about/

5. Note that in January 2017, NIST published draft updates to the original framework, and these can be viewed at: https://www.nist.gov/sites/default/files/documents/cyberframework/cybersecurity-framework-021214.pdf

APPENDIX B
GOOD PRACTICE GUIDELINES

A man may be very sincere in good principles, without having good practice.

Samuel Johnson

There are many examples of good practice guidelines on the internet, making it an impossible task to list them all. However, the following are of particular note, and will direct the reader to those guidelines of interest that will provide the level of detail required.

GENERAL CYBER SECURITY ADVICE

CPNI has a wealth of information covering all sectors of the CNI at https://www.cpni.gov.uk/advice/cyber/Good-practice-catalogue/

Good practice information on industrial control systems can be found at https://ics-cert.us-cert.gov/Recommended-Practices

The UK's Health and Social Care Information Centre posts good practice information for cyber security at http://systems.hscic.gov.uk/infogov/security/infrasec/gpg

NCSC promotes cyber security good practice information for both public and private sectors, and guidance documents can be found at https://www.ncsc.gov.uk/guidance

For both public and private sectors, warning advice and reporting points (WARPs) can be found at https://www.warp.gov.uk/find-a-warp/

As part of the National Cyber Security Strategy, the UK's CERT has four areas of responsibility:

1. national cyber security incident management;
2. supporting critical national infrastructure companies to handle cyber security incidents;
3. promoting cyber security situational awareness across industry, academia, and the public sector;
4. providing the single international point of contact for coordination and collaboration between national CERTs.

Further information can be obtained from https://www.cert.gov.uk

Organisations that are members of the Information Security Forum (ISF) have access to the Forum's Standard of Good Practice, the most recent version being from 2013. See https://www.securityforum.org/tool/the-isf-standardrmation-security/

UK GOVERNMENT CYBER SECURITY ADVICE

The following are a selection of useful advice and guidance documents from the UK government for both small and larger businesses:

Help small businesses stay safe online: https://www.cyberstreetwise.com

What small businesses need to know about cyber security: https://www.getsafeonline. org/media/pdf/bis-13-780-small-business-cyber-security-guidance.pdf

The UK Cyber Essentials and Cyber Essentials Plus schemes: https://www.cyberaware. gov.uk/cyberessentials/

Cyber security guidance for business: https://www.gov.uk/government/collections/ cyber-security-guidance-for-business

Advice and guidance from NCSC: https://www.ncsc.gov.uk/guidance

10 Steps to Cyber Security: https://www.gov.uk/government/uploads/system/uploads/ attachment_data/file/395717/10_steps_infographic.pdf

10 Steps: Executive Companion: https://www.gov.uk/government/publications/cyber-risk-management-a-board-level-responsibility/10-steps-executive-companion

APPENDIX C
CYBER SECURITY LAW

Law and order exist for the purpose of establishing justice and when they fail in this purpose they become the dangerously structured dams that block the flow of social progress.

Martin Luther King Jr., 'Letter from Birmingham Jail', 16 April 1963

There are a number of pieces of UK legislation that are specifically concerned with cyber security, and also regulations and directives from the EU that have or may be placed with the UK's legislative framework.

UK LAW

The Computer Misuse Act 1990

This was introduced in response to a High Court decision to overturn the conviction of Robert Schifreen and Steven Gold, who in 1985 gained unauthorised access to BT's Prestel electronic mail system, and eventually accessed the mailbox of HRH the Duke of Edinburgh.

It is generally considered as the primary means of prosecuting cyber-attackers in the UK, provided that there is a warning notice on the computer system concerned requiring a user to confirm they are authorised to access the computer.

Download at: www.legislation.gov.uk/ukpga/1990/18/contents

The Copyright, Designs and Patents Act 1988

The 1988 Act amends previous legislation, and establishes the period of time over which copyright of work exists – mostly for 70 years following the death of the author or creator if known, or 70 years after the creation or publication of the work, but 50 years for computer-generated works.

In order for something to be protected by copyright it must fall within one of the following categories of work:

- literature;
- drama;
- music;
- art;
- film;
- sound recording;

- broadcasts;
- typographical arrangement of published works.

Download at: www.legislation.gov.uk/ukpga/1988/48/contents

The Data Protection Act 1998

Derived from the EU Data Protection Directive, this is the primary legislation under which all information privacy issues are managed. In April 2016, the EU agreed a major overhaul to the legislation, the GDPR, and this will come into force in 2018. As it is a regulation, and not a directive, it does not require changes to UK law.

Download at: www.legislation.gov.uk/ukpga/1998/29/contents

Data Retention and Investigatory Powers Act 2014

In 2014, a ruling by the European Court of Justice removed the obligation of communications service providers (CSPs) to store communications data, upon which the police and security services rely heavily. The government passed emergency data retention legislation known as the Data Retention and Investigatory Powers Act (DRIPA) that made it UK law again.

Download at: www.legislation.gov.uk/ukpga/2014/27/pdfs/ukpga_20140027_en.pdf

The Digital Economy Act 2010

In particular, this act addresses media policy issues related to digital media, including copyright infringement and internet domain names

Download at: www.legislation.gov.uk/ukpga/2010/24/contents

The Intellectual Property Act 2014

This Act introduced a number of measures and made changes to the law in order to make design law simpler, clearer and more robust. It also introduced changes to patent law, which simplified complex areas and made it less costly and easier to use and defend patents.

Download at: www.legislation.gov.uk/ukpga/2014/18/contents/enacted

Investigatory Powers Act 2016

This Act is frequently referred to as the 'Snooper's Charter', since it extends the powers of the security services and police much further than any previous legislation.

It contains a number of key points:

- It allows the security services and law enforcement agencies to undertake targeted interception of communications, the bulk collection of communications data and the bulk interception of communications.

- It creates the Investigatory Powers Commission (IPC) to oversee the use of all investigatory powers, alongside the oversight provided by the Intelligence and Security Committee of Parliament and the Investigatory Powers Tribunal.

- It requires CSPs to retain for one year UK internet users' internet connection records. This includes which websites were visited but not the individual pages or the full browsing history.

- It allows police, intelligence officers and government department managers to view the internet connection records, without a warrant.

- It permits the police and security services to carry out 'targeted equipment interference'. This means hacking into computers or devices (such as smartphones, tablet computers, etc.) to access their data.

- It places a legal obligation on CSPs to provide assistance with supplying targeted interception of data, and communications and with equipment interference in relation to investigations.

- It requires CSPs in the UK to remove encryption applied within their network.

- It creates new criminal offences for the unlawful access of internet data, and also for a CSP who reveals that data has been requested.

However, at the time of writing (January 2017), although the Act had become law, there had previously been a ruling by the European Court of Justice that what it called 'indiscriminate' collection of data was against EU law, and that data could only be retained if it was used to fight serious crime. The matter has now been referred back to the UK Court of Appeal, and time will tell whether the Act will require serious modification. In the meantime of course, the security services and law enforcement agencies are quite entitled to insist on the co-operation of CSPs.

The Malicious Communications Act 1988

This act makes it an offence to 'send or deliver letters or other articles for the purpose of causing distress or anxiety'. Its application in the cyber security environment is that it also applies to electronic communications, and has been used successfully to prosecute internet trolls and people posting malicious or offensive remarks on social media.

Download at: www.legislation.gov.uk/ukpga/1988/27/contents

The Regulation of Investigatory Powers Act 2000

Regulation of Investigatory Powers Act (RIPA) sets out (in theory at least) how public bodies (including the police and security services) may monitor the communications of individuals with the purpose of investigating acts of crime or terrorism.

Download at: www.legislation.gov.uk/ukpga/2000/23/contents

Additionally, the campaign group Liberty is launching a crowd-funded challenge to the legislation, which it calls 'an assault on our freedom'.[1]

The Act can be downloaded at: http://www.legislation.gov.uk/ukpga/2016/25/contents/enacted

EU DIRECTIVES AND REGULATIONS

The Network and Information Security (NIS) Directive

This was proposed as part of the European Union's cyber security strategy, created to enhance data security throughout member states. The Directive is intended to foster co-operation between EU nations whilst legislating expected security requirements for all essential services. It was formalised in July 2016, and must be implemented by all member states by April 2018.

There are broadly four key areas to the Directive:

1. Member states are required to adopt a national strategy that sets out concrete policy and regulatory measures to maintain a level of network and information security. This includes designating a national competent authority for information security and setting up a CERT that is responsible for handling incidents and risks.

2. The competent authorities in EU member states and the European Commission will form a co-operation network to coordinate against risks and incidents affecting network and information systems. The network will exchange information between authorities, provide early warnings on information security issues and agree on a coordinated response in accordance with an EU NIS co-operation plan.

3. EU member states must ensure that public bodies and certain market operators take appropriate technical and organisational measures to manage the security risks of networks and information systems – these must guarantee a level of security appropriate to the risks and should prevent and minimise the impact of security incidents affecting the core services they provide.

4. Public bodies and selected private sector companies must also notify the competent authority of incidents that have a significant impact on the continuity of these services. The competent authority may decide to inform the public about the incident. The significance of the incident should take into account the number of users affected, the duration of the incident and the geographical spread of the area affected by the incident. Hence, these requirements apply not only to private sector companies set out in the next paragraph but also to public bodies.

The Directive would currently apply to the following private sector industries:

- key internet companies (such as large cloud providers, social networks, e-commerce platforms, search engines);

- banking sector and stock exchange;

- energy (such as electricity and gas);

- transport (operators of air, rail and maritime transport and logistics);

- health (such as electronic medical devices and online/electronic personal health and financial information);

- public administrations (such as e-government and e-participation services);

- ISPs are already required to provide incident notification under the current EU Telecom Framework Directive.

Download further details at: https://ec.europa.eu/digital-single-market/en/network-and-information-security-nis-directive

EU General Data Protection Regulation (GDPR)

The EU GDPR effectively extends the current data protection legislation. It applies both to data controllers and data processors, and, additionally, data controllers will be required to ensure that data processors comply with contractual terms and conditions. Data controllers and data processors must also be able to demonstrate compliance with the GDPR.

It adds to the definitions of personal data, which now include artefacts that can be linked to a person's identity, such as IP addresses, and to sensitive personal data, with artefacts such as genetic or biometric information.

It also extends the rights of the individual:

- the right to be informed about what data is held about them and why;

- the right of individuals' access to their data;

- the right of rectification of incorrect data;

- the right of erasure of data that is out of date;

- the right to restrict the processing of data;

- the right to move their data from one organisation to another;

- the right to object to the processing of their data;

- rights related to the automated processing and profiling of their data.

The GDPR also tightens up the requirements for notifications of data breaches, and deals with the transfer of data outside the EU.

Download further information at: https://ico.org.uk/for-organisations/data-protection-reform/overview-of-the-gdpr/

Additionally, the international law firm Allen & Overy has produced a useful guidance document, which can be downloaded at: http://www.allenovery.com/SiteCollectionDocuments/Radical%20changes%20to%20European%20data%20protection%20legislation.pdf

OTHER RELEVANT LEGISLATION

EU-US Privacy Shield

The EU-US Privacy Shield has been designed to replace the Safe Harbor agreement (see under 'Why we should care' in Chapter 2).

Download further information at: http://ec.europa.eu/justice/data-protection/files/factsheets/factsheet_eu-us_privacy_shield_en.pdf

Four areas are of interest:

1. For the commercial sector, there will be strong obligations on companies and robust enforcement:

- greater transparency;

- oversight mechanisms to ensure companies abide by the rules;

- sanctions or exclusion of companies if they do not comply;

- tightened conditions for onward transfers.

2. There will be several possibilities for redress:

- directly with the company. Companies must reply to complaints from individuals within 45 days;

- alternative dispute resolution. Free of charge;

- with the Data Protection Authority, they will work with U.S. Department of Commerce and Federal Trade Commission to ensure unresolved complaints by EU citizens are investigated and swiftly resolved;

- Privacy Shield Panel. As a last resort, there will be an arbitration mechanism to ensure an enforceable decision.

3. There will be clear safeguards and transparency obligations regarding US government access:

- For the first time, written assurance has been provided by the US that any access by public authorities to personal data will be subject to clear limitations, safeguards and oversight mechanisms.

- US authorities affirm the absence of indiscriminate or mass surveillance.

- Companies will be able to report approximate number of access requests.

- New redress possibility through EU-US Privacy Shield Ombudsperson mechanism, independent from the intelligence community, handling and solving complaints from individuals.

4. *The annual joint review mechanism:*

- monitoring the functioning of the Privacy Shield and US commitments, including access to data for law enforcement and national security purposes;
- conducted by the European Commission and the US Department of Commerce, associating national intelligence experts from the US and European data protection authorities;
- annual privacy summit with non-governmental organisations (NGOs) and stakeholders on developments in the area of US privacy law and its impact on Europeans;
- public report by the European Commission to the European Parliament and the Council, based on the annual joint review and other relevant sources of information (for example, transparency reports by companies).

Further information can be downloaded at: https://www.privacyshield.gov/Program-Overview

NOTE

1. See https://www.liberty-human-rights.org.uk/news/press-releases-and-statements/people-vs-snoopers'-charter-liberty-launches-crowdfunded-legal

APPENDIX D
CYBER SECURITY TRAINING

A man, though wise, should never be ashamed of learning more, and must unbend his mind.

Sophocles

Generic cyber security training can cover a number of areas, such as:

- Certified Information Systems Security Professional (CISSP);[1]
- information security governance;
- Payment Card Industry Data Security Standard (PCIDSS);[2]
- information risk management;
- ISO/IEC 27001;[3]
- Sarbanes–Oxley[4] (for organisations listed on the New York Stock Exchange);
- Basel III (banking sector);[5]
- Control Objectives for Information and Related Technologies (COBIT 5);[6]
- Certificate of Cloud Security Knowledge (CCSK);[7]
- governance, risk and compliance;
- information security audit;
- business continuity;
- NCSC Certified Practitioner (CCP) Scheme;[8]
- Systems Security Certified Practitioner (SSCP);[9]
- Certified Cloud Security Professional (CCSP);[10]
- information assurance (IA).

BCS, The Chartered Institute for IT, offer a number of training courses and accreditations. At foundation level:

- Certificate in Information Security Management Principles (CISMP);[11]
- Foundation Certificate in Data Protection;[12]
- Foundation Certificate in Cyber Resilience (RESILIA™).[13]

At practitioner level:

- Practitioner Certificate in Information Risk Management (PCIRM);[14]
- Practitioner Certificate in Business Continuity Management (PCBCM);[15]

- Practitioner Certificate in Data Protection;[16]
- Practitioner Certificate in Freedom of Information;[17]
- Practitioner Certificate in Information Assurance Architecture;[18]
- Practitioner Certificate in Cyber Resilience (RESILIA™).[19]

Additionally, there are a number of universities that offer computer and information security management courses at both bachelor's and master's levels, including:

- Edinburgh Napier University: MSc in Advanced Security and Digital Forensics;
- Lancaster University: MSc in Cyber Security;
- University of Oxford: MSc in Software and Systems Security;
- Royal Holloway: MSc in Information Security;
- University of York: MSc in Cyber Security;
- Cranfield University: Cyber Defence and Information Assurance MSc/PgCert/PgDip;
- University of Birmingham: MSc in Cyber Security;
- University of Southampton: MSc Cyber Security;
- University of Surrey: MSc in Information Security;
- University of Warwick: MSc in Cyber Security and Management.

Rather more specialised cyber security training can take place at several levels, depending upon the nature of the individuals' roles, and is likely to be in any of the following disciplines:

- firewall configuration and management;
- systems hardening;
- secure software development;
- VPN technologies;
- access control, including authentication devices;
- IDSs;
- ethical hacking and penetration testing;
- database security;
- wireless security;
- security incident investigation;
- digital forensics;
- public key infrastructure (PKI) and Transport Layer Security (TLS).

NOTES

1. See https://www.isc2.org/cissp/default.aspx

2. See https://www.pcisecuritystandards.org/pci_security/

3. See www.iso.org/iso/iso27001

4. See www.soxlaw.com/

5. See www.bis.org/bcbs/basel3.htm

6. See www.isaca.org/cobit/pages/default.aspx

7. See https://cloudsecurityalliance.org/education/ccsk/# info-video1

8. See https://www.ncsc.gov.uk/articles/about-certified-professional-scheme

9. See https://www.isc2.org/sscp/default.aspx

10. See https://www.isc2.org/ccsp/default.aspx?utm_campaign=ccsp&utm_source=csa&utm_medium=certtopnav

11. See http://certifications.bcs.org/category/15735

12. See http://certifications.bcs.org/category/18107

13. See http://certifications.bcs.org/category/18472

14. See http://certifications.bcs.org/content/conWebDoc/53082

15. See http://certifications.bcs.org/content/conWebDoc/53085

16. See http://certifications.bcs.org/category/15742

17. See http://certifications.bcs.org/category/15745

18. See http://certifications.bcs.org/category/17270

19. See http://certifications.bcs.org/category/18473

APPENDIX E
LINKS TO OTHER USEFUL ORGANISATIONS

The trouble with finding quotes on the Internet is that you never know if they are genuine.

Abraham Lincoln

The Copyright Licensing Agency
www.cla.co.uk

The UK Copyright Service
https://www.copyrightservice.co.uk

The Performing Rights Society
www.prsformusic.com/Pages/default.aspx

The British Association of Picture Libraries and Agencies
www.bapla.org.uk/en/page/show_home_page.html

The Intellectual Property Office
https://www.gov.uk/government/organisations/intellectual-property-office

The Motion Picture Licensing Corporation
www.themplc.co.uk

The Design and Artists Copyright Society
https://www.dacs.org.uk

The Federation Against Software Theft
www.fast.org

FURTHER READING

Books don't just go with you; they take you where you've never been.

Anonymous

There are many books on cyber security-related topics. Here is a sample of those that you might find of interest:

Alexander, D., Finch, A., Sutton, D. and Taylor, A. (2013) *Information Security Management Principles, Second edition.* Edited by A. Taylor. BCS, Swindon, UK. ISBN 978-1-78017-175-3

Bartlett, J. (2015) *The Dark Net.* Windmill Books, London, UK. ISBN 978-0-09959-202-0

BCS, The Chartered Institute for IT. (n.d.) *Personal Data Guardianship Code.* BCS, Swindon, UK. Retrieved from www.bcs.org/upload/pdf/pdgc.pdf

Day, P. (2014) *Cyber Attack: The Truth About Digital Crime, Cyber Warfare and Government Snooping.* Carlton Books, London, UK. ISBN 978-1-78097-533-7

Goodman, M. (2016) *Future Crimes: Inside The Digital Underground and the Battle For Our Connected World.* Corgi, London, UK. ISBN 978-0-55217-080-2

Green, J.S. (2015) *Cyber Security: An Introduction for Non-Technical Managers.* Routledge, London, UK. ISBN 978-1-47246-673-0

Hafner, K. and Lyon, M. (1998) *Where Wizards Stay Up Late: The Origins of the Internet.* Simon & Schuster, New York, USA. ISBN 978-0-68483-267-8 [This book covers the beginnings of the ArpaNet and its eventual transition to the internet.]

IT Governance Institute. (2006) *Information Security Governance: Guidance for Boards of Directors and Executive Management, 2nd Edition.* Retrieved from www.isaca.org/knowledge-center/research/documents/information-security-govenance-for-board-of-directors-and-executive-management_res_eng_0510.pdf

Lohr, S. (2015) *Data-ism: Inside the big data revolution.* Oneworld, London, UK. ISBN 978-1-78074-518-3

Rowlingson, R. (2011) *The Essential Guide to Home Computer Security.* BCS, Swindon, UK. ISBN 978-1-90612-469-4

Schneier, B. (2015) *Data and Goliath: The hidden battles to collect your data and control your world.* W W Norton, New York, USA. ISBN 978-0-39335-217-7

Singer, P.W. and Friedman, A. (2014) *Cybersecurity and Cyberwar: What everyone needs to know.* Oxford University Press, Oxford, UK. ISBN 978-0-19991-811-9

Stoll, C. (1991) *The Cuckoo's Egg. Tracking a Spy Through the Maze of Computer Espionage.* Bodley Head, London, UK. ISBN 978-1-41650-778-9 [This book describes the first major incidence of cyber espionage.]

Sutton, D. (2014) *Information Risk Management.* BCS, Swindon, UK. ISBN 978-1-78017-265-1

Sutton, D. (2015) Trusted Information Sharing for Cyber Security Situational Awareness. *Elektrotechnik und Informationstechnik.* 132, 2, pp. 113–116. DOI 10.1007/s00502-015-0288-3. ISSN 0932-383X.

The European Network and Information Security Agency. (2010) *The New User's Guide: How to raise information security awareness.* ENISA, Luxembourg. ISBN 978-92-9204-049-9

INDEX

Diagrams and tables are in *italics*